The Polygamy Question

THE POLYGAMY QUESTION

Edited by
JANET BENNION
LISA FISHBAYN JOFFE

UTAH STATE UNIVERSITY PRESS
Logan

© 2016 by the University Press of Colorado

Published by Utah State University Press
An imprint of University Press of Colorado
5589 Arapahoe Avenue, Suite 206C
Boulder, Colorado 80303

The University Press of Colorado is a proud member of
The Association of American University Presses.

The University Press of Colorado is a cooperative publishing enterprise supported,
in part, by Adams State College, Colorado State University, Fort Lewis College,
Metropolitan State College of Denver, Regis University, University of Colorado,
University of Northern Colorado, Utah State University, and Western State College of
Colorado.

ISBN: 978-0-87421-980-7 (paper)
ISBN: 978-0-87421-997-5 (e-book)

Library of Congress Cataloging-in-Publication Data

Names: Bennion, Janet, 1964– I Joffe, Lisa Fishbayn.
Title: The polygamy question / edited by Janet Bennion, Lisa Fishbayn Joffe.
Description: Logan : Utah State University Press, [2015]
Identifiers: LCCN 2015000659I ISBN 9780874219807 (pbk.) I ISBN 9780874219975
   (ebook)
Subjects: LCSH: Polygamy. I Polygamy—Religious aspects.
Classification: LCC HQ981 .P654 2015 I DDC 204/.41—dc23

LC record available at http://lccn.loc.gov/2015000659

Contents

The Polygamy Question

INTRODUCTION

Janet Bennion and Lisa Fishbayn Joffe

PLURAL MARRIAGE AND MARRIAGE PLURALISM

Polygamy is tolerated to some degree by almost half of the world's societies. It is practiced by only 2 percent of North Americans from a range of religious and national backgrounds. Some participants in polygamous marriages have immigrated to North America from countries where such marriage is permitted and recognized under the law. Others are members of local fundamentalist Mormon religious sects, which practice polygamy outside the bounds of secular law. However, questions regarding the legal and ethical permissibility of plural marriage occupy a disproportionately large space in the public and legal imagination. This collection seeks to trace the genealogy of contemporary interest in the institution of polygamous marriage, explore arguments for and against its recognition under North American legal systems, and consider how such recognition might operate in practice.

The term *polygamy* is a gender-neutral one that denotes a state of marriage to many spouses. Polyandry, marriage of one woman to multiple husbands, is uncommon. While it may have been more widespread in hunter-gatherer societies, contemporary polyandry is practiced by a relatively small number of groups living in harsh environments. Brothers may share a wife to prevent a family's land from being subdivided between families into units too small to support them. A man may nominate a brother to be a second husband to protect his wife during a long absence. Polyandry rarely comes about through the choice of the wife (Starkweather and Hames 2012).

Though we use "polygamy" throughout this volume, we are referring to "polygyny," where one man is married to several women. Polygyny dates back to the initial practice of shifting horticulture in sub-Saharan Africa in order to maximize fertility and produce young dependent males (Goody 1976, 27–29). In 1970, Esther Boserup suggested polygyny's true purpose was for men to be able to monopolize women's productive labors and the children they bore (Boserup 1970). The biblical

DOI: 10.7330/9780874219975.c000

patriarchs practiced polygamy, and Jewish law permitted it. It was abolished for Ashkenazi Jews in the eleventh century but persisted as a permitted, if frowned upon, alternative for Sephardic Jews into the modern era (Goldfeder 2016). Classical Chinese and ancient Roman societies all once embraced polygamy. It was also encountered sporadically among Native Americans and in the West African continent, Polynesia, India, and ancient Greece. In North America—both Canada and the United States—polygamy emerged in both Native American and Mormon contexts, with recent Muslim immigrant and convert societies adding to these numbers.

The history of Mormon polygamy in the United States is a short but eventful one that offers a unique perspective on its appeal to adherents and the anxieties it raises among outsiders. Mormonism is a young religion, founded in the United States in the 1820s. In 1852, Brigham Young, leader of the Mormon church (Church of Jesus Christ of Latter Day Saints, or LDS church), revealed the practice of plural marriage as a Mormon doctrine. When Mormons received the revelation regarding polygamy, its supporters argued that while monogamy was associated with societal ills such as infidelity and prostitution, polygamy could meet the need for sexual outlets outside marriage for men in a more benign way (Gordon 2001). Politicians in Washington did not welcome this innovation. In 1856, the platform of the newly founded Republican Party committed the party to prohibit the "twin relics of barbarism," polygamy and slavery. In 1862, the federal government outlawed polygamy in the territories through passage of the Morrill Anti-Bigamy Act. Mormons, who were the majority residents of the Utah territory, ignored the act.

However, prosecutions for polygamy proved difficult because evidence of unregistered plural marriages was scarce. However, in 1887, the Edmunds-Tucker Act made polygamy a felony offense and permitted prosecution based on mere cohabitation. The spouses did not need to go through any ceremony to be accused of polygamy. Scores of polygamists, including Bennion's ancestors, Angus Cannon and his brother George Q. Cannon, were each sentenced to six months in prison in 1889. The final blow to the viability of nineteenth-century Mormon polygamy came that same year when Congress dissolved the corporation of the Mormon church and confiscated most of its property. Within two years, the government also denied the church's right to be a protected religious body. This policy of removal of church resources meant that polygamous families with limited funding had to abandon extra wives who had been deemed illegal under the Edmunds Act. This abandonment created a large group of single and impoverished polygamous women who were no longer tied to their husbands religiously or economically. As a result of the pressures brought on by the Edmunds-Tucker Act, the LDS church renounced the practice of polygamy in 1890 with church president Wilford Woodruff's manifesto. Utah was admitted into the Union in 1896.

At the beginning of the twentieth century, the legal status of polygamy in Utah was still not clear. In 1904, the US Senate held a series of hearings after LDS apostle Reed Smoot was elected as a senator from Utah. The controversy centered on whether or not the LDS church secretly supported plural marriage. In 1905, the LDS church issued a second manifesto that confirmed the church's renunciation of the practice, which helped Smoot keep his senate seat. Yet the hearings continued until 1907, the Senate majority still interested in punishing Smoot for his association with the Mormon church. By 1910, Mormon leadership began excommunicating those who formed new polygamous alliances, targeting underground plural movements. From 1929 to 1933, Mormon fundamentalist leadership refused to stop practicing polygamy and was subject to arrest and disenfranchisement. In 1935, the Utah legislature elevated the crime of unlawful cohabitation from a misdemeanor to a felony. That same year, Utah and Arizona law enforcement raided the polygamous settlement at Short Creek after allegations of polygamy and sex trafficking.

In 1944, fifteen Utah fundamentalist men and nine of their wives were arrested on charges of bigamy and jailed in Sugarhouse, Salt Lake City. Then, in 1953, officials again raided Short Creek and removed 263 children from their parents in Arizona and Utah. Two years later the Utah Supreme Court held in *Utah v. Black* that a polygamous family was an immoral environment for rearing children because of the parents' practice and advocacy of plural marriage, upholding the decision of the Juvenile Court to remove children from polygamous families (Smith 2011).

After the 1953 raid on Short Creek and the hostile public reaction to images of children forcibly removed from their parents, most polygamists went underground or fled to Mexico or Canada. However, many stayed in the United States and sought to practice their religious beliefs in the open. For the most part, the police did not enforce the antipolygamy law. Although state courts occasionally convicted individuals of polygamy, in the last fifty years, government officials have more often focused on other crimes committed by polygamists, such as child abuse, statutory rape, welfare fraud, and incest. The official position of the Utah attorney general's office was not to pursue cases of bigamy between consenting adults. This tolerant approach is exemplified by the 1991 case, *In the Matter of the Adoption of W. A. T., et al.*, in which the Utah Supreme Court ruled that a polygamous family could adopt children, essentially reversing *Utah v. Black*. In spite of this era of relative tolerance, in April 2008 the state of Texas raided the Eldorado FLDS (Fundamentalist LDS) compound, removing 460 children from their families based on accusations of child abuse. A subsequent investigation found that one-quarter of girls between age twelve and fifteen residing in the compound had been entered into spiritual marriages, and some had given birth to children. Twelve men were prosecuted for sexual assault on children as a result. This case also resulted in a public backlash based on the removal of young children from their parents' custody for extended periods during the investigation.

Currently, most American polygamists—numbering approximately 40,000 to 50,000—are associated with fundamentalist Mormonism. These can be sorted into four groups: the Fundamentalist Latter-Day Saints and three groups named for their dominant families—the Allreds, the LeBarons, and the Kingstons. It is difficult to assess how many immigrants from countries that recognize polygamy live in the United States in polygamous families. Estimates for Muslims alone range from 50,000 to 100,000 people (Hagerty 2008). This would bring the total number of possible polygamists in the United States to approximately 50,000 to 150,000.[1]

Like mainstream Mormons, fundamentalists believe that God is a mortal man who has become exalted and that if they are worthy, they too will become gods and goddesses of their own worlds. Yet, unlike the mainstream Mormon church, fundamentalists still practice polygamy, which they believe will offset the imbalance in sex ratios related to the abundance of religious women and the dearth of good men, as recorded in Isaiah 4. They see it as not only a direct commandment of God but as a catch-all solution for prostitution, infidelity, homosexuality, spinsterhood, and childlessness.

LEGAL AND SOCIAL HISTORY

The practice of polygamy occupies a unique place in American history, with surprising resonance for other Anglo-American legal systems. Mormon polygamy, the product of a small home-grown religious faith, has disproportionately affected legal and social history. *Reynolds v. US* (1879), a central judgment in American constitutional law, interprets the First Amendment to protect freedom of religious belief but not of religiously motivated actions. The ruling was prompted by a challenge to a bigamy conviction by Mr. Reynolds, a Mormon who had argued that his faith required him to take multiple wives. Chief Justice M. R. Waite, a founder of the Republican Party, said of polygamy, "To permit this would make the professed doctrines of religious belief superior to the law of the land, and in effect to permit every citizen to become a law unto himself . . . government could exist only in name under such circumstances" (Reynolds v. US).[2]

The classic definition of marriage in English law as "a voluntary union for life of one man and one woman to the exclusion of all others" in *Hyde v. Hyde* (1886) was prompted by an attempt by a polygamous spouse who had married in Utah to seek a divorce in the United Kingdom.[3] The English court refused to accept jurisdiction, holding that a polygamous marriage could not be recognized as a valid marriage. While recent debates in the United Kingdom over the recognition of same-sex marriage have emphasized reading this clause as "one *man* and one *woman*," the statement was originally drafted to emphasize *only one* man and *only one* woman.

The nineteenth-century precursors to the provisions of the Criminal Code of Canada which prohibit polygamy, recently at issue in the British Columbia Polygamy Reference (Reference re: Section 293 of the Criminal Code of Canada), were passed to ward off the possibility that Mormon polygamists, subject to persecution for their practices in the United States, might seek refuge to practice them in Canada.[4] Canada's Parliament returned to the issue of polygamous immigrants in 2015 with passage of the Zero Tolerance for Barbaric Practices Act, which bans them from entry into Canada and allows for their deportation if they engage in polygamy while residing there. When the US government began its assault on polygamy in 1887, a small community of members of the Mormon church fled to Canada. They sought permission from Parliament in 1888 to bring their plural wives with them. The Canadian government refused and in 1890 passed its first legislation against plural marriage. The law sought to convict Mormons "on the basis of cohabitation, attacking the Mormons' private ceremonies" (Macintosh, Herbst, and Dickson 2009).[5]

The regulation of Mormon polygamy and its implications for the definition of marriage in Utah continue to roil political and legal waters today. In December 2013, the United States District Court in Utah struck down a provision of Utah's bigamy law that made it an offense for a legally married person not only to purport to marry a second spouse but also to cohabit with someone in a marriage-like relationship (Brown v. Buhman).[6] A week later, a different judge of the same court struck down an amendment to the Utah state constitution that prohibited the recognition of same-sex marriage as a violation of the Fourteenth Amendment due process rights of same-sex couples (Kitchen v. Herbert).[7] Both judgments emphasized that the state required compelling reasons to refuse recognition to the marriage choices of its citizens.

For centuries, polygamy has played a role in the public imagination as metaphor and catalyst for discussing other challenging marital practices. Indeed, the history of regulation of polygamy evokes legacies of religious and cultural intolerance. The court in *Brown v. Buhman*, for example, found that Utah's prohibition was rooted in orientalist racism. The social harm it protected against was introducing a practice perceived to be characteristic of non-European people—or non-White races—into white society because it is "almost exclusively a feature of the life of Asiatic and of African people" that had been adopted by Mormons.[8]

Justice Antonin Scalia of the United States Supreme Court warned in his dissent in *Lawrence v. Texas* that decriminalization of homosexual practices and the recognition of same-sex marriage have now put America on a slippery slope toward affirming polygamy (Lawrence v. Texas).[9] It would appear, based on the recent decision in *Brown v. Buhman*, that he might be right. The time has therefore come to determine what sort of impact such recognition might have. To what extent would the decriminalization of plural marriage endanger the values that underlie traditional American heteronormative marriage? Which of these values deserve to be perpetuated? Further, if plural marriage is decriminalized, what would be the relative costs to women and children, and society as a whole?

Scholars have come at the question of the relative benefits and harms of polygamy in different ways. Some look at the reasons women give for entering into polygamy. Anthropologists Robin Fox (1993) and Phil Kilbride (1994) were both interested in showing the benefits polygamy offers in solving the crises of American modernity; they emphasized how women might choose alternative family forms as a way to cope with the socioeconomic obstacles they confront. Kilbride applauded the adaptive measures of polygamists that help them share resources and provide protection from the harsh realities of urban life. For Mormon women not born into polygamy, it is considered a last resort for those facing poverty or limited marital prospects after having been abandoned by their husbands or if they are unable to find a mate. Female converts in the Montana Allredite order are attracted to the commune because of the socioeconomic support it offers, replacing a rather difficult life in the mainstream where their status as divorcees, single mothers, widows, and "unmarriageables" limits their access to good men and the economic and spiritual affirmation that comes from a community of worship (Bennion 1998). Women may choose polygamy when resource inequalities among men are more pronounced, when they perceive being the subsequent wife of a wealthy/good man to be better than being the only wife of a "rogue" male (Kanazawa and Still 1999). Women in some polygamous communities hold positions of independent religious or political power in the community. They can raise their children with minimal oversight by their husband, manage their household, and work in the all-important female support networks. Finally, Mormon fundamentalism balances the deprivations and difficulties of the lives of polygamous wives with a promise of an afterlife as "queens and priestesses." Polygamous women enjoy autonomy and freedoms associated with the multifaceted ties established between married women of the same patriarchal kingdoms. For example, women may unite in opposition to a husband who "gets out of line." Women have a greater chance of halting or changing the behavior of males by expressing their dissatisfaction collectively (Forbes 2003). When women are isolated, the need for a strong female support network becomes increasingly significant. Furthermore, as Bennion's research indicates, when this network is present, it may be more difficult for abuse to go unnoticed as community members are more likely to be engaged in and aware of daily events in the lives of their peers (Bennion 1998). These networks also provide women with a protective emotional and financial safety net that reduces the need for women to rely exclusively on their husbands for these resources.

Women may also find emotional and economic sustenance in their relationships with their sister wives. Patricia Dixon-Spear challenges us to rethink plural marriage as a vehicle for coping with the shortage of good men and fostering a "womanist ethic of care for sisters" (Dixon-Spear 2009). This ethic of care is especially vital during the prolonged absences of husbands when women must work together to create a large co-op of domestic and mechanical skills as well as childcare for the children of women who work. It reduces the number of hours per day that women labor, contributing to increased leisure and contentment; it alleviates anxieties, providing a mechanism for support in times of illness or hardship; and it mediates disputes. Women develop a strong interdependence with each other and, in doing so, create a large repertoire of domestic and mechanical skills. By contrast, monogamous women may not experience this type of shared skill set, especially if they are isolated from their friends, sisters, or community networks. Polygamous women also say that they value being surrounded by women in an environment where emotions are not suppressed, as they perceive them to be among men, and that they can escape from the demands of their husband in ways a monogamous woman cannot.

Assuming the marriage is otherwise tolerable, polygamy has also been offered as an alternative to divorce and may—in some instances—lead to greater stability in the marital relationship. Anastasia Gage-Brandon, who did research on polygamous marriages in Nigeria in the late 1980s and early 1990s, found that marriages involving two wives were the most stable unions and were much less likely to end in divorce than both marriages involving more than two wives and monogamous unions (Gage-Brandon 1992). In addition to these potential benefits, polygamy may enhance family life by providing a greater number of loving parents for children and a wider range of supportive siblings (Jankowiak and Diderich 2000).

Harmful behaviors are present within some polygamous groups, but the causation is unclear. Many scholars highlight a correlation between polygamy and attitudes of male supremacy in Mormon and Muslim fundamentalist households (Jankowiak and Allen 1995). Among some fundamentalist Mormons, a duty of adoration of the father is supported by a strict code that requires obedience from all children and wives. The punishment for breaking this code is known as the *blood atonement*, corporal punishment through whipping or cutting of the skin to atone for the sins against the father. Male supremacy or dominance stifles female decision making and autonomy and creates an environment of alienation, ridicule, and, possibly, battery. The husbands in such households insist on restricting the ability of females to travel, pursue an education, or even go to a hospital for medical care. This mistreatment of women is not necessarily a factor of polygamy itself but rather a manifestation of the husbands' extreme fundamentalist beliefs. These men abuse their priesthood powers and present themselves as the sole guardians of the family's spiritual welfare. Studies of polygamous Muslim households have also linked abuse and unequal treatment to extreme patriarchal beliefs. In Dena Hassouneh-Phillips's examination of US Muslim women who were victims of abuse, the majority of participants reported that their husbands' "misuse" of polygamy rather than polygamy itself constituted the abuse and that this abuse occurred when their husbands "strayed from Islamic dictates in their pursuit of other wives" (Hassouneh-Phillips 2001). Similarly, the majority of participants expressed a belief that the unjust treatment of wives, not polygamy itself, was abusive and emotionally destructive to women.

The criminalization of polygamy does not resolve this abuse; rather, it leads to families "often practicing polygamy clandestinely and inconspicuously," creating the potential for loss of perspective and abuse within the group (Campbell et al. 2005). The conditions under which polygamy is practiced in North America may, in fact, allow domestic violence to thrive. Abusers may deliberately choose to settle in remote places in order to maintain control over their victims without being observed, and women in such isolated locations are unable to leave the community easily. It is also important to note that the correlation between isolation and abuse is not limited to polygamous family relationships. Examples of abuse within monogamous relationships related to isolation have been found in northern Maine, the state with the highest rate of sexual abuse in the United States, and remote areas of midwestern states (Keller 2006).

Underage girls may be subjected to coercion to enter into polygamy in FLDS communities. Should a girl refuse, she is told she could jeopardize her salvation and let the whole community down as well as lose financial and social security. She is encouraged to have as many children as possible and to get pregnant very soon after marriage. Forcing a fifteen-year-old into a "spiritual union" with an older male is statutory rape of a minor incapable of giving valid consent to sexual activity. In some groups, a plural wife is apt to lack a high-school diploma because of her early motherhood. She is also likely to have little or no financial support from a husband who has other families as well and to be surviving economically only through the formal assistance of the church and informal support networks of sister wives and other plural wives in similar situations. She may well lose these critical sources of support if she seriously reconsiders plural marriage and has no connections outside the isolated community that makes plural marriage "its defining ideology and practice" (Strassberg 2010). Having many children of her own may make her feel that she cannot escape the group, especially without independent socioeconomic resources to help her obtain a divorce, custody of her children, and child-support payments from the biological father. In extreme cases, if a woman does have the courage to try to leave an abusive situation, she knows she may have to leave her children behind under fundamentalist religious doctrine.

Even women who claim to support polygamy may be harmed by it. Alean Al-Krenawi's study of Bedouin women (Slonim-Nevo and Al-Krenawi 2006) raises additional questions about wife order, differential treatment, and mental stability. He sought to compare how satisfied "senior wives" (the first wives in polygamous marriages) and women in monogamous marriages were in the West Bank, Palestine. Al-Krenawi found significant differences with regard to family functioning, marital satisfaction, self-esteem, and life satisfaction. Though the senior wives approved of polygamy over monogamy, they expressed more psychological problems than their monogamous counterparts.

The contributions to this volume come from multiple disciplines, including anthropology, sociology, women's studies, history, and law, and they focus on two related issues. The first defines both the harms and benefits of polygamy. The second key issue flows from the first. If the alleged harms of polygamy stem from the institution itself in all its instantiations, how could it be regulated by the state? If there are forms of polygamy that respect or even enhance the possibilities for a satisfying life for its participants, could the practices of these groups be separated from abusive forms of polygamy through regulating subsets of abusive behavior rather than the practice of polygamy itself? Should this regulation take place through refusal to recognize polygamous marriages as having any legal effect, through regulating the processes for entry into and dissolution of polygamous marriages, or through criminalization of such unions? The authors seek to disaggregate the diverse forms of polygamy practiced in North America and to chart the variable impacts these models of polygamy have on men, women, and children—whether they are independent individuals or members of relatively coherent fundamentalist communities.

The first section begins with two related pieces by Sarah Song and Lori Beaman. They both trace how the characterization of North American polygamy has, and has not, changed over the last century. In "Polygamy in Nineteenth Century America," Song explains how the nineteenth-century anti-Mormon critique of polygamy protected patriarchy while shielding monogamy from similar criticisms. She posits that opposition to polygamy was a sort of smokescreen for opposition to the political power of the church in Utah. She concludes that the movement against Mormon polygamy was not only concerned with its overt objective to protect women's rights but also with upholding Christian-model monogamy and its associated patriarchal public morals. The threat that Mormon polygamy was seen to pose to monogamous marriage and to Christian civilization itself was heightened by Mormon reforms allowing for easy divorce and for women's suffrage in Utah. In actuality, polygamy served as a handy foil, deflecting attention from the bigger concern of political elites in the nation's capital: the growing political and economic power of the Mormon church. While antipolygamists stressed the importance of saving vulnerable women from the insults of barbaric oriental practices, they also succeeded in holding off a state in which the granting of suffrage to polygamous women would mean polygamy's perpetuation.

In "Opposing Polygamy: A Matter of Equality or Patriarchy?," Lori Beaman analyzes another more recent antipolygamy narrative involving the 2010 British Columbia Polygamy Reference. The Canadian province of British Columbia was grappling with the question of whether to prosecute members of the Bountiful FLDS polygamist community for the crime of polygamy. While there was a criminal law on the books, the province had been reluctant to bring prosecutions for fear that the law would be struck down as unconstitutional. The government sent a reference to the British Columbia Supreme Court, asking them for an opinion on how the law should be interpreted and whether it was permissible to enforce it under the Canadian Constitution. While some women currently residing in Bountiful, and various other groups, filed affidavits testifying to their agency in choosing polygamy, their voices were balanced by those of women who had left the community and rejected polygamy. The court heard extensive testimony from scholars and activists on the nature and extent of harms that might correlate with polygamy. In an exhaustive review of the literature across a range of disciplines, the court concluded that polygamy correlated with harms to women's equality, to the well-being of children in polygamous families and communities, and to the nation as a whole. Polygamy was linked with rises in crime and antisocial behavior by men excluded from marriage, pressure on women to enter into underage marriage, an emphasis on patriarchal control over women and children, which manifested in increased rates of domestic violence and poor maternal and child health, and reduced paternal investment in the well-being of their children as they diverted their resources to acquiring new brides.[10] On this basis, the court decided that the provisions of the Criminal Code of Canada that render polygamy illegal do not violate the Canadian Charter of Rights and Freedoms. While the religious freedom of polygamists was indeed violated by the criminal prohibition, this limitation was justified in order to achieve the public-policy objectives of avoiding the harms associated with it.

Beaman reads the decision through a skeptical lens. She argues that certain ways of imagining polygamy allow policymakers, lawmakers, and others to displace the inequality of women onto the institution of polygamy and behave as though women's equality has been reached in monogamous society. Beaman cautions that contemporary campaigns against polygamy may also be motivated by a desire to demonize the patriarchal practices of the illiberal other while failing to interrogate those of the dominant culture. While not arguing in favor of polygamy per se, she urges a more nuanced and self-conscious examination of the contrasts between polygamy and monogamy that does not take for granted that monogamous family forms are always better for women. A commitment to multicultural toleration entails taking seriously the claims of women within illiberal minority groups, acknowledging that they are capable of meaningfully choosing to commit themselves to a way of life beyond the mainstream.

In Janet Bennion's essay, "The Variable Impact of Mormon Polygamy on Women and Children," she examines factors contributing to well- and poor-functioning polygyny among four Mormon fundamentalist groups in the Intermountain West. Using an ethnographic approach, Bennion asserts that it is the combination of several key variables that contributes to poor-functioning polygamy: (1) illegality, (2) geographic isolation, (3) socio-economic inequality, (4) male supremacy, (5) economic deprivation, (6) absence of female networking, and (7) the presence of sexual, physical, and emotional abuse.

In Debra Majeed's essay, "Ethics of Sisterhood: African American Muslim Women and Polygyny," she too explores why some women might choose polygamy. She demonstrates how African American Muslim women in the Chicago area are drawn to polygamist marriages to cope with a perceived severe shortage of eligible, marriageable men within black America. Further, the higher status routinely afforded married women has led some African American Muslim women to accept plural marriage to obtain resources and prestige. This essay traces how women's agency, exegesis of the Qur'an, and demographic conditions affect how African American Muslims practice polygyny.

Polygamy has been practiced across a range of cultural and religious traditions from time immemorial. Contemporary polygamy in North America involves both immigrants from countries where polygamy is legally recognized and Americans who convert or are born into such societies. In addition to moral objections rooted in religious doctrine and tradition, some theorists develop ethical objections to polygamy based on its failure to generate conditions for autonomy for all its members. If the toleration of minority cultural practices is justified based on their capacity to contribute to the exercise of autonomy by their members, then the practices of groups designed to extinguish the capacity for autonomy in girls and women are problematic.

In "An Economist's Perspective on Polygyny," Shoshana Grossbard writes about the negative economic impact of polygyny. She relies on two assumptions: (1) marriage is an institution that organizes household production, such production including giving birth, raising children, homemaking, and many more activities, and (2) marriage markets exist. Because of the high value of women in marriage markets in polygamous societies, men's incentives to control women by way of political and religious institutions, such as early arranged marriages, will increase. Her primary argument is that polygamy is bad for women because marriage markets are not, in fact, free because the men who institute and control polygyny institute corresponding limitations on women's freedom to exploit the increased value of women under polygyny. Moreover, Grossbard argues, polygynous societies, sometimes implicitly, recognize that polygamy harms women because they institute ways to limit those harms. Grossbard concludes by outlining the parameters for experiments in polygamous marriage that might comport with a commitment to women's freedom to negotiate entry, exit, and the terms of such marriages. Nineteenth-century Mormon women did not have equal input into legal processes, but they did publicly defend and advocate polygamy in a number of different and compelling ways. They participated at least as much as men, if not more, in the public defense of polygamy, and it seems at least possible that they had equal influence in legal processes and may have approved of plural marriage for religious reasons. It is unclear whether modern polygynous women have the same level of participation and advocacy.

Rose McDermott, a political scientist and expert witness in the Polygamy Reference, presents another opposing view of polygamy with her colleague, Jonathan Cowden. She testified about the negative effects of polygamy on the well-being of women and children, and the court mentioned her work as central to its decision. In their piece for this volume, "The Effect of Polygyny on Women, Children, and the State," the authors argue that such violence and suppression of basic rights can be "potentiated by a number of factors, including patriarchy, pastoralism, patri-locality and polygyny" (118). These features of the social structure enhance male control over women and children in ways that allow and encourage "violence and suppression of political rights and liberties" (118). As polygamy increases, the lives of women and children and the associated features of family life will all worsen. In particular, the marriage age of women will decline, the rate of maternal mortality will increase, life expectancy will decrease, and the birthrate will increase. They note that polygamy's effect on children will be devastating, especially at the secondary level.

Given the factors that lead women to choose polygamy and the dangers it poses, do the harms warrant continued *criminalization*? If there are forms of polygamy that are perceived to respect or even enhance the possibilities for a satisfying life for its participants, is it possible to isolate and regulate abusive behavior rather than the practice of polygamy itself? Should this regulation take place through *decriminalization*, in which the state merely tolerates polygamy but refuses to recognize polygamous marriages as having any legal effect, or through *legal recognition* of polygamy as a form of legal marriage in which the state takes responsibility for regulating the processes for entry into and dissolution of polygamous marriages?

Criminal prosecutions of polygamy itself are difficult for both ideological and practical reasons. The obstacles to effective prosecution are well known: (1) family members may be reluctant to testify against each other; (2) children raised in fundamentalist communities are taught to fear and distrust the law; (3) there is no paper trail for underage births or unlawful marriages; (4) it is nearly impossible to obtain accurate evidence about abuse or about which jurisdiction perpetrators should even be prosecuted in; (5) local police and doctors in fundamentalist communities often aid and abet residents engaged in criminal activity; (6) law enforcement and political officials are concerned about acting too aggressively against a practice some see as a protected religious activity, and many Mormon law-enforcement officials are simply unwilling to charge consenting adults for religious beliefs their Mormon ancestors shared; and (7) busy prosecutors place greater focus on more serious offenses, ignoring polygamy (Duncan 2008).

Several of the essays in this volume are devoted to parsing the evidence weighed by the BC Supreme Court and evaluating the decision and its implications. In her chapter, "Testing the Limits of Religious Freedom: The Case of Polygamy's Criminalization in Canada," Melanie Heath analyzes the discourse used by the judge in the case. She writes that the opinion places disproportionate emphasis on the nature of harms associated with polygamy and insufficient emphasis on claims, lodged by men and women, that polygamy allowed them to pursue their own religiously based conception of a good life. Heath's main argument here is that the court's discussion of the harm of polygyny obscures its ability to consider religious freedom and the right to familial and sexual intimacy.

In "Distinguishing Polygyny and Polyfidelity under Criminal Law," Maura Strassberg argues in favor of continuing criminal prohibition, although in a more tailored way. She writes that Mormon fundamentalist polygamy operates in a tyrannical, patriarchal fashion that seeks to eliminate a capacity for independent thought and actions in girls and boys in the community. Plural marriage thus renders community members unfit for participation in civic discourse. Polygyny not only fails to produce critical building blocks of liberal democracy, such as autonomous individuality, robust public and private spheres, and affirmative reconciliation of individuality and social existence, but promotes a despotic state populated by subjects rather than citizens. Strassberg argues that polygamy should be criminalized in order to protect both the individuals involved and the broader society.

In Song's second essay in this collection, "Polygamy Today: A Case for Qualified Recognition," she expresses concern that the mere regulation of polygamy may serve to undermine the equality struggles of women. She also justifies state involvement in order to ensure women autonomy in entry into and exit from the marital bond. Women (and men) are free to exit monogamous relationships, but they are less free to exit polygamous ones, perhaps because of social censure in their communities.

In "Should Polygamy Be a Crime?" Martha Bailey argues against criminalization because the liberal state ought not to intrude into the bedrooms of the nation by imposing criminal sanctions for private, non-commercial sexual activity among consenting adults. She argues also for consistency, as the state does not regulate a range of other distasteful intimacies, such as incest between adults. She also contends that most misconduct will be caught by other criminal laws, not by the ban on polygamy. When polygamy is criminalized, female victims of abuse may be less likely to report their status because they are afraid of being charged or that they will jeopardize the welfare of their entire family with the threat of criminal charges. In this way, a prohibition, which is designed to protect women from abuse may, in fact, put them at greater risk. Criminalizing polygamy is not an effective way to address the harms of certain forms of polygamy to women and children.

Finally, in "(Mis)Recognizing Polygamy," Kerri Abrams asks us to step away from the moral questions involved in regulating polygamy to consider the practical ones. What would such recognition entail in terms of distributing the sorts of social welfare benefits we currently distribute through the family? Would we really be comfortable with the intensity of regulation necessary to ensure fair treatment within polygamous families? The modern state now regulates domestic violence within ongoing families, but traditional forms of marriage regulation have allowed the state to intervene to divide assets and enforce support only after marriages have broken down. Given that polygamous families may have a more fluid and continuing mobility among spouses, this might make government oversight a regular part of polygamous life. For example, South African laws recognizing polygamy require that first wives give their written consent to the husband's marriage to a subsequent wife (Stacey and Meadow 2009). A recent Constitutional Court case held that failure to secure the informed consent of the first wife renders second marriages invalid (Mayelane v. Ngwenyama).[11] Abrams contrasts the merits of an approach that seeks to base welfare entitlements on family relationships with one that simply allows a polygamous spouse to select one family member to receive these benefits. In sum, Abrams's chapter urges readers to consider the ways that legal recognition of polygamy may not be the best solution for those seeking an alternative to the criminalization of plural marriage.

Contemporary modes for regulating polygamy need to be rethought in light of changing demographics, changing mores, and changing legal norms. Laws against polygamy have been called into question on constitutional grounds in both Canada and the United States. The challenge to the Utah criminal law against polygamy in *Brown v. Buhman* was brought by Kody Brown and his four wives, featured performers in the reality television program *Sister Wives*, who felt they had been threatened with prosecution because they had openly extolled the virtues of their polygamous lifestyle. Only Kody and his first wife, Meri, are legally married. The "marriages" between Kody and Janelle, Christine, and Robyn were created through religious rituals only. The court found that this law had initially been drafted to prevent Mormons' polygamous common-law marriages from gaining recognition as legal marriages, a possibility that ceased to exist when Utah abolished common-law marriage in 1898. To continue to use the law to prosecute Mormon fundamentalist polygamists like the Browns who entered into purely religious marriages without any pretense that they were valid legal marriages violated these polygamists' rights to due process under the Fourteenth Amendment and religious freedom under the First. Moreover, the state could not point to a good reason to punish religiously motivated intimacy with multiple partners while making no attempt to regulate adultery motivated by more banal desires.

In the twenty-first century, more progressive forms of plural marriage are emerging, causing many to reexamine the merits of a ban on polygamy. As the *Brown* case shows, openly polygamous families may be encouraging a social shift in society in favor of toleration and decriminalization of polygamy. Primetime television has played no small part in this normative transformation. The drama *Big Love*, which ran on HBO from 2006 to 2011, presented the fictional relationships of the Henrickson family, consisting of one husband, three wives, and their children, with sensitivity and humor. Reality television shows like *Sister Wives* and *Polygamy, USA* may seek to titillate with the details of polygamous family formation and family management among Mormon fundamentalists, but these programs also operate to normalize the polygamous unit, showing seemingly happy, thriving, and relatively self-aware families with little apparent abuse or underage marriage. Viewers are presented with images of a variety of forms of polygamy, including those depicting women as the decision makers who operate in the public sphere with careers and political ambitions and seek to redefine their roles within their religion and within the family. This volume provides multinational, multidisciplinary scholarship on the pros and cons of legalization and the complexities of evaluating polygamy as a workable form of marriage in this new and changing landscape.

Notes

1. Reporting actual number of individuals and families that live a polygamous lifestyle is variable and unclear because standards differ in making this calculation. Do we count children and their parents? Are polyamorists included? Jonathan Turley's estimation mirrors my own estimation of 50,000. See Jonathan Turley, "Polygamy Laws Expose Our Own Hypocrisy," *USA TODAY*, Oct. 4, 2004, available at usatoday30.usatoday.com/news/opinion/columnist/2004-10-3-turley_x.htm. Samuel D. Brunson ("Taxing Polygamy," 91 WASH. U.L.REV. 113, 146 [2013]) estimates the number of polygamists as high as 150,000, though he does not specify the source of his data.
2. Hyde v. Hyde, Courts of Probate and Divorce. L.R. 1 P&D 130 (1886).
3. Reynolds v. US, US Supreme Court, 98 U.S. 145, 133 U.S. 333 (1879).
4. Reference re: Section 293 of the Criminal Code of Canada, BCSC 1588 (2011) (hereafter, Polygamy Reference).
5. Incidentally, only two polygamy convictions have taken place in Canada since 1890; *R. v. Bear's Shin Bone* (1899) 4 Terr. L.R. 173, a case involving First Nations customary law marriages, demonstrates how the law's selective use has tracked understandings of the "barbarous" nature of non-European marital forms (Drummond 2009).
6. Brown v. Buhman, US District Court, District of Utah, Central Division. (December 13, 2013).
7. Kitchen v. Herbert, United States District Court of the District of Utah, December 20, 2013, 961 F. Supp. 2d 1181 (D. Utah). For a little over two weeks, same-sex couples rushed to marry in the state. On January 6, the state attorney general won an injunction from the United States Supreme Court to prohibit same-sex marriages in the state until the case had been appealed to the Tenth Circuit Court of Appeals. Arguments in that case were set to be heard in April 2014. Utah Governor Herbert's decision to instruct the state not to recognize the 1,300 same-sex marriages performed during this period is being challenged in a lawsuit brought by the ACLU. However, the point has been rendered moot by the decision of the United States Supreme Court in Obergefell v. Hodges, June 26, 2015, which found that same sex couples are entitled to legal recognition of their marital unions.
8. *Brown*, at 20.
9. Lawrence v. Texas, 539 U.S. 558 (2003).
10. Polygamy Reference, paras. 770–93.
11. Mayelane v. Ngwenyama and Another, Case CCT 57/12, May 30, 2013, ZACC 14, paras. 770–793.

References

Bennion, Janet. 1998. *Women of Principle: Female Networking in Contemporary Mormon Polygyny.* Oxford: Oxford University Press.

Boserup, Esther. 1970. *Woman's Role in Economic Development.* London: Earthscan.

Campbell, Angela, Nicholas Bala, Katherine Duvall-Antonacopoulos, Leslie MacRae, Joanne J. Paetsch, Martha Bailey, Beverley Baines, Bita Amani, and Amy Kaufman. 2005. *Polygamy in Canada: Legal and Social Implications for Women and Children: A Collection of Policy Research Reports.* Ottawa: Status of Women Canada. http://www .vancouversun.com/pdf/polygamy_021209.pdf.

Dixon-Spear, Patricia. 2009. *We Want for Our Sisters What We Want for Ourselves: African American Women Who Practice Polygyny by Consent.* Baltimore: Black Classic.

Drummond, Susan. 2009. "Polygamy's Inscrutable Criminal Mischief." *Osgoode Hall Law Journal* 47 (2): 317–69.

Duncan, Emily. 2008. "The Positive Effects of Legalizing Polygamy: 'Love Is a Many Splendored Thing.'" *Duke Journal of Gender Law & Policy* 15: 315–337.

Forbes, Stephanie. 2003. "'Why Just Have One?': An Evaluation of the Anti-Polygamy Laws under the Establishment Clause." *Houston Law Review* 39 (5): 1517–47.

Fox, Robin. 1993. *Reproduction and Succession.* New Brunswick, NJ: Transaction.

Gage-Brandon, Anastasia J. 1992. "The Polygyny-Divorce Relationship: A Case Study of Nigeria." *Journal of Marriage and the Family* 54 (2): 285–92. http://dx.doi.org/10.2307 /353060.

Goldfeder, Mark. 2016. *Legalizing Plural Marriage.* Waltham: Brandeis University Press.

Goody, Jack. 1976. *Production and Reproduction: A Comparative Study of the Domestic Domain.* Cambridge: Cambridge University Press.

Gordon, Sarah. 2001. *The Mormon Question: Polygamy and Constitutional Conflict in Nineteenth-Century America.* Chapel Hill: University of North Carolina Press.

Hagerty, Barbara. 2008. "Some Muslims in U.S. Quietly Engage in Polygamy." *NPR,* May 27.

Hassouneh-Phillips, Dena. 2001. "Polygamy and Wife Abuse: A Qualitative Study of Muslim Women in America." *Health Care for Women International* 22 (8): 735–48. http://dx.doi.org/10.1080/073993301753339951.

Jankowiak, William, and E. Allen. 1995. "The Balance of Duty and Desire in an American Polygamous Community." In *Romantic Passion: A Universal Experience?* edited by William Jankowiak, 166–86. New York: Columbia University Press.

Jankowiak, William, and Monique Diderich. 2000. "Sibling Solidarity in a Polygamous Community in the USA." *Evolution and Human Behavior* 21 (2): 125–39. http://dx.doi .org/10.1016/S1090-5138(00)00027-1.

Kanazawa, Satoshi, and Mary C. Still. 1999. "Why Monogamy?" *Social Forces* 78 (1): 25–50. http://dx.doi.org/10.1093/sf/78.1.25.

Keller, James. 2006. "Canada Should Legalize Polygamy: Study." *CTV News,* January 13.

Kilbride, Phil. 1994. *Plural Marriage for Our Times: A Reinvented Option?* Westport, CT: Bergin and Garvey.

Macintosh, George K., Ludmilla B. Herbst, and Tim Dickson, 2009. "Opening Statement of the Amicus Addressing Breach." The Supreme Court of British Columbia, Vancouver Registry, No. S-097767, p. 7.

Slonim-Nevo, Vered, and Alean Al-Krenawi. 2006. "Success and Failure among Polygamous Families: The Experiences of Wives, Husbands, and Children." *Family Process* 45 (3): 311–30. http://dx.doi.org/10.1111/j.1545-5300.2006.00173.x.

Smith, Linda. 2011. "Child Protection Law and the FLDS Raid in Texas." In *Modern Polygamy in the United States: Historical, Cultural, and Legal Issues,* edited by Cardell Jacobson, 301–30. New York: Oxford University Press.

Stacey, Judith, and Tey Meadow. 2009. *Politics and Society.* New York: Sage.

Starkweather, Katherine E., and Raymond Hames. 2012. "A Survey of Non-Classical Polyandry." *Human Nature (Hawthorne, N.Y.)* 23 (2): 149–72. http://dx.doi.org/10.1007/s12110-012-9144-x.

Strassberg, Maura. 2010. "Why the U.S. Should Not Decriminalize Polygamy." Paper presented at the conference Polygamy, Polygyny, and Polyamory, Waltham, MA.

SECTION I

Identifying the Harms and Benefits of Polygamy

1

POLYGAMY IN NINETEENTH-CENTURY AMERICA

Sarah Song

This paper examines how critique of minority norms and practices, even by well-intentioned reformers, can divert attention from the majority culture's own inequalities, shielding them from criticism and perhaps even fueling discourses of cultural superiority within the dominant culture. Such a diversionary effect can be seen in the controversy over Mormon polygamy in nineteenth-century America as well as in contemporary debates over minority cultural practices, including arranged marriage and female circumcision within immigrant communities.[1]

The movement against Mormon polygamy provides an early example of a minority group's demand for accommodation—in this case, a demand for immunity from prosecution, an exemption from generally applicable law—and the dominant culture's overwhelmingly negative response. As one legal historian put it, the federal government pursued the campaign against polygamy with "a zeal and concentration" that was "unequalled in the annals of federal law enforcement" (Linford 1964, 312, 585). Opponents of polygamy called for federal intervention to dismantle what was widely considered a deeply patriarchal practice. Some might look approvingly at the outcome of this case, pointing to it as a model for how liberal democratic states might deal with illiberal and nondemocratic groups. What they would miss, however, is not only how such intervention failed to improve the status of Mormon women but also how condemnation of polygamy helped divert attention from the majority culture's own patriarchal norms. The focus on polygamy helped shield Christian monogamy and the traditional gender roles associated with it from criticism. It also served as a useful tool in the government's assault on what was probably its bigger concern, the political power of the Mormon church.

In this paper, I examine the politics of the American antipolygamy movement to explore the intercultural dynamic of what I call *diversion.* Antipolygamy activists gave two main arguments against polygamy: that

DOI: 10.7330/9780874219975.c001

it violated Christian public morals and that it subordinated women. While antipolygamy activists expressed genuine concern for the plight of Mormon women in polygamous marriages, they did not connect their concern for these women with a broader concern for the status of women in all marriages, which is what leading woman's-rights activists Elizabeth Cady Stanton and Susan B. Anthony sought to do.

THE RISE AND FALL OF MORMON POLYGAMY

In 1830, Joseph Smith, a New York farmer, founded the Church of Jesus Christ of Latter-Day Saints. The Book of Mormon, as translated by Smith, described the Hebrew origins of Native Americans and established America as God's chosen land. In 1843 in Nauvoo, Illinois, Smith had a revelation mandating "plural marriage," but the revelation was not made public until 1852 after the Mormons had settled in Utah.[2] While Mormon leaders began practicing plural marriage in Illinois, it was on the western frontier that the practice grew, offering a systematic alternative to Christian monogamy. Responding to what they perceived to be the increasing secularization of marriage in the dominant culture, Mormon leaders solemnized marriages without state involvement (Foster 1981, 135–36; Hardy 1992, 6). Public outrage against the practice grew. The Republican Party condemned the "twin relics of barbarism—polygamy and slavery" in its party platform of 1856 and asserted the sovereign power of Congress over the territories (Linford 1964, 312).

Efforts by Americans and by government officials to dismantle Mormon polygamy spanned from 1862 to 1890. In 1862, Congress criminalized bigamy in the territories (Morrill Anti-Bigamy Act).[3] The law proved unenforceable since Utah did not register marriages and Mormon juries would not convict polygamists. In 1874, Congress followed up with the Poland Act, which transferred jurisdiction of criminal and civil cases from probate courts in the Utah Territory, whose judges were often Mormon bishops, to federal territorial courts and gave federal judges considerable power over selection of jurors (Poland Act).[4] In 1879, the US Supreme Court upheld a bigamy conviction in *Reynolds v. US*, but the decision did not eliminate the practice since prosecutors could not easily prove plural marriage.[5] Congress followed up in 1882 by changing the name of the offense described as "bigamy" to "polygamy," which made it easier to procure polygamy convictions by criminalizing "unlawful cohabitation." It also denied polygamists the right to vote and hold public office and required a man to swear he was not a polygamist and a woman to swear she was not married to one (Edmunds Act).[6] Some Mormons who were denied the vote in the 1882 election because they refused to take the oath sued the registrar of ballots. Two years later, the US Supreme Court held that it was appropriate for Congress to make marital status "a condition of the elective franchise," adding that a sovereign power could legitimately "declare that no one but a married person shall be entitled to vote" (Murphy v. Ramsey).[7]

In 1887, Congress stepped up the assault by repealing the incorporation of the Mormon church and directing the US attorney general to expropriate its property holdings over $50,000 (Edmunds-Tucker Act).[8] The act also disenfranchised Mormon women, who had had the vote for seventeen years before that point. The Mormons resisted and continued to practice polygamy, but in 1889, the Supreme Court upheld Congress's power to dissolve and expropriate the church's property against the church's claim that it was a protected religious body.[9] Finally, in 1890, Mormon president Wilford Woodruff issued a manifesto accepting the federal prohibition of polygamy and encouraged members to refrain from contracting any further polygamous marriages.

THE ANTIPOLYGAMY MOVEMENT AND THE DIVERSIONARY EFFECT

Why did American citizens, legislators, and judges in the nineteenth century deem polygamy to be intolerable? The leading arguments against polygamy were that it offended Protestant public morals and that it was deeply patriarchal. While patriarchal power was not unique to the polygamous form of marriage, citizens and government officials targeted it because it was seen to embody an extreme form of patriarchy inconsistent with democracy. If we examine the broader social and political context in which antipolygamy activism arose, however, we see that while motivated by a desire to improve the status of Mormon women, the antipolygamy movement was also fueled by a desire to protect traditional monogamous marriage and dismantle the political power of the Mormon church. The focus on polygamy served these latter goals well by shielding monogamy from feminist criticism and gathering support for the federal attack on the political power of the Mormon church.

The broader historical context in which antipolygamy arose was a period of increasing anxiety over sexual values, family structure, and the proper role of women. Social changes in the majority culture—the spread of prostitution, the rising incidence of divorce, and lax morality of the growing cities—stirred anxieties about the preservation of Christian-model monogamy. By the time the issue of polygamy arose on the national political stage, nineteenth-century women's-rights activists had already been unsettling prevailing gender norms. As the historian Michael Grossberg has shown, by the 1840s, family reformers, fearful of utopian experiments and the demands of women's-rights activists, diagnosed a "crisis of the family" and expressed "moral panic" around the issue of marriage reform (Grossberg 1985, 10, 83). The antipolygamy movement's persistent focus on the theme of sexual perversion allowed members of the majority culture to displace its anxieties about these social changes onto subversive minorities. In addition to its subversive sexual practices, Mormonism's association with lenient divorce laws and female enfranchisement fueled fears that all three were part of a plot to undermine the traditional American family and Christian civilization itself (Davis 1960, 214, 216; Gordon 2002, 52–54; Smith 1997, 388).

Polygamy challenged the Christian concept of marital unity and the related common-law concept of coverture. In the eyes of the law, the husband and wife were one legal person represented by the husband, with the legal existence of the wife "covered" by his authority. According to the preeminent expert on common law, William Blackstone, a woman's legal identity was subsumed by her husband's upon marriage.[10] What helped soften the image of the patriarchal nature of monogamy, in contrast to polygamy, was the rising ideology of romantic conjugal love, premised on consent and focused on one person. The metaphor of "one flesh" was recast as spiritual union of the couple based on mutual love and consent, offering a gentler version of coverture (Gordon 2002, 67–68).

The patriarchal nature of polygamy was the focus of the *Reynolds* case. The court held that the establishment and free exercise clauses did not protect local difference in domestic relations. Writing for the majority, Chief Justice Morrison Waite recognized polygamy as a religious doctrine, but he argued that the First Amendment protection of religious freedom extended to belief, not action.[11] In justifying government restrictions on religious action, he did not address Mormon arguments that highlighted questions of jurisdiction and the powers of Congress over the territories, focusing instead on questions of sexual behavior and the connection between marriage structure and political structure.[12] Chief Justice Waite expressed concern for the "pure-minded women" who were the "innocent victims of this delusion" and argued for upholding Congress's proscription on polygamy on the grounds that it "leads to the patriarchal principle . . . which, when applied to large communities, fetters the people in stationary despotism, while that principle cannot long exist in connection with monogamy."[13] Such condemnation of patriarchy seems disingenuous insofar as nineteenth-century opponents of polygamy neither challenged patriarchal power within monogamy nor advocated the equality of women outside marriage. Yet, the court was genuinely concerned with the patriarchal nature of polygamy: Mormon life was seen to embody patriarchy of a nature and degree unmatched by monogamy (Rosenblum 1997, 77). Such extreme patriarchy was seen to be inconsistent with democracy. Considered against notions of romantic conjugal love that (at least in theory) promised marital unions based on consent and mutual love, polygamy was truly a form of bondage.

The court cast the conflict as between a secular state and religion and affirmed the state's civil interest in preserving monogamy. The case for the civil interest in marriage was based on the widely accepted view that marriage structure was intimately connected with political order: "Marriage, while from its very nature a sacred obligation, is nevertheless, in most civilized nations, a civil contract, and usually regulated by law. Upon it society may be said to be built, and out of its fruits spring social relations and social obligations and duties, with which government is necessarily required to deal. In fact, according as monogamous or polygamous marriages are allowed, do we find the principles on which the government of the people, to a greater or less extent, rests."[14] To buttress his claim about the state's civil interest in protecting monogamy, Chief Justice Waite drew on dominant ideas in the political thinking of his day—in particular, the claim that monogamy fostered democracy, whereas polygamy led ineluctably to despotism.

The association between monogamy and freedom, on the one hand, and polygamy and despotism, on the other, can be traced at least as far back as Montesquieu's idea that "domestic government" shaped "political government" (Montesquieu 1989, 270, 316). He also made the connection between family and political order in his 1728 epistolary novel, *Persian Letters*. Although Montesquieu's target had been the despotic elements of the French government and not non-Western cultures, his work initiated the Enlightenment association of polygamy with despotism. The harem signified coercion and despotism, whereas monogamy connoted consent and political liberty. The leading political and legal philosophers of the early-American republic contrasted monogamy with polygamy in order to illustrate the superiority of Christian morality over "oriental despotism." For example, William Paley's (1785) *The Principles of Moral and Political Philosophy*, which became the most widely read college text on the subject in the first half of the nineteenth century, acclaimed the social benefits of monogamous marriage. In contrast, polygamy, he argued, produced the evils of political distrust as well as the abasement of women. Such views linking monogamy with public order were accepted and developed by the jurist James Wilson in the 1790s and by leading antebellum legal thinkers Chancellor James Kent and Supreme Court Justice Joseph Story (Cott 2000, 22–23).

Chief Justice Waite followed in this tradition of associating polygamy with patriarchy and despotism, buttressing this claim with widespread Christian revulsion against polygamy. He combined moral revulsion with racial revulsion by drawing upon the work of Francis Lieber, a German émigré who had become one of America's most influential political scientists (Reynolds v. US).[15] Lieber hailed monogamy as the centerpiece of white Christian civilization. While Justice Waite did not go as far as Lieber in racializing polygamy, he did follow Lieber in mapping polygamy onto non-Christian and non-Western parts of the world: "Polygamy has always been odious among the northern and western nations of Europe, and, until the establishment of the Mormon Church, was almost exclusively a feature of the life of Asiatic and of African people" (Reynolds v. US; see also Gordon 2002, 142; Rosenblum 1997, 75).[16]

The *Reynolds* court reflected the antipolygamy discourse of the 1870s and 1880s, which associated polygamy with non-White and non-European peoples. Americans commonly linked polygamy to places deemed barbarous, including the "Incas of Peru," "Mohammedan countries," or "the Barbary states" (Cott 2000, 116–17). The linkage of monogamy with European culture and Whiteness had begun earlier in the discourse of Christian missionaries. Upon their return from foreign missions, Protestant missionaries supplied America with descriptions of "heathen" societies, such as India and China. Women in these societies were depicted as slaves, degraded by practices such as seraglio, polygamy, and *sati*. In contrast, American women were portrayed as having been emancipated by Christianity (Brumberg 1982, 347–71). Protestant women also organized home missions and benevolent societies to save degraded groups in America, including Native Americans, Roman Catholics, and Mormons (Iversen 1997, 104, 133–57).[17] Antipolygamists associated Mormon polygamy with Turkish harems, and anti-Mormon fiction borrowed from a popular book of the Victorian era, *The Lustful Turk* (1828) (Foster 1993, 115–32). In addition to missionary discourse, the experiences of European imperialism and theories of evolution also contributed to the discourse of "civilization," which suggested a linear path of progress from barbarism to civilization with white Europeans and Americans in the lead. The *Reynolds* court both drew upon and reinforced this discourse of racial and cultural superiority of whites over others, casting the American-born Mormon religion as foreign and "Other."

By using rhetorical questions and analogizing polygamy with human sacrifice and the Hindu tradition of *sati*, the court implied that no reasonable individual could contest the ban on polygamy. As Chief Justice Waite put it,

> Suppose one believed that human sacrifices were a necessary part of religious worship, would it be seriously contended that the civil government under which he lived could not interfere to prevent a sacrifice? Or if a wife religiously believed it was her duty to burn herself upon the funeral pile [*sic*] of her dead husband, would it be beyond the power of the civil government to prevent her carrying her belief into practice? So here, as a law of the organization of society under the exclusive dominion of the United States, it is provided that plural marriages shall not be allowed."[18]

The court saw the deeply patriarchal nature of polygamy—a monstrous practice on par with human sacrifice—as inconsistent with democratic political life, whereas monogamy was viewed as indispensable for civilized society and republican government.[19]

Yet, even as it recast a religious conflict between Christians and Mormons as a conflict between a secular state and religious individuals, the *Reynolds* court endorsed the marriage form of America's dominant religious tradition. The court's conception of marriage and its view of the connection between marriage and public order were undeniably Protestant. Chief Justice Waite drew on the theory and history of state court rulings on religion, which deemed the Christian structure and meaning of marriage as integral to the flourishing of democracy. As the chief justice himself observed, the offense of polygamy was considered an offense against Christianity. Civil courts assumed the authority formerly wielded by ecclesiastical courts, but this did not mean that religious understandings of marriage were then supplanted with secular or more ecumenical understandings. Rather, the court integrated the protection of Christian marriage into the First Amendment (Gordon 2002, 135). In subsequent cases involving the Mormons, the court's religious favoritism was more explicit: polygamy was "a return to barbarism . . . contrary to the spirit of Christianity and of the civilization which Christianity has produced in the Western world."[20] To call polygamy "a tenet of religion is to offend the common sense of mankind" (Davis v. Beason).[21]

The perceived threat of Mormon polygamy to Christian monogamy and civilization was heightened by Mormonism's association with easy divorce and woman's suffrage. On the divorce question, in 1852, the

Utah territorial legislature enacted a divorce statute that simply required the petitioner to demonstrate that he or she was "a resident or wishes to become one." In addition to this lenient residency requirement, Utah's divorce law also included an omnibus clause allowing a divorce "when it shall be made to appear to the satisfaction and conviction of the court, that the parties cannot live in peace and union together, and that their welfare requires a separation." These provisions made Utah the most permissive of any jurisdiction in America on divorce. Some scholars contend that divorce was more prevalent among nineteenth-century Mormons in Utah than in any other jurisdiction in the United States, especially when divorces in polygamous marriages (granted by ecclesiastical courts after plural marriage was made illegal in 1862) are included in the total (Campbell and Campbell 1978, 4–23; Daynes 2001, 141–59; Firmage and Mangrum 1988, 325–27; Gordon 2002, 176). Historians Lawrence Foster and Louis Kern have argued that Mormon women had the primary initiative in determining when to end a relationship, while the husband could not so easily divorce if his wife was opposed. Kern (1981, 168–69) finds that 73 percent of all divorce actions in Utah territory were taken by women and argues that divorce may have served as a means to redress the dissatisfactions of plural wives, suggesting that polygamy actually worked out as serial polyandry (see also Foster 1981, 218). Residents of other jurisdictions also took advantage of the lenient divorce laws. Divorce rates rose in the 1870s after the transcontinental railroad was completed; Utah's lenient residency standard allowed Eastern lawyers to flood local courts with divorce petitions (Gordon 2002, 176).

Antipolygamy activists found common cause with advocates of stringent divorce laws: both polygamy and divorce treated marriage as a capricious thing and threatened to destroy it. Antidivorce activists called divorce "the polygamic principle" or "polygamy on the installment plan" (Gordon 2002, 173). The mobility of the population after the Civil War undercut the ability of state governments to control the laws of marriage and divorce, and there was increasing anxiety over rising divorce rates and abandonment. Antidivorce and antipolygamy reformers joined forces in calling for a "United States marriage law," which would establish uniform marriage and divorce laws. In 1886, Republican senator George Edmunds, Congress's leading antipolygamy spokesman, attempted to get a bill through Congress that would authorize the government to collect divorce statistics as a first step toward restricting divorce (Gordon 2002, 129–30, 177; Iversen 1997, 106–7).

In addition to lenient divorce laws, the Mormon experiment with woman's suffrage heightened women's image as cultural subversives.

In 1870, the Mormon-controlled Utah territorial legislature had unani-mously approved the enfranchisement of women, including all female citizens over twenty-one and all the wives, widows, or daughters of native-born or naturalized men. These women of Utah were among the first women to vote in America, and they had the vote for seventeen years before they were disenfranchised by the Edmunds-Tucker Act (Grimes 1967, 33–40).[22] Mormon leaders seem to have endorsed woman's suf-frage largely out of desire to ensure their own political domination in Utah by "voting their wives," which doubled their constituency in the face of rapid settlement of "gentiles" (Flexner 1975, 165; Gordon 2002, 168–71; Lerner 1971, 139). In the 1870s, suffragists outside Utah also defended the enfranchisement of Mormon women on the grounds that revoking woman's suffrage would aid polygamy. The expectation here was that once women in Utah had a political voice, they would use it to unshackle themselves from polygamy. Indeed, in 1869, a congressman from Indiana had actually introduced a woman's suffrage bill to the Committee on Territories with the hope that female enfranchisement would lead to the abolition of polygamy (Kern 1981, 193).

Instead, Mormon women voted the way their husbands did and mobi-lized in defense of polygamy, and this played into the hands of those who opposed Mormon women's suffrage on the grounds that they were too degraded to exercise an independent political voice. As one observer put it, "Mormon women hold mass-meetings in Salt Lake City that are engineered by the church and assert that they are perfectly satisfied with their condition. Before the abolition of slavery the world was assured that Negroes were happy in their chains, and individual slaves may have said as much" (Gordon 1996a, 830). Even liberal Republicans sympa-thetic to woman's suffrage outside Utah distanced themselves from the issue. The *New York Times*, which had supported federal legislation to enfranchise the women of Utah, argued after the Female Suffrage Bill passed the Utah legislature that "the downfall of polygamy is too important to be imperiled by experiments in woman suffrage" (March 5, 1869). A few prosuffrage Republicans and women's-rights activists argued against revoking female enfranchisement in Utah; they asked why former polygamists should keep the right to vote while their wives lost it. A few southern Democrats, all of whom opposed woman's suf-frage as a matter of federal policy, argued that suffrage was better left to the states and territories.[23] But there was overwhelming support in favor of revocation. Moderate Republicans led the campaign, which met with little resistance in Congress. Republican senator George Edmunds, the sponsor of the bill that disenfranchised the women of Utah, expressed a widely shared sentiment that likened Mormon women to slaves, stating that revocation would "relieve the Mormon women of Utah from the slavehood of being obliged to exercise a political function which is to keep her in a state of degradation" (Gordon 2002, 168–71). The disenfranchisement bill had the support of middle-class evangelical women, who were concerned about protecting Christian-model monogamy. In 1884, Angie Newman, founder of the Woman's Home Missionary Society and a leading antipolygamy spokeswoman, drafted a petition calling for Congress to abolish woman's suffrage in Utah and obtained 250,000 signatures from among the nation's organized Christian women's groups in support of the bill (Iversen 1997, 103–7, 162–63).

Polygamy, easy divorce, and woman's suffrage were all linked in the minds of antipolygamy activists. To condemn these practices by the Mormon minority was to stand with Christian monogamy.

STANTON AND ANTHONY'S VIEWS ON POLYGAMY

Yet some women's-rights activists, including Elizabeth Cady Stanton and Susan B. Anthony, recognized that polygamy and these other "subversive" Mormon measures served as a handy foil that deflected criticism of monogamy and downplayed the limited but not inconsequential improvements in women's status brought about by Mormon-led reforms on divorce and suffrage. While the enfranchisement of women in Utah may not have been intended to advance women's rights, it had the consequence of encouraging women's political participation, especially as Congress's assault against polygamy gained momentum. Shortly after they were enfranchised, Mormon women began publishing the *Woman's Exponent*, which ran articles criticizing the inequitable treatment of women in all domains of life and defended polygamy in the name of women's rights. They also established contact with leading women's-rights activists, and by 1872, Mormon women held office in the National Woman Suffrage Association (NWSA), the suffrage organization led by Stanton and Anthony. Emmeline B. Wells, the editor of the *Woman's Exponent*, printed news of suffrage activities, and Mormon women helped gather signatures for the NWSA in support of the woman's suffrage amendment (Iversen 1997, 4–5, 28, 61).[24]

Stanton and Anthony were invited by Mormon suffragists to speak in Salt Lake City in 1871. In her lecture from the pulpit of the Mormon Tabernacle, Stanton attacked patriarchal power and the subordination of women by organized religion and argued that there was just as good a reason for polyandry as there was for polygyny. Accompanied by NWSA members, two prominent Mormon women, Emmeline B. Wells and Zina Young Williams, delivered a memorial from the House Judiciary Committee on behalf of all Mormon women, defending their practice of polygamy and asking Congress to repeal the Morrill Act of 1862. They maintained that Mormon women were contented wives and mothers and the effect of enforcing antipolygamy legislation would make 50,000 women outcasts and their children illegitimate (Iversen 1997, 25–26, 29–30). The alliance between the NWSA and Mormon women was possible in part because NWSA members questioned women's status within all forms of marriage and within all religious communities. Unlike many public officials and citizens of their day, they did not see the *form* of marriage as the key to women's emancipation, emphasizing that women were subordinated within all forms of marriage.

It is within this larger context of mainstream gender practices that Stanton and Anthony viewed the controversy over Mormon polygamy. Stanton herself distinguished among three kinds of "polygamy": Mormon polygamy, bigamy based on fraud, and polygamy involving one wife and many mistresses "everywhere practiced in the United States" (Weisbrod and Sheingorn 1978, 841). Rather than condemn Mormon polygamy and defend Christian monogamy, Stanton criticized all contracts of marriage as oppressive for women: "In entering this contract, the man gives up nothing that he before possessed—he is a man still; while the legal existence of the woman is suspended during marriage, and henceforth she is known but in and through the husband." She sought to improve women's status within marriage by arguing for greater equality within marriage and greater freedom to divorce (Stanton, Anthony, and Gage 1848–1861, 738–40).[25]

Similarly, Anthony urged suffragists to avoid "shouts of puritanic horror" against polygamy and offer a "simple, loving, sisterly clasp of hands" in order to help abolish "the whole system of woman's subjection to man in both polygamy and monogamy" (Iversen 1997, 35). As she would stress many years later, what was important was women's independence, regardless of marriage form: "What we have tried to do is to show . . . that the principle of the subjection of woman to man is the point of attack; and that woman's work in monogamy and polygamy is one and the same—that of planting her feet on the ground of self-support" (Weisbrod and Sheingorn 1978, 842). The NWSA was careful to separate support for Mormon women from support for the Mormon religion and polygamy, but it did not focus its efforts on attacking Mormon polygamy, as many middle-class evangelical women did, in part because it saw all forms of marriage as subordinating women and because Mormons had enfranchised women and provided women with greater freedom to divorce. When the federal government moved to disenfranchise the women of Utah with the Edmunds-Tucker bill, NWSA activists argued against the use of "federal power to disenfranchise the women of Utah, who have had a more just and liberal spirit shown them by Mormon men than Gentile women in the States have yet perceived in their rulers" (Stanton, Anthony, and Gage 1876–1885, 128).

Antipolygamists who sought to defend Christian monogamy in the face of attacks by women's-rights activists found a convenient diversion in Mormon polygamy. As legal historian Sarah Barringer Gordon (2002) puts it, "The popular appeal of anti-polygamy gave legislators a convenient out—here was a form of marriage that *truly* replicated 'slavery' for white women. By enacting laws to prohibit the 'enslavement of women in Utah,' congressmen could deflect attention from domestic relations in their own states and direct it toward a rebellious territory. In this sense, Utah became a handy foil" (53–54). Antipolygamists attacked what they believed to be a deeply patriarchal practice, but the focus on polygamy served the cause of those who defended Christian-model monogamy and the patriarchal roles associated with it. Both Anthony's and Stanton's remarks on Mormonism and their emphasis on women's subordination within all forms of marriage suggest that they saw through the diversionary rhetoric.

The focus on polygamy was not only a handy foil against critiques of monogamy but also a diversion from the federal government's attack on what was probably its bigger concern: the political power of the Mormon church in Utah. In contrast to other nineteenth-century American communal experiments, such as the Shakers and Oneida Perfectionists, the Mormon church had grown too politically powerful to be ignored. As President Hayes recorded in his diary in 1880, "Laws must be enacted which will take from the Mormon Church its temporal power. Mormonism as a sectarian idea is nothing, but as a system of government it is our duty to deal with it as an enemy of our institutions, and its supporters and leaders as criminals" (Hansen 1981, 144). Reverend Josiah Strong put it more colorfully: Mormonism was "an *imperium in imperio* ruled by a man who is prophet, priest, king and pope, all in one . . . he out-popes the Roman by holding familiar conversations with the Almighty, and getting, to order, new revelations direct from heaven." The real danger of Mormonism was "ecclesiastical despotism"; polygamy is "not a root, but a graft" (Strong 1981, 112–15). The Mormons were not merely a small separatist community seeking a free-exercise exemption from civil marriage laws; they challenged the political authority of the American state by claiming a right to self-government in the Utah Territory. In 1849, Mormons established an autonomous state of Deseret and envisioned a western empire in the Great Salt Lake basin of Utah that was to encompass all of Nevada and Utah and parts of California, Oregon, Arizona, New Mexico, Colorado, and Wyoming. Mormons petitioned for statehood for the Utah Territory in 1850, and when the federal government rejected it, Brigham Young, the first governor of the territory, continued to rule the territory as a theocracy. They had to accept federally appointed judges, but the Mormon-dominated legislature appointed probate judges in each county with jurisdiction over divorce, alimony, guardianship, and property cases. Children of polygamous wives were recognized and permitted to inherit property, and the courts upheld a variety of living and support arrangements for polygamous families (Foster 1981, 216–20).

Supreme Court Justice Bradley summed up the political threat of Mormonism by pointing to "the past history of the sect, to their defiance of the government authorities, to their attempt to establish an independent community, to their efforts to drive from the territory all who were not connected with them in communion and sympathy." Mormonism was more than a deviant religious group; it was also an "immense power in the Territory of Utah" which was "constantly attempting to oppose, thwart and subvert the legislation of Congress and the will of the government of the United States."[26]

Polygamy proved an effective weapon for those whose real concern was Mormon political power. As Senator Frederick T. Dubois of Idaho explained,

> Those of us who understand the situation were not nearly so much opposed to polygamy as we were to the political domination of the Church. We realized, however, that we could not make those who did not come actually in contact with it, understand what this political domination meant. We made use of polygamy in consequence as our great weapon of offence and to gain recruits to our standard. There was a universal detestation of polygamy, and inasmuch as the Mormons openly defended it we were given a very effective weapon with which to attack. (Hansen 1981, 145)

Scholars of Mormon history disagree about whether polygamy or Mormon political power was the real issue behind federal intervention.[27] What is clear is that the use of polygamy as the federal point of attack proved politically effective, not only for dismantling Mormon power but also for deflecting attention from monogamy and the patriarchal norms associated with it.

CONCLUSION

In the case of nineteenth-century Mormon polygamy, the dominant culture's opposition to polygamy appears to have been motivated less by a concern to empower women and more by a desire to uphold the gendered public morals of the dominant culture. Citizens and public officials opposing polygamy sought to protect Christian-model monogamy, and the focus on Mormon polygamy helped shield the dominant culture's own patriarchal practices from criticism.

This diversionary effect can be seen beyond the case of Mormon polygamy. Contemporary feminist critique of domestic violence and forced marriage in immigrant communities has sometimes served to reinforce a false dichotomy between oppressive minority cultures on the one hand, and egalitarian Western majority cultures on the other, deflecting attention from the reality of domestic violence and underage marriage within the latter. Marriage practices within immigrant communities should be evaluated alongside practices common to the majority culture: parental pressure over whom to marry and parent-arranged blind dates. Mainstream marriage practices should receive the same kind of scrutiny as the marriage practices of minority communities, with the issue of a woman's consent to marriage and a minimum age for all marriages at the forefront of these considerations.

As Stanton and Anthony emphasized in seeking solidarity with Mormon women in nineteenth-century America, the focus of those concerned about the rights of women should be on the entire system of women's subjection to men, within monogamous and polygamous marriage and within majority and minority cultures. A religious or cultural minority group's practices should be analyzed alongside comparable practices of the dominant culture and in the broader historical context of past reaction to such practices, lest we overlook the diversionary effects that can reinforce gender hierarchies across groups. My discussion of Mormon polygamy also suggests the need for social and political critics to guard against reproducing colonial discourses of cultural and racial superiority while voicing feminist concerns. One way to do so is to examine the particular contexts of ritual practices and the national and international discourses surrounding them, with special attention to the power inequalities among the groups involved.

Notes

1.   This paper was originally published as "Polygamy in America" in *Justice, Gender, and the Politics of Multiculturalism*, 142–68. Permission granted by Adam Hirschberg,

Cambridge University Press, October 2013. For discussion of the contemporary cases, see chapter 9 of this volume.

2. The revelation, as dictated by Smith, endorsed polygyny and implies a restriction on polyandry: "If any man espouse a virgin, and desire to espouse another, and the first give her consent, and if he espouse the second, and they are virgins, and have vowed to no other man, then he is justified: he cannot commit adultery. . . . If one or either of the ten virgins, after she is espoused, shall be with another man, she has committed adultery, and shall be destroyed; for they are given unto him to multiply and replenish the earth" (Van Wagoner 1989, 56).

3. Morrill Anti-Bigamy Act, 12 Stat. 501 (1862).

4. Poland Act, 18 Stat. 253 (1874).

5. Reynolds v. US, 98 US 145 (1879).

6. Edmunds Act, 22 Stat. 30 (1882).

7. Murphy v. Ramsey, 114 US 15 (1884), 43.

8. Edmunds-Tucker Act, 24 Stat. 635 (1887).

9. Late Corporation of the Church of Jesus Christ of Latter-day Saints (Mormon Church) v. US, 136 US 1 (1889). For further discussion of these statutes and court cases, see Linford (1964) and Sarah Barringer Gordon (2002).

10. Nineteenth-century American legal treatise writers, including James Kent and Joseph Story, sustained the importance of coverture (Basch 1982, 49, 62, 64–65).

11. *Reynolds,* at 162.

12. For a detailed account of the lawyers' arguments in the case, as well as how the *Reynolds* court drew on the jurisprudential lessons of the states in its decision, see chapter 4 of Gordon (2002).

13. *Reynolds,* at 167–69.

14. Ibid., at 165–66.

15. Ibid., at 164–66. Justice Waite found Lieber's statements on polygamy in Chancellor Kent's *Commentaries on American Law,* a treatise from the 1820s used by generations of American lawyers and judges. Lieber's (1838–1839, 1853) major works—*Manual of Political Ethics, Designed Chiefly for the Use of Colleges and Students at Law* and *On Civil Liberty and Self-Government*—became popular college texts. Politicians and judges, including President Lincoln during the Civil War, drew on his advice, and his work was regarded as authoritative well into the 1870s and 1880s (see Cott 2000, 114–15; Weisbrod and Sheingorn 1978, 833).

16. *Reynolds,* at 164.

17. On antipolygamy discourse in the popular fiction of the day, see Gordon 1996b, 295–350.

18. *Reynolds,* at 165–66.

19. In *Murphy,* at 43, 45, the court explicitly linked monogamy with republican government. It argued that monogamy was "wholesome and necessary" to a "free, self-governing commonwealth" and that on these grounds Congress could take political power away from those who were hostile to monogamy.

20. Corporation of the Church of Jesus Christ of the Latter Day Saints v. US, 136 US 1 (1890), at 49.

21. Davis v. Beason, 133 US 333 (1890). Martha Minow has argued that the Supreme Court in the 1920s, 1960s, and 1970s used state regulation of the family as an arena for struggles between competing groups over religion, morality, and different ways of life. She points to *Reynolds v. US* as a "foreshadowing" case (Minow 1987, 962–67).

22. Both the New Jersey Constitution, written in 1776, and a New Jersey election law passed in 1790 granted the vote to all "inhabitants" who were otherwise qualified to vote, permitting property-owning women to vote. But in 1807, the state legislature

restricted the vote to "free, White male citizens," disenfranchising the women of New Jersey. After this retrenchment, women everywhere in the nation were barred from the polls (Keyssar 2000, 54; Smith, 1997, 106, 110). Wyoming was the first among the territories and states to pass a bill granting women suffrage in 1869, but women in Utah actually went to the polls first (Foster 1981, 214).

23.   Congressional Record (1885–1886), 49th Cong., 1st. Sess., v. 17, pt. 1, 406–7.

24.   The *Woman's Exponent*, which was published between 1872 and 1914, was largely managed and produced by women; it was not officially sponsored by the Mormon church. Its masthead slogan was "The Rights of the Women of Zion, The Rights of the Women of All Nations," and it criticized the unequal treatment of women in politics, education, and the professions, while defending polygamy (Foster 1981, 214–15).

25.   On Stanton's views on divorce, see Elizabeth B. Clark (1990).

26.   *Mormon Church*, at 63–64.

27.   Klaus J. Hansen (1967) argues that the theocracy established by the Mormon church was the primary concern of anti-Mormon action, whereas Lyman argues that polygamy was at the heart of the matter (see also Lyman 1986, 2–5). Gordon contends that both these views are essentially correct since polygamy and church authority were seen to be mutually dependent (Gordon 2002, 260–61, n. 6).

References

Basch, Norma. 1982. *In the Eyes of the Law: Women, Marriage, and Property in Nineteenth-Century New York*. Ithaca: Cornell University Press.

Brumberg, Joan. 1982. "Zenanas and Girlless Villages: The Ethnology of American Evangelical Women, 1870–1910." *Journal of American History* 69 (2): 347–71. http://dx.doi.org/10.2307/1893823.

Campbell, Eugene E., and Bruce L. Campbell. 1978. "Divorce among Mormon Polygamists: Extent and Explanations." *Utah Historical Quarterly* 46: 4–23.

Clark, Elizabeth B. 1990. "Matrimonial Bonds: Slavery and Divorce in Nineteenth-Century America." *Law and History Review* 8 (1): 25–54. http://dx.doi.org/10.2307/743675.

Cott, Nancy. 2000. *Public Vows: A History of Marriage and the Nation*. Cambridge, MA: Harvard University Press.

Davis, David Brion. 1960. "Some Themes of Counter-Subversion: An Analysis of Anti-Masonic, Anti-Catholic, and Anti-Mormon Literature." *Mississippi Valley Historical Review* 47 (2): 205–24. http://dx.doi.org/10.2307/1891707.

Daynes, Kathryn M. 2001. *More Wives Than One: Transformation of the Mormon Marriage System, 1840–1910*. Urbana: University of Illinois Press.

Firmage, Edwin B., and Richard Collin Mangrum. 1988. *Zion in the Courts: A Legal History of the Church of Jesus Christ of Latter-Day Saints, 1830–1900*. Urbana: University of Illinois Press.

Flexner, Eleanor. 1975. *Century of Struggle: The Woman's Rights Movement in the United States*. Cambridge, MA: Harvard University Press.

Foster, Craig. 1993. "Victorian Pornography Imagery in Anti-Mormon Literature." *Journal of Mormon History* 19 (1): 115–32.

Foster, Lawrence. 1981. *Religion and Sexuality: The American Communal Experiments of the Nineteenth Century*. Oxford: Oxford University Press.

Gordon, Sarah Barringer. 1996a. "'The Liberty of Self-Degradation': Polygamy, Woman Suffrage, and Consent in Nineteenth-Century America." *Journal of American History* 83 (3): 815–47. http://dx.doi.org/10.2307/2945641.

Gordon, Sarah Barringer. 1996b. "'Our National Hearthstone': Anti-polygamy Fiction and the Campaign against Moral Diversity in Antebellum America." *Yale Journal of Law and Humanities* 8: 295–350.

Gordon, Sarah Barringer. 2002. *The Mormon Question: Polygamy and Constitutional Conflict in Nineteenth-Century America.* Chapel Hill: University of North Carolina Press.

Grimes, Alan P. 1967. *The Puritan Ethic and Woman Suffrage.* Oxford: Oxford University Press.

Grossberg, Michael. 1985. *Governing the Hearth: Law and the Family in Nineteenth-Century America.* Chapel Hill: University of North Carolina Press.

Hansen, Klaus J. 1967. *Quest for Empire: The Political Kingdom of God and the Council of Fifty in Mormon History.* East Lansing: Michigan State University Press.

Hansen, Klaus J. 1981. *Mormonism and the American Experience.* Chicago: University of Chicago Press.

Hardy, B. Carmon. 1992. *Solemn Covenant: The Mormon Polygamous Passage.* Urbana: University of Illinois Press.

Iversen, Joan Smyth. 1997. *The Antipolygamy Controversy in US Women's Movements, 1880–1925: A Debate on the American Home.* New York: Garland.

Kern, Louis J. 1981. *An Ordered Love: Sex Roles and Sexuality in Victorian Utopias—the Shakers, the Mormons, and the Oneida Community.* Chapel Hill: University of North Carolina Press.

Keyssar, Alexander. 2000. *The Right to Vote: The Contested History of Democracy in the United States.* New York: Basic Books.

Lerner, Gerda. 1971. *The Woman in American History.* Menlo Park, CA: Addison-Wesley.

Linford, Orma. 1964. "The Mormons and the Law: The Polygamy Cases, Part I." *Utah Law Review* 9:308–70.

Lyman, E. Leo. 1986. *Political Deliverance: The Mormon Quest for Utah Statehood.* Urbana: University of Illinois Press.

Minow, Martha. 1987. "We, the Family: Constitutional Rights and American Families." *Journal of American History* 74 (3): 959–83. http://dx.doi.org/10.2307/1902161.

Montesquieu. 1989. *The Spirit of the Laws.* Translated by Anne M. Cohler, Basia Carolyn Miller, and Harold Samuel Stone. Cambridge: Cambridge University Press.

Rosenblum, Nancy. 1997. "Democratic Sex: Reynolds vs. US, Sexual Relations, and Community." In *Sex, Preference, and Family: Essays on Law and Nature*, edited by David M. Estlund and Martha C. Nussbaum, 63–85. Oxford: Oxford University Press.

Smith, Rogers M. 1997. *Civic Ideals: Conflicting Visions of Citizenship in US History.* New Haven: Yale University Press.

Stanton, Elizabeth Cady, Susan B. Anthony, and Matilda Joslyn Gage, eds. 1848–1861. *History of Woman Suffrage.* Vol. 1. New York: Fowler and Wells.

Stanton, Elizabeth Cady, Susan B. Anthony, and Matilda Joslyn Gage, eds. 1876–1885. *History of Woman Suffrage.* Vol. 3. New York: Fowler and Wells.

Strong, Josiah. 1981. *Our Country: Its Possible Future and Its Present Crisis.* New York: Baker and Taylor.

Van Wagoner, Richard S. 1989. *Mormon Polygamy: A History.* Salt Lake City: Signature Books.

Weisbrod, Carol, and Pamela Sheingorn. 1978. "Reynolds v. US: Nineteenth-Century Forms of Marriage and the Status of Women." *10 Connecticut Law Review.* 828–58.

2

OPPOSING POLYGAMY
A Matter of Equality or Patriarchy?

Lori G. Beaman

Repealing the prohibition of polygamy in the Criminal Code may violate the equality rights of women in Canada, and would affect Canada's international commitments.

(Federal Minister of Justice, Martin Cauchon)[1]

I will teach [her] to be realistic. There's [sic] all these books out nowadays about romance and love but there's more to life than that. There's hard work, there's raising your children and it takes work to make a marriage. It takes a lot of work and effort. Good communication skills with your husband. And I could teach her by my example, by loving my sister wives, and show them that I like plural marriage but I'm not going to force it on [my kids]. If they choose to do that when they get older then that's their choice, but I just want them to show, from me living it right, that they could see the beauty in it, but I'm not going to force them to do it. And another thing is that, for Bountiful they say that there are so many underage marriages. There's not. And my daughter, I don't want her getting married till at least forty. Just joking, but I want her to be at least 20 because it feels like they're at least a little bit smarter going out to the marriage life. I was 21.

Bountiful woman[2]

On November 23, 2011, the Supreme Court of British Columbia released its judgment in the *Reference re: Section 293 of the Criminal Code of Canada* (2011) (hereinafter referred to as the *Reference re: Polygamy*), in which the court decided that the provisions of the Criminal Code of Canada that rendered polygamy illegal did not violate the Canadian Charter of Rights and Freedoms.[3] The case in itself is interesting for a variety of reasons, not least of which is the court's self-proclaimed commitment to protect monogamy for the good of society. Perhaps more interesting, though, is the role the notion of women's equality played in framing

DOI: 10.7330/9780874219975.c002

the public presentation of the case. Much of the buzz around the case dealt with the ways in which women in the polygamous community of Bountiful, British Columbia, were women at risk. Reasoned discussion about whether polygamy is inherently harmful to women was, in my experience at least, almost impossible.[4] There were few people with whom one could engage in such explorations without encountering a terse "of course polygamy is bad for women" reply. When the women of Bountiful themselves declared their agency, their voices were muted by the much louder voices of other women, policymakers and politicians, and activist groups ranging from LEAF West Coast to the Evangelical Fellowship of Canada, all of whom focused on the ill effects of polygamy. When researcher Angela Campbell presented the voices of women who live in Bountiful in her court testimony, her evidence was countered by videotapes of ex-polygamist women who recounted the horror stories of their experiences.[5] There was no space for doubt that polygamy was inherently harmful.

One of the astounding facts about the polygamy discussions, if they can be called that, is the range of people and groups who deployed the rhetoric of women's equality to condemn the practice of polygamy. These unusual bedfellows spanned the political spectrum and part-nered with feminist groups and state interests in a stunning broad-based coalition. While some might argue that surely this is evidence of the inherently harmful nature of polygamy, I argue that it signals a need for a closer examination of the near-hysterical and moralistic response generated by the suggestion that polygamy might be decriminalized. Otherwise, is the potential for women's inequality within polygamous family forms a sufficient reason to criminalize it? From my vantage point as a feminist researcher who has studied religion, religious freedom, and women's agency for my entire career, the reaction to polygamy fit within a framework that has consistently denied agency to some religious women. Women who are religious, especially fundamentalist, orthodox, observant, or practicing (as they are variously labeled and label them-selves) are not imagined to make choices in the same way as the "free" women of the sexually liberated neoliberal market-capitalist world.

In this paper I examine some of the vectors that produced the almost unequivocal condemnation of polygamy in the name of women's equal-ity. The discussion that follows does not focus on the legal decision but rather on some of the themes that framed the debates. To illus-trate these I turn to some of the affidavits of the expert witnesses in the British Columbia case. First, I explore some of the literature that takes up the postfeminist myth of women's equality in the hope of revealing the tenuousness of claims that juxtapose Canadian society/values with those of the inhabitants of Bountiful and others who practice polygamy. My main claim will be that women's equality is far from real or achieved. This observation is important because much of the antipolygamy discourse positions itself as being on the side of women, and particularly as championing women's equality. Second, I will consider the strange and troubling coalition of interests of state, policy, and feminist groups who are exhibiting what French sociologist and researcher Nicolas Dot-Pouillard (2007) describes as "republican feminism."[6] Third, I will argue that the rhetoric of women's equality and the harm polygamy causes to women have diverted attention from an equally if not more prevalent line of argument and evidence that emerged in public discourse and in the submissions of expert witnesses, namely, harm to men. Bluntly put, the lack of availability of women for men is a dominant concern. Feminist groups would do well, therefore, to pay more attention to those with whom they find themselves in bed.

THE MYTH OF EQUALITY

Two interrelated themes emerge in relation to women's equality and polygamy. The first is the "fact" of women's equality as an achieved goal or as a goal that is nearly accomplished. The second is that the state has a special duty to protect this (perceived) status quo of equality from threat, which is often imagined as being posed by an "Other" who does not understand the nature of citizenship or Canadian values. The second—the state as defender of women's equality—works to reinforce the truth of the first and to displace queries about whether women are really equal and whether the state is a defender of women's equality, or whether its actions might be related to other goals.

In discussions about polygamy, women enter in two related ways: the first is that women (and usually children are mentioned in the same breath to create a "women-and-children" merger) suffer harm in polygamous relationships and need to be protected from them; the second is that polygamy flies in the face of women's equality, and thus modern society and the nation-state must be defended against it. I will discuss more fully the intertwining of women and the nation in the next sections, but for now I simply note that the protection of women becomes equated with the protection of nation. Arguments about women's equality contain the core premise that women's equality has in fact been achieved and that polygamy represents a practice that threatens to undermine that equality. The circulation of the myth of women's equality works to frame the discussion about polygamy in particular ways, diverting attention from the myriad ways women have not, in fact, achieved either material or symbolic equality.

The fiction of equality in Western democracies can be marked in any number of ways, including a review of domestic violence against women, sexual assault against women, the murder of women, women's inferior rates of pay in the paid labor force, women's overrepresentation in statistics about division of domestic labor, the representation of women in the media, women's self-mutilation through cosmetic surgery, the control of women's reproduction, and so on (Beaman 2012). How is it possible, in the face of overwhelming evidence to the contrary, that the fiction of women's equality is maintained? Anna Tsing (2005) observes that the process of generalization, which transforms the particular into the universal, requires "a large space of compatibility among disparate particular facts and observations" (89). Axioms of unity, she argues, allow for disparate facts and observations to be reconciled to form convergences, which in turn "offer legitimacy and charisma to nascent categories" (89). "Women's equality" offers an axiom of unity that in turn reproduces women's equality as a given and as an achieved reality. This axiom of unity also renders it extremely difficult for other facts to challenge the truth of the claim that, for example, women are equal to men. Further, it creates a framework within which patterns of abuse, for example, are understood as exceptions and within which even the most ridiculous is normalized as representative of women's equality.

Angela McRobbie (2009) elaborates on the fiction of equality in her research, noting the ways in which governments, markets, and postfeminists collude in the perpetuation of the myth of women's equality even in the face of almost overwhelming evidence of its fiction: "Drawing on a vocabulary that includes words like 'empowerment' and 'choice,' these elements are then converted into a much more individualistic discourse, and they are deployed in this new guise, particularly in media and popular culture, but also by agencies of the state, as a kind of substitute feminism" (1). She identifies a "resurgent patriarchal attempt to undo the achievements of the women's movements in [the] spheres of work and home" (48). While McRobbie maps the contours of the fiction of equality in culture, Cordelia Fine (2010) examines the ways in which neuroscientific claims about differences between women and men are being used to reify women's inequality. In her unravelling of so-called scientific facts about the essential differences between men and women, Fine points out that the scientific proof used to support such differences (and very often women's inequality) is often more majority opinion than fact.

In addition, there is an important body of literature that specifically addresses the place of Muslim women in contemporary discussions of women's equality. That literature highlights the dependence of narratives of equality on a bifurcation of Us and Them and a reliance on the "Other" to convince Us of our own (superior) equality and freedom. This is very much the case in the example of polygamy, which has racist and colonial undertones that divide the world into a civilized Us and a barbaric Them. This bifurcation has a long history, as early opposition to polygamy among Latter-Day Saints was very much dependent on the displacement of those who would practice polygamy into the category of "exotic other" (Barringer Gordon 2001; Denike 2013; Ertman 2010) that forms a part of the broader story of Western colonialism (Razack 2008; Said 1978). The opposition of equality, freedom, and cultural majorities has seen some heated debates within feminism as well, as is illustrated by the famous article by Susan Moller Okin (1999) and the responses to it (Cohen, Howard, and Nussbaum 1999). These debates have implications beyond women specifically. Sarah Bracke and Nadia Fadil argue that "gender operates as a critical terrain in the processes of constituting cultural differences and constructing the national self and its others" (Bracke and Fadil 2012, 38).

The myth of the equality of men and women (not to be petty, but women rarely get first place in this duo—i.e., women and men) has pervaded the social landscape such that there is little room for counter-narratives or evidence to the contrary. Public discourse and public processes depend on the truth of the narrative of equality to sort through policy questions about diversity. The social fact of women's equality, entangled in the religious "Other," can be seen, for example, in the Bouchard-Taylor report (Bouchard and Taylor 2008, which contains a number of assumptions about gender equality [for a detailed discussion of these, see Beaman and Lefebvre 2012]), including the "fact" of male-female equality in Quebec and a narrative of that equality having been achieved in opposition to the church (which, in the case of Quebec, was the Roman Catholic Church).[7] The threat to equality identified by submissions to the commission and taken up by the commission itself is sourced as being from religious practices, which are largely framed as potentially undermining an established and achieved equality. Although religious freedom is taken seriously by the commission, it must not, in their view, trump gender equality. The notion that one might trump the other plays into the oppositional positioning of religion and equality.

The imagining of how women's equality might look and the identification of women's inequality specifically in the context of polygamy take a number of forms in the polygamy case evidence. One expert (Rebecca Cooke), for example, intertwines the argument that women's equality and women are in need of protection in her expert report. One of the themes that runs through her report is that because women can't also have multiple husbands, polygamy is inherently wrong.[8] This failure of formal equality—men and women should both be able to have multiple spouses—is identified as a decisive factor in proving polygamy's harm. This approach rests on a number of assumptions—that the male-female relationship is primary within polygynous relationships (there is ample evidence that it may not be); that female polyamory is not possible in other contexts (in other words, outside of the specific religious world-view of the Fundamentalist Church of Jesus Christ of Latter-Day Saints [FLDS] or some Muslim practice); and that women desire to have multiple husbands. This same expert notes that polygamy is a form of discrimination against women because women are "confined to specified sex roles, by virtue of the fact that they are wives, and not husbands" (Cooke n.d., para. 163). Although there is ample evidence to suggest that this discrimination is also the case in nonpolygamous relationships, women outside the polygamous context are imagined to be equal and free to define their own roles aside from their status as wives (see Johnson 2002 and West 1988 for their analyses of the "choices" women make in relation to family).

An argument that monogamous marriage has helped women achieve equality was also presented in the expert evidence. The idea that marriage is good for women has long held purchase despite the fact that its development has been more likely associated with an attempt to guarantee paternity of offspring (Lerner 1986).

> Finally, I speculate that the spread of monogamous marriage, which represents a kind of sexual egalitarianism, may have created the conditions for the emergence of democracy and political equality, including women's equality. Within the anthropological record, there is a strong statistical linkage between democratic institutions and monogamy. (Henrich n.d., 6/25)

Polygamy, in contrast, was imagined as precluding women's equality and as interfering with their freedom: "Amongst other harms, the provision recognizes that the practice of polygamy deprives women and girls of the ability to freely choose when to engage in sexual activity, when to get married, when to leave marriages and when to have children" (West Coast Women's Legal Education and Action Fund n.d., para. 26).

Although there is evidence from women living in polygamous relationships that they negotiate or take charge of the frequency and timing of their sexual relations, childbearing, and so on (Campbell 2008, 2009), a more monolithic version of women's lives emerged in the evidence and in the public discourse. The freedom created by monogamous marriage contrasted with the lack of freedom of polygamous women was a core theme, with no attention paid to the ways monogamy creates its own inequalities for women. Women's "choice" regarding sexual relations and around childbearing is much more complex than is presented in the choice/no-choice model used to illustrate the harms of polygamy (Johnson 2002; MacKinnon 1990, 1989, 1987). Despite the fact that there is almost no research on the actual lives of women who live in polygamous relationships in North America,[9] the fact of nonpolygamous women's equality and freedom was juxtaposed with the fact of polygamous women's inequality and oppression to justify criminalization. This bifurcation serves to divert attention from the possibility that women's equality has made little advancement during the past four decades and that it is, in fact, as Fine (2010), Hemmings (2011), and McRobbie (2009), among others, argue, suffering a decline.[10]

The argument can be made that even though equality has not been realized, it is an important goal that justifies the criminalization of polygamy. There is no disputing that women's equality is an important goal, but I take issue with the idea that criminalizing a particular family form will further the advancement of women's equality. If this were the case, there is sufficient evidence of women's continuing inequality (unequal division of labor, disadvantages women face in the paid labor force as a result of their inequality in the home, and violence against women in the domestic setting) within monogamous family forms to consider criminalizing it as well.

The argument I am making here is not that because women continue to be unequal in so many respects, we might as well give up and accept polygamy too. The continuing fact of women's inequality should not be used as a justification for supporting polygamy if it is in fact harmful to women. In raising the fact of women's inequality, one must be careful not to fall into a sort of trap that supports the continuation of women's inequality. First, I have no doubt that abuses happen in polygamous families (Johnson 2002, 2013) or that the abuse some women have suffered and reported on in public statements, such as those before the court in the *Reference re: Polygamy* (2001) or in Debbie Palmer and Dave Perrin's book, are not real (Palmer and Perrin 2004). However, for every story of abuse in polygamous families, there are matching ones in monogamous families. This should signal a need for deeper questioning about family forms and functions and the abuse of women more generally (Calder 2009, 2013). However, the fear that such a query generates is of such a magnitude that it paralyzes further discussion and exploration.

REPUBLICAN FEMINISM AND THE GOOD OF THE NATION

One of the curious and troubling aspects of polygamy discussions is the partnering of feminist groups with state interests, both of which frame their objection to polygamy as being in the interests of women. This rather paternalistic approach by both the state and feminists is not limited to Canada or to the polygamy issue. In the French context, Dot-Pouillard (2007) has reflected on the transformation of feminism in France in the context of the controversy over the *hijab*, *niqab*, and *burqa*. He identifies three types of feminist responses to this issue:

> Un nouveau féminisme républicain, fondé sur le paradigme assimila-tionniste et sur l'idée d'un espace public lisse et homogène, condition d'une véritable égalité; un courant féministe historique, critiquant tout à la fois le voile comme instrument réactionnaire et la loi sur les signes religieux comme répressive et contre-productive; un féminisme métisse enfin, dénonçant la vision coloniale de l'islam en France, et prêt à créer une transversalité entre féminisme occidental et féminisme musulman emergent. (14)

Multiple similar feminist responses have emerged in the Canadian context. Distinctive types of feminism such as liberal feminism, radical feminism, and socialist feminism have imagined equality in different, although sometimes overlapping, ways. Further, feminism's relationship with religion has always been complex, sometimes including the belief that women who adopt a religious worldview have a false consciousness. So too, religious women have engaged with feminism in multiple ways (Beaman 1997, 1999, 2001), ranging from complete rejection to acceptance of and alliance with feminist goals, indeed sometimes even identifying as both religious and feminist. Polygamy in particular has engendered a range of feminist responses (Bailey and Kaufman 2010; Campbell 2008, 2009; Campbell et al. 2005).

The identification of republican feminism has perhaps been seen as being most relevant to the Quebec context, in part because the Bouchard-Taylor Commission has pushed feminists to enter into the public debate about religion in ways feminist groups in other parts of Canada have not had to do. The Conseil du statut de la femme in Quebec adopted a republican feminist approach in its submission to the Bouchard-Taylor Commission and again in its 2010 report on polygamy.[11] This is not to deny the unique history of Quebec in relation to religion, particularly as it relates to the Roman Catholic Church; however, the feminist-state alliance, with its peculiar joint identification of national values (especially the equality of women and men), is not relegated to Quebec. Opposition to polygamy among feminist organizations outside Quebec certainly exists, as was evidenced during the public discussions on polygamy and in the expert evidence and submissions made during the trial. This republican feminism, which aligns itself with the state, is assimilationist, homogeneous, and rooted in formal rather than substantive notions of equality.

In the *Reference re: Polygamy* (2001), one of the foremost feminist organizations in Canada, West Coast LEAF (West Coast Women's Legal Education and Action Fund), submitted opening statements that clearly aligned the state, West Coast LEAF, and the equality of women and girls in the fight against polygamy, stating that the polygamy provisions of the Criminal Code are "firmly situated in the constitutional context of equality rights for women and girls" (West Coast Women's Legal Education and Action Fund n.d., para. 1). West Coast LEAF's general alliance with the state, its approval of the state, and its partnering on equality with the state, is evidenced in multiple statements, including

> Parliament is entitled to legislate to affirmatively protect the constitutional interests of vulnerable groups. Section 293 must be read down to prevent the practice of polygamy where such practice is exploitative of the women and children involved, and the section is justifiable to the extent that it prohibits unacceptably harmful conduct. (West Coast Women's Legal Education and Action Fund n.d., para. 7)

> The state has a positive obligation to protect equality rights, and therefore section 293 fulfills the Crown's obligations to consider the equality rights of women and girls of faith in polygamous communities and ensure that they are not exploited. In addition, the government is required not to revoke legislation that is necessary to protect equality rights. (para. 30)

> Any limitations on freedom of religion, religious or marital equality, or the rights to liberty and security of the person can be justified because the state is entitled to legislate to prevent the exploitation of women and children. (para. 38)

Surprisingly, the voices of women themselves, as evidenced by Angela Campbell (2008, 2009), for example, who lived in the polygamous relationships under scrutiny did not enter into the conceptualization of the effects of polygamy or the sort of response that the state might engage in. As with the case of the Muslim women who choose to veil, women's reasons for engaging in particular practices found little space in the discussions of women's equality and harm to women. In both cases the interests of women were intricately linked to the future of the nation-state.[12]

The range of potential harms to the nation identified by experts was astonishing: one expert suggested that she had shown conclusively that "states with higher amounts of per capita defense expenditures are more likely on average to have higher degrees of polygyny" (McDermott n.d., para. 131), and further, "A polygynous state spends more on average on defense, leaving fewer potential resources available for building domestic infrastructure, including projects devoted to health and education. This is quite a diverse set of effects, confirming the wide-ranging consequences of polygyny" (McDermott n.d., para. 157). Sweeping summaries of the harms were included in expert statements, reflecting a broader discourse about the harms of polygamy and lending expert credibility to the "common sense" of polygamy's wrongs. For example, one expert summarized Western writers' (the *they* in the following statement) litany of harms:

> Polygamy, they have argued, is unnatural and unjust to wives and children. It is the inevitable cause or consequence of sundry harms and crimes. And it is a threat to good citizenship, social order, and political stability, and, in some more recent formulations, an impediment to the advancement of civilizations toward liberty, equality, and democratic government. (Witte n.d., para. 289)

Polygamy was noted to violate the principle of the separation of church and state, to cause economic underdevelopment in sub-Saharan Africa, to increase savings and output, to impact children's development, which in turn impacts productivity, to impact female life expectancy, to impact domestic and international politics and the distribution of political rights and freedoms, and to increase crime rates.[13] Although the data relied on for many of these conclusions originated in isolated studies from Africa (longitudinal studies were rare), and there was conflicting data when all of the research was taken as a whole, the translation of the horrors of polygamy was made to the North American context *tout court*.[14]

Not only was polygamy identified as harming the nation, but monogamy was cited as potentially being responsible for democracy itself:

> The anthropologically peculiar institutions of imposing monogamous marriage may be one of the foundations of Western civilization, and may explain why democratic ideals and notions of human rights first emerged as a Western phenomenon. (Henrich n.d., 6/25)

These authors, and others (Herlihy 1995), suggest that monogamy may impact the emergence of democratic governance at all levels by (1) dissipating the pool of unmarried males that were previously harnessed by despots in wars of aggression and (2) focusing males, especially high-status males, on investing in their offspring and their current wife (in lieu of pursuing additional wives). Historically, we know that universal monogamous marriage preceded the emergence of democratic institutions in Europe and the rise of notions of equality between the sexes. In Ancient Greece, we do not know which came first but we do know that Athens, for example, had both monogamous marriage and elements of democracy. In this sense, the peculiar institutions of monogamous marriage may be part of the foundations of Western civilization and may explain why democratic ideals and notions of human rights first emerged as a Western phenomenon. (Henrich n.d., 41/80)

The worry, then, was about male aggression and competition between men rather than about any inherent "rightness" of monogamy. This theme of concern about competition between men repeats again in contemporary discussions about polygamous societies.

POLYGAMY'S HARM TO MEN

Although women's equality and the protection of women and children were at the forefront of antipolygamy discourse, there were other justifications circulating in both public and legal discourses that bear mentioning. Specifically, an equally powerful and persuasive rhetoric developed around the harm to men. While publicly it was the harm to women and children that was the most pervasive rhetoric, harm to nation and harm to men were important drivers behind the push to maintain polygamy's harm.

My objection is not about the exploration of potential harm to men and boys within polygamous relationships; rather, the point is that the front-stage presentation of harm to women and women's equality has engaged feminist support of opposition to polygamy, has further perpetuated the myth of women's equality, and has diverted attention from broader questions about the harm women suffer in monogamous relationships (Calder 2013). A narrative emerges from the discussions of harm to men and boys: polygamy is harmful to boys because if they are ostracized from their communities (based on anecdotal evidence), they grow up with no women to marry (if they have been ostracized from their communities, presumably they are loose in nonpolygamous communities where there is a free market of women), and thus they become dangerous loners or part of gangs of men without purpose.[15] Since women are the moral guardians of society, maintaining their availability for men, and thus reducing the numbers of unmarried men, is key to minimizing male aggression and violence.

The dangers posed by unmarried men, those who could not "find" a wife (also referred to as "surplus" men), was an important theme in the expert evidence:[16]

> Because many junior males in polygynous societies will not be able to find a wife, polygyny therefore has the consequence of generating a class of largely poor, young, unmarried men who are statistically predisposed to violence. For example, most homicides in Canada and the United States result from the actions of males aged fifteen and thirty-five. And among those murders, the majority is committed by men between the ages of twenty and twenty-nine; of that pool of homicides, the majority is committed by unmarried men (Daly and Wilson 1999). In ninety preindustrial societies, the structural causes of internal violence were found to be associated with polygyny as well (Ross 1986). (McDermott, n.d., para. 34)

> This relationship has a social and physiological as well as economic basis. Mazur (Mazur and Booth 1998) reports that men with high levels of testosterone, including unmarried men, are more likely to exhibit violent and antisocial behaviors, such as law breaking, substance abuse, and other forms of aggressive behavior. In addition, he shows that age-adjusted testosterone is not constant over time. Rather, male testosterone increases in the years surrounding divorce and decreases in the years surrounding marriage, independent of age. Indeed, male testosterone drops in the time surrounding courtship and marriage and drops further with the birth of each child (Gray et al. 2000). Thus, men married to women receive beneficent effects on their propensity toward violence and aggression relative to unmarried men. (McDermott n.d., para. 35)

> A non-trivial increase in the incidence of polygamy, which is quite plausible if polygamy were legalized given what we know about both male and female mating preferences, would result in increased crime and antisocial behaviour by the pool of unmarried males it would create" (Henrich n.d., 2/21).

Like the "distraction" of women's equality, the notion of surplus men distracts from larger economic, race, and class inequalities that in fact produce the surplus men of such concern. Moreover, the propensity to engage in war among nations that are not polygamous is not addressed.

Fear of the "Other," and particularly of terrorism, was also linked to the single man:

> Even terrorist groups understand the threat posed by large numbers of unmarried men. One of the most notorious terrorist groups ever, the Black September movement, was responsible for the seizure of Israeli athletes at the Munich Olympics in 1972. When Arafat's organization sought

to dismantle this group out of fear that their violence would undermine broader political objectives, military leaders decided to simply marry them off. Through a system of financial incentives and structured "mixers," members of Black September married attractive young Palestinian women. When such men were later asked to leave the country with legal passports, not a single one agreed to go, for fear of losing his family because of past terrorist activities" (Hoffman 2001). (McDermott, Expert report, para. 151)

The Northern Ireland Prison Service used similar strategies when they offered early release to former IRA and loyalist terrorists. None of the men offered early parole through a system designed to reaffirm family ties ever returned to prison (Hoffman 2001). Unmarried men simply have less to lose by engaging in violence, destruction, and mayhem. They also have more incentive to seek dominance through less conventional, riskier, and more dangerous means in hopes of garnering the resources required to attract a wife. (McDermott n.d., para. 153)

The male "Other," often racialized, associated with wildness and lack of civility or progress, was also identified as being linked to polygamy, continuing, as argued in the last section, an ongoing link between the oriental or racialized "Other" and the dangers of polygamy. The identification of the "Other" begins with the distinction between Christian and Jewish approaches to polygamy:

While mainstream Judaism took until the early second millennium of the common era to renounce polygamy, Christianity renounced it from the start. Indeed, it was the presence of occasional Jewish polygamists in their midst that first prompted early Christians to speak out against the practice. Jews "have four or five wives" and marry "as many as they wish," complained Justin Martyr early on. (Witte n.d., para. 106)[17]

But the narrative continues to unfold in a broader direction:

David Courtwright (1996) argued that, "(w)here married men have been scarce or parental supervision wanting, violence and disorder have flourished, as in the mining camps, cattle towns, Chinatowns, black ghettos, and the small hours of the morning" (p. 280). Similarly, in India, districts with higher ratios of men to women have higher rates of homicide (Dreze and Khera 2000). (McDermott n.d., para. 151)[18]

And finally, the surplus men of China garner more detailed mention:

In China, sex ratios (males to females) rose markedly from 1.053 to 1.095 between 1988 and 2004, nearly doubling the unmarried or "surplus" men (Edlund et al. 2007). At the same time, crime rates nearly doubled—90% of which were committed by men. The increase in sex ratio was created by the gradual implementation of china's one-child policy. (Henrich n.d., 25/44)

Narratives of risk, dependent in part on the idea that men are bigger risk takers than are women, also ran through the story of polygamy's harms. Men as risk takers has been a theme in the gender differences challenged by Cordelia Fine (2010), among others. The acknowledgment of risks taken by women, including childbearing, walking the streets at high-risk times, and willingness to experience change are simply not part of the calculation of risk viewed as noteworthy:

> When women want men who are rich and have high status and men want younger, more attractive women the result is that "This makes males the 'risky' sex, and predicts they have a corresponding psychology. A male who finds himself without access to females should be dramatically more likely to take substantial risks aimed at increasing his opportunities for sex (e.g., theft, murder, etc.). Ample empirical evidence indicates that males have a much greater propensity for taking risks of all kinds, especially when status is at stake (Daly and Wilson 1983, 1988, 1990; Buss 2007). This means that social factors that severely limit or restrict the reproductive options for low-status males will shift them into this risk-taking mode." (Henrich n.d., 9/28)[19]

This expert's review of other research resulted in the conclusion that "unmarried men gather in groups, engage in personally risky behaviour (gambling, illegal drugs, alcohol abuse), and commit more serious crimes than married men, including rape, murder, theft, property crimes, and assault" (Henrich n.d., 21/40).

The assumptions underlying the narrative created by these pieces of expert observation are that married men are not aggressive (statistics on domestic violence would suggest otherwise); that women are responsible for male aggression and have a duty to "tame them" for the sake of society, or, alternatively, even if they are not responsible, they are valuable commodities in the control of men and thus access to them must be appropriately regulated; that men are inherently aggressive rather than socialized to aggression; that monogamy is in fact the dominant model of family (there is plenty of evidence to suggest that a wide range of family forms exist—see for instance Calder 2009 and 2013, Emens 2004, and Klesse 2005); that monogamy as a normative force, rather than a lived reality, is key (thus we can ignore the pervasiveness of serial monogamy and adultery); that heterosexual desire is normative; that men are incapable of being a civilizing force; that when women are not readily available, men must waste precious time, energy, and resources competing for women;[20] that women have no agency and make no decisions around marriage;[21] and that monogamy represents civilized society while polygamy is part of uncivilized or barbarian societies.

CONCLUSIONS

The discursive workup of polygamy as harmful depends on a clear dividing line being established between those who practice polygamy and
those who do not. That line demarcates an Us who is dedicated to wom-
en's equality, nonviolent, committed to monogamy, and progressive and
a Them who perpetuates women's oppression, is violent both toward
women and other groups and nations, and who represent a barbaric way
of life (from which the We has progressed). This paper has argued that
the dividing line is not clear and that women's inequality remains a pervasive fact of social life. One of patriarchy's greatest achievements has
been to fold feminism into gender concerns in the production of the
myth of women's equality. To be able to point to an "Other" who acts as a
"poster child" for women's oppression and inequality effectively shields
one from accusations of perpetuating the same thing.

What result is produced by the argument that women are not
equal and that opposition to polygamy is based on fears about men
rather than about harm to women? Is it possible that one single family
form such as polygamy can wreak the havoc attributed to it? Perhaps.
However, a number of factors should offer a sufficient caution and
invite a closer examination and more exhaustive discussion of this family arrangement. This paper is not a call to accept polygamy, or to reject
monogamy, or to endorse any particular family form either socially or
through institutional action like criminalization. Rather, it urges a more
careful examination of the myriad ways in which patriarchy circulates to
perpetuate women's inequality. That inequality does not rest in a family
form but in broader patterns that implicate race, class, and economic
injustices that impact both women and men.

Although the site of attention has been on criminal law, the conversation about polygamy cannot be understood solely as a matter of criminalization. The more interesting conversation is one that considers the ways
in which reactions to polygamy are situated in broader social and cultural
contexts that require a close examination. While criminalization has been
acting as a lightning rod of sorts, the various coalitions that have come
together to object to polygamy's decriminalization reveal a profound
societal anxiety across a number of fronts. This anxiety invites deeper
investigation, particularly around the concept and goal of the equality of
women. It requires a deeper examination of the ways in which that equality is imagined, by whom, and the ways in which it is actualized, or not.
The lack of progress, indeed in some cases regression, around women's
equality should press us to reinvigorate the feminist project and to insist
that the notion of postfeminism be abandoned.

The myth of women's equality that circulates in this "postfeminist" era is in many ways a repeat of the history of feminism. The end of the first wave of feminism saw its collapse into humanism, yet some important remnants of that first wave remain and repeat. Two sets of motivations animated first-wave feminism. The first was the achievement of an equality that was at the very least formal in terms of opportunities for women, based on women's inherent worth. The second set was rooted in the belief that women were morally superior to men and as such had an obligation to be involved in public life. This obligation, though, was still tied to women's primary duty to be mothers and wives and was understood in the context of ideas like "the hand that rocks the cradle rules the world." This approach held that while women should have basic rights that allow them some participation in political and public realms, the heavy lifting should be left to men.[22] This idea of women's moral superiority and taming abilities repeats in ideas about "surplus men" and ensuring that the marketplace of women from which men can choose remains "free."

Notes

1. See the British Columbia Statement from the Ministry of Attorney General: Province to Seek Supreme Court Opinion on Polygamy (http://www2.news.gov.bc.ca/news _releases_2009-2013/2009AG0012-000518.htm).

2. See Angela Campbell (2009).

3. *Reference re: Section 293 of the Criminal Code of Canada*, BCSC 1588 (2011). I would like to acknowledge the support of the Religion and Diversity Project in the preparation of this article as well as the ongoing financial support of my research through my Canada Research Chair in the Contextualization of Religion in a Diverse Canada. I would also like to thank Karine Henrie and Marianne Abou-Hamad for their meticulous attention to editorial detail. My friend and colleague Sally Cole has been unwavering in her support of this work and has offered numerous suggestions for resources that have proven to be fundamental to the development of the arguments in this paper. I am grateful for the extremely competent research assistance of Lauren Forbes. This article was originally published in 2014 as "Opposing Polygamy: A Matter of Equality or Patriarchy?" in *Of Crime and Religion: Polygamy in Canadian Law*, edited by David Koussens, Stéphane Bernatchez, and Marie-Pierre Robert (Sherbrooke: Éditions Revue de Droit de l'Université de Sherbrooke, 2014). Permission granted via e-mail by David Gilles, Professeur de Droit, Université de Sherbrooke, October 2013.

4. I became aware of these pieces of evidence, which are publicly available, because of my own involvement as an expert witness in this trial.

5. I equate this cherry picking of horror stories to going to a transition house for abused women and asking them what they think of marriage and monogamy and then basing one's conclusions on what (we hope) is a skewed sample.

6. For an elaboration of republican feminism in the Quebec context, see Jocelyn Maclure (2008) and Daniel Weinstock (2007).

7. There is certainly a case to be made that women's equality in Quebec is different than it is in the rest of Canada. Quebec has a state-funded day-care program,

arguably the most progressive access in Canada to reproductive technology as well as to abortion and the so-called morning-after pill. At a slightly more superficial but not insignificant level, Quebec women do not (cannot) legally take their husband's name when they marry.

8.   This point is also made by LEAF: "Therefore, the common form of polygamy is inherently unequal in that it allows husbands to take multiple wives, but not wives to take multiple husbands" (West Coast Women's Legal Education and Action Fund n.d., para. 14[a]).

9.   See Campbell (2008, 2009, 2013). See also Altman and Ginat (1996), Bradley (1993), Jacobson and Burton (2011), Pelland and Casoni (2010), and Wright and Richardson (2011).

10.   See also the edited collection by Faraday, Denike, and Stephenson (2009), which offers a critical and somewhat disheartening assessment of the law's ability to offer substantive equality for women.

11.   See Conseil du Statut de la Femme (2010).

12.   See Sarah Carter (2008) for a discussion of early regulation of polygamy in Canada and its links to nation building.

13.   The range of polygamy's evils is astounding. Some of the expert statements noted that polygamy violates the separation of church and state (Witte n.d., para. 331); polygamy causes economic underdevelopment (McDermott n.d., para. 25); banning polygamy decreases fertility and increases output per capita (para. 25); polygamy lowers female life expectancy and decreases rights and freedoms (para. 132); and polygamy increases crime (Henrich n.d., 27/46). In addition, "polygyny can also exert effects on various aspects of domestic and international politics for a given nation state. First, to the extent that junior boys who have been excised from polygynous communities become wards of the state, the cost of educating, socializing, housing, feeding and job training for them gets transferred from the family to taxpayers. Second, to the extent that secondary wives can obtain aid from the state under laws designed to help women with dependent children, financial costs for such support can escalate as well" (McDermott n.d., para. 126).

14.   There are obvious problems with such a translation, but there are two specific points of interest. First, the discourse repeated a similar discussion that took place in the late 1800s and early 1900s, creating a dividing line that distinguished between the civilized Us and the uncivilized (and unchristian) Them. Second, the racial implications of this cannot be overemphasized (See Denike, 2013. See also Barringer Gordon 2001 and Ertman 2010).

15.   For elaboration see Cooke (n.d., para. 64) and McDermott (n.d., para. 32).

16.   For similar statements see also McDermott (n.d., paras. 38, 150).

17.   The theme of Christian versus Jewish approaches to polygamy recurs several times: "While mainstream Judaism took until the early second millennium of the common era to renounce polygamy, Christianity renounced it from the start. Indeed, it was the presence of occasional Jewish polygamists in their midst that first prompted early Christians to speak out against the practice" (John Witte n.d., para. 106). Witte observes that Christians held that "with the earth filled with people, roughly equally divided between male and female, polygamy is both 'unnatural' and 'unjust'" (paras. 124, 256, 272).

18.   Similarly, in his review of the literature, Henrich (26/45) finds violence in India and the American West when unmarried men migrated there.

19.   Also: "It will increase the pool of unmarried men psychologically primed to take risks and compete fiercely with other males to obtain reproductive opportunities (this increases crime and risky behaviour)" (Henrich n.d., 5/24).

20.   "Greater degrees of polygynous marriage may reduce national wealth (GDP) per capita both because of the manner in which efforts are shifted to obtaining more wives and because of the increase in female fertility" (Henrich n.d., 2/21). "Recent research indicates that 53 percent of the variance in sex differences in mortality can be uniquely explained by a combination of polygyny and economic inequality (Kruger 2010). This work demonstrates that increased male mating competition in polygynous areas leads to riskier behavior on the part of adult men seeking mates" (McDermott n.d., para. 37).

21.   In this statement, for example, the power hierarchies of men are the decisive factors in the organization of marriage: "As this complaint makes manifest, marriage competition in communities where a statistically significant number of men practice polygyny can have especially pernicious effects on adolescent boys. Power hierarchies among men determine which men are afforded the opportunity to take multiple wives and which are necessarily excluded" (Cooke n.d., para. 65).

22.   See Gorham (1976), Kealey (1979), and Matheson and Lang (1976).

References

Altman, Irwin, and Joseph Ginat. 1996. *Polygamous Families in Contemporary Society.* New York: Cambridge University Press.

Bailey, Martha, and Amy J. Kaufman. 2010. *Polygamy in the Monogamous World.* Santa Barbara, CA: Praeger.

Barringer Gordon, Sarah. 2001. *The Mormon Question: Polygamy and Constitutional Conflict in Nineteenth-Century America.* Chapel Hill: University of North Carolina Press.

Beaman, Lori G. 1997. "Collaborators or Resistors?: Evangelical Women in Atlantic Canada." *Atlantis* 22 (1): 9–18.

Beaman, Lori G. 1999. *Shared Beliefs, Different Lives: Women's Identities in Evangelical Context.* St. Louis: Chalice.

Beaman, Lori G. 2001. "Molly Mormons, Mormon Feminists and Moderates: Religious Diversity and the Latter Day Saints Church." *Sociology of Religion* 62 (1): 65–86. http://dx.doi.org/10.2307/3712231.

Beaman, Lori G. 2012. "The Status of Women: The Report from a Civilized Society." *Canadian Criminal Law Review* 16 (2): 223–46.

Beaman, Lori G., and Solange Lefebvre. 2012. "Protecting Gender Relations: The Bouchard-Taylor Commission and the Equality of Women." *Canadian Journal for Social Research* 2 (1): 95–104.

Bouchard, Gérard, and Charles Taylor. 2008. "Building the Future: A Time for Reconciliation." In *Commission de consultation sur les pratiques d'accommodement reliées aux différences culturelles.* Quebec, QC: Quebec Government Printing Office.

Bracke, Sarah, and Nadia Fadil. 2012. "Is the Headscarf Oppressive or Emancipatory? Field Notes on the Gendrification of the 'Multicultural Debate.'" *Religion and Gender* 2 (1): 36–56.

Bradley, Martha 1993. *Kidnapped from That Land: The Government Raids on the Short Creek Polygamists.* Salt Lake City: University of Utah Press.

Calder, Gillian 2009. "Penguins and Polyamory: Using Law and Film to Explore the Essence of Marriage in Canadian Family Law." *Canadian Journal of Women and the Law* 21 (1): 55–89. http://dx.doi.org/10.3138/cjwl.21.1.55.

Calder, Gillian. 2013. "'To the Exclusion of All Others': Polygamy, Monogamy and the Legal Family in Canada." In *Polygamy's Rights and Wrongs: Perspectives on Harm, Family, and the Law,* edited by Gillian Calder and Lori G. Beaman, 215–33. Vancouver: University of British Columbia Press.

Campbell, Angela. 2008. "'Wives' Tales: Reflecting on Research in Bountiful." *Canadian Journal of Law and Society* 23 (1–2): 121–41. http://dx.doi.org/10.1017/S082932 0100009601.

Campbell, Angela. 2009. "Bountiful Voices." *Osgoode Hall Law Review* 47 (2): 183–234.

Campbell, Angela. 2013. "Plus ça Change . . .? Bountiful's Diverse and Durable Marriage Practices." *Polygamy's Rights and Wrongs: Perspectives on Harm, Family, and the Law,* edited by Gillian Calder and Lori G. Beaman, 21–45. Vancouver: University of British Columbia Press.

Campbell, Angela, Nicholas Bala, Katherine Duvall-Antonacopoulos, Leslie MacRae, Joanna J. Paetsch, Martha Bailey, Beverley Baines, Bita Amani, and Amy Kaufman. 2005. *Polygamy in Canada: Legal and Social Implications for Women and Children—A Collection of Policy Research Reports.* Calgary: Alberta Civil Liberties Research Centre.

Carter, Sarah. 2008. *The Importance of Being Monogamous: Marriage and Nation Building in Western Canada to 1915.* Edmonton: University of Alberta Press.

Cohen, Joshua, Matthew Howard, and Martha C. Nussbaum, eds. 1999. *Is Multiculturalism Bad for Women?* Princeton, NJ: Princeton University Press.

Conseil du Statut de la Femme. 2010. *Polygamy and the Rights of Women: Opinion Summary.* Quebec: Conseil du Statut de la Femme.

Cooke, Rebecca J. n.d. (2011). "State Obligations to Eliminate Polygamy under International Law." Expert report for the attorney general of Canada, submitted to the Supreme Court of British Columbia July 16, 2010. (Vancouver Registry No. S-097767).

Denike, Margaret. 2013. "Polygamy and Race-Thinking: A Genealogy." In *Polygamy's Rights and Wrongs: Perspectives on Harm, Family, and the Law,* edited by Gillian Calder and Lori G. Beaman, 142–69. Vancouver, BC: University of British Columbia Press.

Dot-Pouillard, Nicolas. 2007. "Les recompositions du mouvement féministe Français au regard du hijab. Le voile comme signe et révélateur ces impensés d'un espace public déchiré entre identité républicaine et héritage colonial." *SociologieS.* sociologies .revues.org/document246.html.

Emens, Elizabeth F. 2004. "Monogamy's Law: Compulsory Monogamy and Polyamorous Existence." *New York Review of Law and Social Change* 29 (2): 277–376.

Ertman, Martha. 2010. "Race Treason: The Untold Story of America's Ban on Polygamy." *Columbia Journal of Gender and Law* 19 (2): 287–366.

Faraday, Fay, Margaret Denike, and M. Kate Stephenson, eds. 2009. *Making Equality Rights Real: Securing Substantive Equality under the Charter.* Toronto: Irwin Law.

Fine, Cordelia. 2010. *Delusions of Gender: How Our Minds, Society, and Neurosexism Create Difference.* New York: W. W. Norton.

Gorham, Deborah. 1976. "The Canadian Suffragists." In *Women in the Canadian Mosaic,* edited by Gwen Matheson, 23–56. Toronto: Peter Martin.

Hemmings, Clare. 2011. *Why Stories Matter: Grammar of Feminist Theory.* Durham, NC: Duke University Press.

Henrich, Joseph. n.d. (2010). Affidavit #1. Supreme Court of British Columbia (Vancouver Registry No. S-097767).

Jacobson, Cardell, and Lara Burton. 2011. *Modern Polygamy in the United States: Historical, Cultural, and Legal Issues.* New York: Oxford University Press.

Johnson, Rebecca. 2002. *Taxing Choices.* Vancouver: University of British Columbia Press.

Johnson, Rebecca. 2013. "Reflecting on Polygamy: What's the Harm?" In *Polygamy's Rights and Wrongs: Perspectives on Harm, Family, and the Law,* edited by Gillian Calder and Lori G. Beaman, 97–119. Vancouver: University of British Columbia Press.

Kealey, Linda. 1979. *A Not Unreasonable Claim: Women and Reform in Canada in 1880s–1920s.* Toronto: Women's Press.

Klesse, Christian. 2005. "Bisexual Women, Non-Monogamy and Differentialist Anti-Promiscuity Discourses." *Sexualities* 8 (4): 445–64. http://dx.doi.org/10.1177 /1363460705056620.

Lerner, Gerda. 1986. *The Creation of Patriarchy.* Oxford: Oxford University Press.

Maclure, Jocelyn. 2008. "Le malaise relatif aux pratiques d'accommodement de la diversité religieuse: une thèse interprétative." In *L'accommodement raisonnable et la diversité religieuse à l'école publique. normes et pratiques,* edited by Marie McAndrew, Micheline Milot, Jean-Sébastien Imbeault and Paul Eid, 215–42. Montréal: Fides.

MacKinnon, Catharine A. 1987. "Feminism, Marxism, Method, and the State: Toward a Feminist Jurisprudence." In *Feminism and Methodology,* edited by Sandra Harding, 169–79. Bloomington: Indiana University Press.

MacKinnon, Catharine A. 1989. *Toward a Feminist Theory of the State.* Cambridge: Harvard University Press.

MacKinnon, Catharine A. 1990. "Legal Perspectives on Sexual Difference." In *Theoretical Perspectives on Sexual Difference,* edited by Deborah Rhodes, 213–25. New Haven: Yale University Press.

Matheson, Gwen, and V. E. Lang. 1976. "Nellie McClung: 'Not a Nice Woman.'" In *Women in the Canadian Mosaic,* edited by Gwen Matheson, 1–20. Toronto: Peter Martin.

McDermott, Rose. n.d. Expert report prepared for the attorney general of Canada. Supreme Court of British Columbia (Vancouver Registry No. S-097767).

McRobbie, Angela. 2009. *The Aftermath of Feminism: Gender, Culture and Social Change.* Los Angeles: Sage.

Moller Okin, Susan. 1999. "Is Multiculturalism Bad for Women?" In *Is Multiculturalism Bad for Women?* edited by Joshua Cohen, Matthew Howard, and Martha C. Nussbaum, 9–24. Princeton, NJ: Princeton University Press.

Palmer, Debbie, and Dave Perrin. 2004. *Keep Sweet: Children of Polygamy.* Creston, BC: Dave's Press.

Pelland, Marie-Andrée, and Dianne Casoni. 2010. "Vicissitudes de l'identité sociale et allégations d'entorses aux lois chez un groupe de Mormons polygames Canadiens." *Déviance et Société* 34 (1): 49–69. http://dx.doi.org/10.3917/ds.341.0049.

Razack, Sherene H. 2008. *Casting Out: The Eviction of Muslims from Western Law and Politics.* Toronto: University of Toronto Press.

Said, Edward W. 1978. *Orientalism.* New York: Vintage Books.

Tsing, Anna L. 2005. *Friction: An Ethnography of Global Connection.* Princeton, NJ: Princeton University Press.

Weinstock, Daniel. 2007. "La 'crise' des accommodements au Québec: Hypothèses explicatives." *Revue éthique publique* 9 (1): 20–27.

West, Robin L. 1988. "Jurisprudence and Gender." *University of Chicago Law Review. University of Chicago. Law School* 55 (1): 1–72. http://dx.doi.org/10.2307/1599769.

West Coast Women's Legal Education and Action Fund (West Coast LEAF). n.d. Opening Statement of West Coast LEAF. n.d. Supreme Court of British Columbia (Vancouver Registry No. S-097767).

Witte, John, Jr. n.d. Expert report for the attorney general of Canada, submitted to the Supreme Court of British Columbia (Vancouver Registry No. S-097767).

Wright, Stuart A., and James T. Richardson, eds. 2011. *Saints under Siege: The Texas State Raid on the Fundamentalist Latter Day Saints.* New York: New York University Press.

3

THE VARIABLE IMPACT OF MORMON POLYGYNY ON WOMEN AND CHILDREN

Janet Bennion

Based on twenty years of ethnographic field research (participant-obser-vation and interview) and abuse prevalence data from the attorney general and child protection services offices in four states, the predicting variables linked to poor-functioning polygamy are (1) illegality, (2) geographic isolation, (3) socioeconomic inequality, (4) male supremacy, (5) economic deprivation, (6) absence of female networking, and (7) the presence of sexual, physical, and emotional abuse. It is asserted that the combination of these factors within contemporary millenarian fundamentalist movements practicing plural marriage contribute to the expression of child sexual molestation, under-age marriage, domestic violence, and gendered marginalization of women, children, and young men. Such analysis of factors is necessary to better intervene and prevent mistreatment of women and children within poor-functioning polygamy.

As polygyny becomes a primetime phenomenon, scholars are drawn to the question of viability and the protection of women and children, especially in North America, where such variability in the expression of plural marriage exists. Currently, approximately 50,000 fundamentalist Mormons practice polygyny in defiance of the law (Wilde 2010). They believe that God is an exalted man and that if they are worthy, they can become gods and goddesses of their own worlds. Polygyny is seen as a mechanism of fulfilling the gospel, "a divine principle dedicated by the Gods for the perpetuation of life and birth of earths." Polygyny washes away the filth of the "daughters of Zion," as recorded in Isaiah 4:4, a catch-all solution for prostitution, infidelity, homosexuality, spinster-hood, childlessness, and various types of sexual sin (Bradley 1990).

Converts to fundamentalism consecrate all their properties and assets to be "worthy to have their names written in the book of the law of God" (LeBaron 1981). Men and boys are expected to be "kings in the

DOI: 10.7330/9780874219975.c003

making," taking up the mantle of religious priesthood leadership, economic stewardship, and absolute purity. Women play a minor role in this formal priesthood scheme as auxiliaries. A woman may, if she is worthy and married to a high-ranking Melchizedek priesthood holder, tap into his power when she is sealed to him. Her primary duties, however, are to bear and raise "righteous seed" for her husband's kingdom, reinforcing the respective marital roles of ruler and subject based on a particular interpretation of the teachings of Joseph Smith. Husbands must be instructional and dominating, and wives must be obedient and respectful, as depicted in Genesis 3:16: "Thy desire shall be to thy husband, and he shall rule over thee."

Women should "respect and revere themselves, as holy vessels, destined to sustain and magnify the eternal and sacred relationship of wife and mother." A wife is the "ornament and glory of man; to share with him a never fading crown, and an eternally increasing dominion" (Musser 1948, 134). Men must fight the political and physical battles while a woman "adorns the home, conserves the larder and renders the habitation an earthly heaven where love, peace, affection, gratitude, and oneness shall abound, she the queen and he the king" (134).

Although the patriarchs of the households are not usually permanent residents, spending time with their other wives and working outside the order, they can exert enormous control over their wives and children, typically presiding over three to four wives and twenty to forty children. In some families, the women live in separate dwellings and meet all together only once a week. In others, up to five or six wives live under one roof and share bathrooms, kitchen, and dining areas, with a separate bedroom for each wife. In general, sexuality is considered a necessary evil—a force man must learn to control and from which pregnant, lactating, and menstruating women must be protected. Because women's primary role is motherhood, a task associated with celestial rewards and kingdoms of glory, barrenness is seen as a reproach—God's curse on the woman and her husband.

Most female recruits to fundamentalism have faced serious marginalization in the orthodox Mormon church as single women, single mothers, divorced and widowed women, and unmarriageables, and they are often socially and economically deprived of the resources available to the rest of the membership. Women are typically drawn to polygyny to find a husband, bear children, and access priesthood resources tied to their salvation. They are baptized and integrated into an already established polygynous extended family. While many women find greater access to valued resources and are quite content in polygyny, other women are dissatisfied because of abuse, abandonment, poverty, or co-wife jealousy. The decision to disengage is serious, and often disengagement is too threatening for women to make an effort to leave. Many are told that they will lose their children, face economic hardship, and be damned, their skin turning as dark as Cain's.

This variation in experience requires us to examine the exact criteria that contribute to both well-functioning and abusive conditions. The data on variability and function are drawn from twenty years of anthropological fieldwork conducted among four groups: the Apostolic United Brethren (AUB) of Utah and Montana, the LeBarons of Mexico, the Kingstons of Utah, and the Fundamentalist Church of Jesus Christ of Latter-day Saints of the southwest. I have lived and worked with twenty-two extended polygamous families and have interviewed more than 355 individuals about their conversion to the movement, their living arrangements, and their lifestyles. My data is also drawn from my autoethnography, a study of my lived experience as a descendant of Mormon polygyny, from participant observations I collected while living among the AUB, and from scores of interviews and observations made over ten years of living in Zion. This data also includes reports produced out of attorney generals' offices and child protection agencies in western states. Inspired by social psychologist Alean Al-Krenawi, who studied "well-functioning" among polygamous families in a Bedouin village south of Israel (Slonim-Nevo and Al-Krenawi 2006), I use the Anna Karenina principle as a heuristic to provide clarity about favorable and unfavorable practices often associated with polygamy. By identifying the risks associated with dysfunctional polygamy, we can better inform law-enforcement agencies and child-protection services about where to seek out and regulate cases of harm-based plural marriage.

The Anna Karenina principle states that "happy families are all alike; every unhappy family is unhappy in its own way" (Tolstoy, qtd. in Diamond 1999). Thus, a deficiency in any one of a number of factors associated with well-functioning dooms that family to failure. Successful polygynous families are not so because of a particular positive trait but because of a lack of the following negative traits: (1) illegality, causing most polygamists to hate and fear mainstream and law officials; (2) circumscription, promoting social, geographic, and religious isolation; (3) inequality between husband and wives and among wives; (4) male supremacy, where men are in control of all valued resources, including women and children; (5) economic deprivation, where much of the community lives below the poverty line, relating to the father's absence, overcrowded households, and substance abuse;

(6) lack of female networking, contributing to marginalization and depression; and (7) abuse.

These traits discourage well-functioning in Mormon fundamentalist polygyny in many overlapping ways. First, illegality forces polygynists to hide their lifestyle, putting wives and children at risk for abuse, economic hardship, and alienation from mainstream resources and protection. The legal ban pushes the practice further underground, exactly where potential abuses are likely to occur, outside public scrutiny in isolated communities fearing incarceration. If fear is dispelled, polygamists are freer to live in the mainstream, where women and children can access counseling, education, and opportunities for economic and emotional autonomy. Illegality also promotes discrimination against polygynous families generated by media, local neighborhoods, schools, and the larger mainstream. Legal recognition would legitimize polygyny as a faith-based lifestyle, which would make it more acceptable to neighbors, employers, and the state and contribute to Al-Krenawi's second wellness factor, that polygamy be religiously sanctioned. This legal protection for religious rights would greatly serve Mormon fundamentalists as well as the growing number of Muslims who believe they are allowed four wives according to the Qur'an. Most important, legal recognition would bring abuses into the light by encouraging victims to seek nearby agencies and counseling centers for help. If polygyny is legalized, "spiritual" wives will be transformed into legal wives, able to gain access to their husband's work-related health benefits and pensions as well as hospital visiting rights and life insurance. Illegality renders polygyny unmonitored and unregulated, preventing women and children from accessing the typical socioeconomic resources that monogamous American families now enjoy: societal recognition, life insurance and health benefits, public education, full employment, protection from criminal abuse, and access to legal recourse for dealing with divorce and child support.

Second, some polygyny is associated with isolation. In a Utah Valley study, 95 percent of the abuse cases gathered from county abuse-relief centers occurred in rural environments (Bennion 2006). Isolation can be used as a means of cloaking sexual and physical abuses against women and children (Chamberlain 2002). Remote places are deliberately chosen by an abuser to maintain control over their victims. When a woman is isolated, she also experiences circumscription, referring to the physical or social environment's blockage of dissident emigration (Carneiro 1988). The desert's geographic barriers of heat, drought, natural predators, poor soil, and imposing sierras together create a physical barricade against apostasy and escape. People who leave their abusive environments risk hunger, economic hardship, and possibly even death on the outside. This geographic hindrance is associated with a harsh social mechanism that keeps people from leaving, including fear of ostracism and spiritual death and of betraying the family. Women, especially, face this type of circumscription because they have been raised to value relationships, loved ones, and solidarity. They also risk losing their children if they attempt to leave (the offspring of a man belong to his patrilineage in the next life). Thus, if a mother is aware of her daughter's abuse, she is not likely to tell anyone about it for two reasons: (1) her husband and the brethren would condemn her for it; and (2) she would have to travel a great distance to locate an appropriate sounding board for such a grievance. For example, Warren Jeff's speech to young ladies cautions them against betraying family in times of abuse. "What do many people do? They run to their friends or someone they think can give them counsel. You run anywhere else besides your Priesthood head, you could run into trouble—don't ever go beyond your bounds and try to rule over him" (Brook Adams, *Salt Lake Tribune*, Aug. 30, 2007). Jeffs sanctions the abuse of vulnerable individuals by powerful ones, denying his actions are abusive. He further circumscribes women by denying them access to help; they are not allowed a driver's license or outside employment.

According to Al-Krenawi, another factor of poor-function is unequal allocation of resources to all wives. Equality should be expanded to all stakeholders: between men and their wives, between wives, and between alpha and rogue males. For fundamentalist Mormons, men must treat each wife equally or lose that wife to a better man. For Muslims, the Qur'an restricts the practice to only those who can truly live it correctly: "If you fear that you will not do justice between them, then marry only one or what your right hands possess: this is more proper that you may not deviate from the right course" (4:3). In South Africa, the law requires that a man show economic proof of his ability to care equitably for all wives before the marriage is sanctioned, requiring men to gain written permission from the first wife and proof that they have adequate finances to take care of any new wives. This law is an insurance policy for women against poverty in the future if their husband begins to prefer one wife over the other. The neglected wife has legal recourse to demand equity in the law (Stacey and Meadow 2009).

If a man treats his wives equally, it is easier for wives to treat each other with love and respect. Equality among women translates to each wife being provided with equal resources and time with their husband as well as collaboration among wives for the benefit of the whole. When a woman enters a polygamous relationship, she can expect to initially experience fear of sharing her husband and fear of the sacrifices involved in not getting anything for herself. The husband gets another wife, gets to feel love for two women, and experiences twice as much intimacy, but a wife may suffer from an acute sense of injustice and jealousy until she overcomes her jealousies and builds strong friendships, gaining access to the valuable economic and emotional network available in many polygamist groups. The frequent absence of men can actually give rise to strong interdependence among the women, leading to female bonding and satisfaction. Women use economic transactions with other women to their advantage in the form of reciprocal exchanges. One wife provides garden produce, another provides childcare, and yet another provides profits from crafts and tourism.

Co-wife rivalries are often based on the desire of a wife to obtain resources for her own children versus allowing resources to be given to another wife's children. When one wife accesses all the favored resources, the other wives are disadvantaged, as in the case of the wives described by Saitoti in Kenya (Achebe 1959; Saitoti 1988). When this divisiveness occurs, the children suffer mistreatment and become ranked in a relentless hierarchy based on the ranking of wives. If, on the other hand, the husband creates an atmosphere of equality and the co-wives do not argue over resources among themselves but rather share freely and exhibit reciprocity and respect, the family has greater chances of success and longevity. Children, seeing their mothers getting along beautifully, witness a cooperative parenting coalition. They will exhibit the same sharing paradigm with their stepsiblings and halfsiblings as true brothers and sisters.

Sororal, or cousin, polygamy is found to be conducive to an environment of widespread sharing. Such a system benefits the woman, who can get household help from a member of her family with whom she can likely form a coalition, retaining significant power in her own household based on kin selection and familiarity (Bennion 1998). Just as important to evolutionary fitness is a woman's ability to share with another woman. Nancy Leis (1974) found that in the Ijaw tribe, disenfranchised women actually cling to each other, forming an opposing unity against their husband should he ever treat any one of them poorly. This unity empowers them and fosters solidarity. Robert Netting (1969) also studied polygamy among Kofyar women, finding that where women share a residence, their status increases (collective opposition to patriarchy). My own studies show how female bonding in Mormon fundamentalist communities is the most vital foundation for the existence of successful family and community economies (Bennion 2004). Without the collaboration of these women, the community of selfish, isolated, and competitive patriarchs would fail.

The plural wives in the Irwin Altman and Josef Ginat study experienced such co-wife jealousy. There was a sense of "loneliness, sometimes to the point of feeling abandoned" and "feelings of inadequacy and low self-esteem" for senior wives, while new wives also experienced jealousy and feelings of inadequacy. Altman and Ginat (1996) identified several strategies used by the wives to manage jealousy. They wrote that wives said they turned to prayer "for solace, guidance, and the strength to help them adjust to the new family situation and abide by their religious beliefs" (170). Husbands became more sensitive to their wives' feelings of loss and inadequacy and made greater efforts to give them love, and support. Wives "aired their adjustment stresses with husbands, sometimes only after suffering frustration and emotional turmoil alone" (170). And wives reached out to one another, learning that they all experienced similar negative feelings and provided mutual support. The women interviewed seemed to find it possible, with much personal and interpersonal work, to establish and maintain romantic dyadic relationships with their husbands despite sharing them with other wives, thus accomplishing the fantasy of monogamy within a polygamous setting. Negative experiences were primarily the result of either a lack of coping strategies or the ineffectiveness of these strategies, due in large part to individual personalities, the interaction of these personalities, and the ethos and experience of the family and its members. Consequently, negative experiences were the result of particularly dysfunctional plural families rather than inherent and inevitable experiences of plural marriage in general.

Another factor of poor-functioning is male supremacy and the subjugation of women. Men are taught they have sole responsibility for the leadership of the family and control of the household; they are in charge of the spiritual and economic well-being of their families. They use their priesthood powers and the biblical blueprint of the Abrahamic Covenant, with its promise of infinite progeny, as the exemplary tool for building up their progeny and keeping their wives in check. Male supremacists dominate others by coercion; they invoke God's authority to sanction sexual abuse and threaten damnation, the removal of economic resources, and physical abuse to any who challenge them. The victims become strongly convinced that their father or husband is justified in abusing them, refusing to equate it with incest or marital rape. Male supremacists may also require that their children be homeschooled, avoiding the evil of the secular schools of the mainstream world. They also keep rogue males under control, marginalizing them in order to access reproductive and economic resources.

Elite polygyny (Nakanike 1991) is defined as a male supremacist method of maintaining reproductive and productive control by a handful of powerful, blood-related patriarchs. This device effectively alienates younger, rogue males while placing the control of all marriageable, or fertile, women in the clan into the hands of the elite. This process includes a mechanism of wife capture (or in the fundamentalist case, conversion) that ensures a continual flow of fecund women into the community. Along with accessing women, patriarchs must control financial stewardships, which are placed in the hands of the reigning brethren (e.g., top pureblood families like the Jessops, Allreds, or LeBarons). These stewardships are further funded with the contributions of new converts through the Law of Consecration. All members give total deference and obedience to the prophet and the brethren, who then make decisions on the members' behalf, including where they will live, how much money they earn, what clothes they will wear, how they will worship, and who they can marry. The elite brethren, because of their access to valued resources, use polygamy to build strategic multiple alliances and maintain control over land, buildings, and manufacturing.

For this control to be upheld, some heads of families are given favorable stewardships in order to keep them from rebelling; these men are also used as officers to protect the rights and properties of the Priesthood Council. Rogue males, who cannot gain favored stewardships and wives, work for the alpha males as "servants on Mt. Zion," or they are disenfranchised through excommunication. In addition, women and children must not be allowed to easily leave the group as they are the "resources" of the family kingdom. They represent the glory and magnificence of the corporate lineages and therefore are cloistered from the outside world. To achieve this segregation, the brethren can use nonsecular education via homeschooling and a rurally isolating environment with natural borders.

Negative consequences affecting women and children within elite polygyny include sexual abuse of children, underage marriage, financial abuse (extracting obedience in exchange for food and shelter), wife rape and battery, megalomania or narcissism, blood atonement, and the alienation of teenage males. Men can also experience abusive conditions through alienating competition for valued resources and the threat of excommunication by the Priesthood brethren. These men, who may be ousted to rid the community of excess males, often leave the group and

experience depression, drug abuse, or alcoholism. Related to male alienation is insufficient father-son contact, which affects the development of
the son's masculine identity. Males are more likely to be separated, segre-
gated, and marginalized at puberty, a situation directly tied to the fierce
competition over scarce wives between fathers, uncles, sons, and nephews. A further consequence of elite polygyny is that it can breed jealousies between wives for the right to their alpha husband's wealth and the
inclusion of their sons in his stewardships. Also, the unequal treatment
of wives is a way for patriarchs to rid themselves of unwanted wives and
make way for younger, more fertile wives (Hassouneh-Phillips 2001).

Warren Jeffs is a prime example of elite polygyny. He successfully
controlled all aspects of people's lives. The worst thing to happen to a
woman, according to Jeffs, is for her to become educated and seek to
rule over her husband. Jeffs's words sound like a 1950s marriage manual: a woman should wake up each morning yearning to please her husband, "rejoicing in his will towards" her. He quotes Brigham Young in
stating, "The very nature of women in their desires shall be to their husband . . . completely submit where he shall rule over you . . . true woman-
hood is attained through Priesthood" (Brook Adams, *Salt Lake Tribune*,
Aug. 30, 2007). These are all phrases designed to persuade women to
submit and defer to men, muting their own voices and desires. If all
actions and thoughts are "centered in him," the men are better able to
control the women and financial resources. In his diary, Jeffs recounts
reassigning the wives of three men, including his brother David, because
God had shown him that they "couldn't exalt their ladies, had lost the
confidence of God." One of his brother's wives had difficulty accepting
the news and could barely bring herself to kiss her new husband. "She
showed a great spirit of resistance, yet she went through with it," Jeffs
records. "She needs to learn to submit to Priesthood" (Brook Adams,
Salt Lake Tribune, Aug. 30, 2007).

More recently, according to the trustees of the FLDS estate, Warren
Jeffs has now sanctioned polyandry as well from his prison cell. It is not
clear whether this development is an advantage for women or not, but
it is certainly striking panic into the hearts of men. He has ordained five
to ten of his brethren to be mated with all the women in the community of marriageable age, whether or not they already have husbands.
These women will be linked to new saviors on Mt. Zion of higher ranking, tied to the apostles of the prophet of God rather than their current
husbands. It has yet to be seen whether this arrangement will succeed in
stopping the flow of apostates out of the FLDS that has been occurring
since Jeffs's imprisonment.

Yet another factor relating to success or failure in polygyny is the presence of poverty. Thornhill and Palmer (2000) wrote that most male abusers are raised in poverty and use sexual force to gain access to women with good genes. They predicted that combating the poverty of males would combat sexual abuse and rape. In my Utah Valley study (Bennion 2006), abuse occurred in lower socioeconomic households where the offender was either unemployed or underemployed. In the case of the polygamous orders, most people live well below the official United States poverty level of $17,000 a year for a family of four. For example, John Ray was a self-proclaimed scholar with little to no income, Chevral Palacios was in and out of construction work, and Ervil LeBaron was a sometime penniless farmer.

Poverty produces many disadvantages for plural wives, who are often dependent on their husband's priesthood stewardships or the charity of the community to gain access to food and clothing for their children. Such women are not likely to leave an abusive situation unless they have an outside relative who can provide them with economic support. If they have a job of their own, they are more able to leave the sect. Impoverished parents often share their frustration with their children through beatings and verbal, as well as sexual, abuse. In an overcrowded, poor household, sibling abuse may occur, and the violence a father doles out to his wife and other children is often ignored. And finally, in poor families the father often goes farther from home for work, at longer and longer intervals, in order to access better jobs, which leads to the father-absence issue. Male/father absence creates opportunities for sexual abuse since the man is not often present during the imprinting years of his children's lives (Parker 1976). He becomes sexually attracted to his daughters as they "blossom."

Economic difficulties also limit individual personal living space, causing discord and malaise. Another Al-Krenawi criterion of wellness is that women must have separate households for each wife. Ideally, this also translates to space for the children so that the various households provide ample bedrooms and space for development of personal identity and autonomy. Each woman and each child should feel they are important and not just a number, or as one wife in my study put it, "one of his many wives."

It is well known in anthropological studies that women suffer in isolated households because there are few other women around with whom to talk and work. Where a female solidarity network is present, it may be harder for abuses to go unnoticed as everyone knows each other's business and the women are "always watching." The network can provide additional childcare for women who need to work outside the community and economic aid for women who are not able to work or who have young children at home. It can help reduce the number of hours per day that women must work to provide for their families, which can contribute to increased leisure and, therefore, contentment (Kimmel 2008). Women are more likely to opt for divorce because of overwork than are men. If women do not have a protective emotional and financial safety net, they are more dependent on their husbands for these resources.

A network can also provide the means for open communication about any number of issues: the family budget, the sexual rotation schedule, the division of labor in the households, and interpersonal grievances. Women need to talk things out in order to get through the feelings of low self-worth and jealousy. As Slonim-Nevo and Al-Krenawi (2006) write, successful polygynous families create intra-familial discourse to avoid discord and resolve conflict. A female network can help alleviate anxieties, provide a mechanism for support in times of illness or hardship, and mediate disputes. Of great importance is its role in providing an opposing unity structure for women in cases where men are abusing their wives' rights. If one or even two women complain against an abusing husband, their complaint may not carry much weight in a rigid patriarchal system, but if ten to fifteen women stand up for the victim, their voices will most definitely be heard.

Finally, the most vital challenge to well-functioning is the presence of abuse. Although no group is more systematically and egregiously labeled as abusive as the FLDS, virtually every other polygamous sect practicing in Utah today has been somehow linked to financial, sexual, or spiritual improprieties (Scharnberg and Brachear, *Chicago Tribune*, Sept. 4, 2006). Yet true and accurate statistics about abuses within polygamy are hard to come by. How do we know reported abuses are valid? The initial call that was the catalyst for the recent Texas raid on the Yearning for Zion compound was discovered to be a hoax. A young woman from Colorado who was not connected in any way to the sect reported the existence of sexual abuse by members of the FLDS. Texas officials and the FBI immediately acted on that false call by placing the children into a foster care program that had a reputation for being extremely abusive itself. Another obstacle to accuracy is that many women and children may be prevented from contacting outside help in situations of abuse; therefore we can never truly know the extent to which abuse takes place in secretive settings.

From the data linked directly to newspaper reports and government agency data, I estimated that more than 158 different cases of abuse have been brought up in the last decade in reference to the FLDS group alone. According to Child Protective Services, from April 2000 to April 2008, 61 reports of abuse involving children have been recorded. Of the 21 reports from 2006 to 2008, only three were sexual in nature; the rest involved physical abuse or neglect (Ken Deibert, press statement in *Arizona Republic*, April 11, 2008). In July 2008, Texas Rangers investigated 20 additional cases of abuse and 50 cases of bigamy tied to Warren Jeffs and five other FLDS men (Ben Winslow, *Deseret News*, Aug. 21, 2008); 131 cases have been brought against the Texas/Colorado City orders, not to mention the 15 reports related to the "lost boys" and the 12 cases reported against Winston Blackmore in British Columbia.

In contrast, for the period of 1996 to 2008, I counted 27 reported offenses linked to the Kingstons (predominantly related to the Mary Ann Kingston case) and only 15 reports filed against the AUB. In the LeBaron clan, there were less than a handful of cases in the last ten years and 17 reports of abuse reported from 1969 to 1977, primarily in relation to Ervil LeBaron's "reign of terror."[1]

In an independent fundamentalist case, a father indoctrinated and "groomed" his twelve-year-old biological daughter and thirteen-year-old stepdaughter to marry him. After having sexual intercourse with both of them, the father was turned into the police by the first girl's mother; yet the twelve-year-old refused to testify against her father (Myers and Brasington 2002). Where polygamy is linked to sexual molestation, the families tend to be large, overcrowded, and rigidly controlled by a patriarchal figure (Bennion 2012). These groups are also generally isolated with little to no secular education for the children. With approximately 50,000 fundamentalists practicing polygamy, it is difficult to gauge how many families are incestuous. What is possible, however, is a thorough scrutiny of perpetrator profiles of men who had already been arrested or publicly identified as sexual offenders. In 2003, I began gathering surveys of sex-offender profiles in the state of Utah, finding that 30 percent of the perpetrators were associated, somehow, with one of the fundamentalist organizations. Seventy percent were associated with monogamist living conditions.

In some cases, abuse is manifested by forced marriage, statutory rape, and co-wife cruelty. In several groups, blood atonement is used as a vehicle of harm, a way to deal with certain sins not covered by Jesus's atonement plan. To attain salvation, a person must spill their blood so that the "smoke thereof might ascend to heaven as an offering for their sins" (Young 1856). It was first taught around 1850 in the Utah Territory by Brigham Young, which some believe led to such practices as execution by firing squad and the Mountain Meadows massacre. Although belief in blood atonement created a negative image for the AUB in the 1970s under the direction of John Ray, since his excommunication, it is no longer practiced. Under the leadership of Warren Jeffs, however, members accused of grievous sin are required to atone with physical punishment or even death. Ervil LeBaron also practiced blood atonement in Colonia LeBaron during his reign of terror in the mid-70s.

Although the AUB has fewer problems with abuse (Llewellyn 2004), I am more familiar with their stories, which I have heard in interviews, from the pulpit, and in cottage meetings. Patriarch John Ray was married to twelve women and was said by his son, a lawyer in the Salt Lake area, to have molested three young women outside his family and at least eight of his own children. To Ray, this abuse was a natural, sacred enterprise. He traveled a great deal on priesthood business and then would come home to find that a daughter had blossomed "as a rose." He would then ask her to join him in the shed out back, where he would rape her and "school" her in two vital areas: (1) she was now connected to him through blood and sex, which meant he would be her savior on Mt. Zion; and (2) if she told anyone, he would torture her through blood atonement.

In 1994, Joseph Thompson was charged by fellow councilman Lamoine Jensen with several counts of child sexual abuse and was then excommunicated from the AUB (Hales 2006). George Maycock was likewise accused of sex abuse in 1998, but no proof was provided for this charge. In both cases, evidence was presented to the AUB priesthood council, but the two councilmen were never prosecuted by the state because the victims would not testify, and Owen Allred would not allow any evidence to be turned over to the officials. The state of Utah closed the case, claiming the AUB had started false rumors. The AUB-council-generated charges were grounded in the testimonies of several of Joseph Thompson's daughters while under hypnosis and the discovery of soft porn and "girly" magazines in his home. One daughter said he lifted her dress when she was twelve years old. His eldest daughter said her abuse was confirmed by Abraham, Isaac, and Jacob in a dream. A former member of the AUB suggests that this removal was a witch hunt designed to allow Jensen to take over the priesthood. Thompson also was said to have joined a few other councilmen in setting up a torture enterprise in Oregon with a fellow councilman in the 1960s, which led to his temporary arrest. He allegedly took young brides and joined in beating prepubescent children (Cantera, *Salt Lake Tribune*, Nov. 20, 2001).

It is still unclear whether Thompson actually abused children or not; he died in 1998, shamed and excommunicated from the Salt Lake order. I witnessed Thompson rationalizing incest at the pulpit during Sunday meetings. He believed that God asked him to mate with his own daughters. He referred to the Law of Lot, stating that Lot was asked by God to have sex with his children in order to build up a more righteous seed after his own wife had been turned to salt outside of Sodom. Lot and his daughters sought refuge in a cave near Zoar; his daughters got him drunk with wine and lay with him in order to preserve their family line (Genesis 19:31–32). Incidentally, the Kingston Clan has often used this same scripture to justify incestuous relationships. Thompson said that as a direct descendant of Joseph Smith and Jesus Christ, he had to keep the blood lines pure via inbreeding. He knew his daughters were pure; therefore, if they could produce a child who was also pure, he would ensure the continuation of the Thompson family kingdom. I also heard Thompson use the story of Sarah and Abraham to sanction incest. Abraham said, "Because I thought, surely the fear of God is not in this place; and they will slay me for my wife's sake. And yet indeed she is my sister; she is the daughter of my father of my mother; and she became my wife" (Genesis 20:11–12).

I met Chevral Palacios, seventy, a councilman in the AUB, years after he had left the Mexico order. A few years later, I read in the *Salt Lake Tribune* that he was charged with four counts of child rape, which included three counts of sodomy on a child and one count for having sex with his young stepdaughters (Cantera, *Salt Lake Tribune*, Nov. 20, 2001). I learned from an informant that he had also given two other daughters away to other councilmen as payment for favors that they had done for him and encouraged his young son of thirteen to have sex with his youngest wife, who was twenty-four. He was excommunicated from the Salt Lake order in 2002.

Ervil LeBaron of Galeana, Mexico, was convicted of murdering his own brother, Verlan LeBaron, and many other members of the Firstborn order. He used the doctrine of penitence and blood atonement to justify his killing spree. In addition, he was identified as having taken young, teenage women to bed, whom he later married in the "covenant." LeBaron's daughter confessed her father's actions in the film *The Godmakers* (Hunt and Decker 1980), stating that her father's thirteen wives created a house full of jealousy and perversion, "as he would take several women to bed with him at one time." She claimed that young preteens were often reserved for older men who would have a harder time securing wives because of their age. LeBaron considered himself to be the "Lamb of God" and used physical punishment to keep his wives, children, and other members of the group in line. He believed that he was the right hand of God with the authority to pass judgment on all sinners of the order; that right also gave him the authority to mate with young adolescent girls as compensation for his good deeds and to build up his mighty family kingdom if the mating resulted in pregnancy. Like King Solomon with his 800 concubines, Ervil LeBaron believed his eleven wives represented his power and authority to spread his seed in righteousness. Walking in his shoes is a recent polygamist, Orson W. Black, who has several wives, including two teenage brides, the youngest just thirteen (Kocherga, *San Antonio Press*, Feb. 22, 2005). Like LeBaron, Black claims to be following Joseph Smith when he sanctioned the law of polygamy in his own household in 1835, the same year that Fanny Alger, a seventeen-year-old orphan living in Smith's home, became pregnant (Cairncross 1974).

In the FLDS group, the most publicized perpetrator is their former prophet, Warren Jeffs, who was sentenced to life plus twenty years in 2011 for sexually assaulting two teenage girls. An audio recording played out the sexual assault of the twelve-year-old, which instructed other child brides in how to please Jeffs sexually. Jeffs told the girls that when they please their prophet sexually, they are pleasing God, atoning for the sins of the FLDS. Jeffs frequently raped young women in his home, indoctrinating them to hold each other down during the "heavenly" sessions of sexual assault, as shown in a video tape. During his trial, a photograph emerged of fifty of his wives, most of whom had been "sealed" to him as minors. His home was said to be a warehouse for hundreds of sexual consorts. Jeffs's nephew and niece testified that he raped them as small children, threatening them to keep the "godly" assaults secret or risk their salvation. DNA evidence showed that Jeffs had fathered a child with a fifteen-year-old girl. Women were taught to be submissive to Jeffs because they believed he was a prophet of God but also that it was their birthright to be abused by him. The assaults were always initiated with a fervent prayer by Jeffs and admonitions that the girls please him or be rejected by God.

In short, I suggest that key factors combine with polygamy to produce a greater risk for poor-functioning or failed family environments. The results of this current research, and future studies of contemporary polygamous lifestyles, may help identify the presence of detrimental conditions, which can then inform policy for the protection of victims and prevention of future abuses. In some cases, research may show the lack of evidence of abuse, which can provide data on the viability of polygamy and inform policy on legalization rights and procedures and antidiscrimination laws for the protection of all nonnormative marriages. As is often the case in monogamy, polygamy may also intensify additional risk factors, such as wife abuse, sexually transmitted diseases, sibling battery, and psychosexual problems inherited by victims of sexual incest. Any investigations of abuse should be conducted on a case-by-case basis rather than targeting a whole religious community or cultural enclave. To buttress my argument that legalization of polygamy will facilitate well-functioning, let me reiterate the legal recognition advantages: (1) the legal right to marry multiple spouses, (2) the right to employment, (3) the right to adopt a child or gain custody, (4) the right to gain child support and inheritance, (5) the right to exit a union with full spousal rights, (6) the right to buy a home, (7) the right to immigrate as polygamists, and (8) the right to run for public office. I suggest that laws should be redrafted to acknowledge cultural integrity, context, and diversity, reflecting the human right to culture as a fundamental principle that "inheres in such constitutional guarantees as equal protection, freedom of association and religion, the right to counsel, and the right to fair trial" (Renteln 2004). This doesn't mean polygynists are exempt from the law but that their culture should be seen as a mitigating circumstance that is weighed against the seriousness of the offense, and their behavior should be viewed in the context of the strength of people's ties to their cultural norms.

In spite of all the potential negative factors associated with polygyny, women are still drawn to the polygynous lifestyle. According to Mormon scholar Rex Cooper (1990), women often face serious obstacles in the mainstream Mormon church. Single women, single mothers, divorced and widowed women, and unmarriageable women are often socially and economically deprived of the resources available to the rest of the membership. Women who convert are typically drawn to polygamy to find a husband, bear children, and access priesthood resources tied to their salvation. Women in polygamous relationships are baptized and integrated into an already established network. During my AUB/ Allred research, I learned that the female converts came from the LDS (Church of Jesus Christ of Latter-Day Saints, or Mormon) church. The majority, 68 percent, spoke to me of being stigmatized for the reasons Cooper lists: lack of husband or abandonment issues. In some cases women had been ostracized in their home wards for being unable to fulfill their roles as described in The Family: A Proclamation to the World[2] (Hinckley 1995). They were drawn to plural marriage—despite the fact that polygamists' views of God are different from mainstream

Mormon beliefs and in spite of the male dominance typical of polygamous households, the illegality of polygamous marriages, and the focus
of polygamous groups on communal sharing—often as a last resort
because their social situation didn't match the mainstream reality of
monogamy. In my analysis of conversion histories, I discovered that
after entering the groups, convert women experienced upward social
and economic mobility (at least temporarily). The greatest mobility
occurred among single, educated women in their thirties who entered
the group and married into the priesthood hierarchy. This increased
their employment advancement and access to economic stewardships
from 26 percent as LDS women to 43 percent as fundamentalist women
in the branch. One could thus argue that the options for some disenfranchised women in the mainstream Mormon world are relatively few.
Women who *do* convert to Mormon fundamentalism see polygyny as
the only viable way to become incorporated into the family model that
ensures Mormon exaltation.

Once within the fundamentalist group, the converts in my study
were often instantly incorporated into a family as a third or fourth wife
and had access to their husband's sperm, his priesthood powers, and
the valuable economic and emotional network established by his wives.
They were suddenly given affirmation and told that they were queens
in the making, as opposed to being called spinsters and single moms in
their old congregations, or wards, in the LDS church. Their children,
if they had any, were promised a home in an already established family
kingdom with several "aunts" to help meet their needs. Some Mormon
women experience more individual satisfaction within the dynamics of
a polygamous family than they would in any other marital form, which
may partially account for the extremely high rate of female conversion.
Advocates of polygamy, such as Anne Wilde, say that it can be seen as
a "viable alternative lifestyle between consenting adults" (Wilde, qtd.
in Lee, *New York Times*, March 28, 2006). Anthropologist Phil Kilbride
states that plural marriage can help rebuild a strong sense of family for
specific groups of Americans, especially in times of socioeconomic crisis.
He suggests that we ask ourselves whether monogamy is perfect. Many
monogamous women suffer under the thumb of a dominant man with
no one nearby to help them. At least polygamous women have their co-
wives to talk to and potentially protect them from a tyrannical husband.
This benefit coincides with one plural wife's opinion that most people
want to outlaw polygamy yet treat adultery and divorce as commonplace.
Some feel that America is all about polygamy—"It's just that they do it
one person at a time—serial polygamists" (Kilbride 1994).

According to Adriana Blake (1996), the sex ratio in America has been skewed in favor of women, especially in the 1980s and 1990s. Among people aged forty-five, there were 200 single women for every 100 available men. She thinks a return to plural marriage could be the best alternative to divorce because it would provide husbands for women, fathers for children, and an end to loneliness. Samuel Chapman, a supporter of polygamy, agrees, stating that the surplus of women in the US population creates competition for good men, which requires men to strive to show their best traits. Women then select the best men instead of settling for leftovers (Chapman, qtd. in Gray 2001). As Randy Maudsley has stated, reinforcing one method of dealing with these skewed sex ratios, if a man is in love with two women, he should just marry them both (Maudsley 1997).

Another polygamous family popularized by the media is the Alex Joseph clan of Big Water, Utah. One of Alex Joseph's wives, Elizabeth Joseph, writes that if polygamy didn't exist, "the modern American career woman would have invented it—because, despite its reputation, polygamy is the one lifestyle that offers an independent woman a real chance to 'have it all'" (Joseph 1997). Elizabeth, who worked as a journalist, relied on her co-wives to help her with child care and meal preparation. She called it a "free-market approach to marriage" that allowed her to pick the best man available, regardless of his marital status. Her husband's other wives actually enhanced her marriage to her husband. Alex, she said, had vast experience as a good husband long before he married her, so he was skilled; he didn't need to be trained like most husbands do. When Elizabeth became a lawyer, she introduced her beautiful and talented secretary, Belinda, to her husband. He married Belinda shortly afterward, uniting the two women as friends and wives. When I met Elizabeth Joseph at the same-sex marriage/plural marriage forum at the Salt Lake library, I found her to be very strong and outspoken. Ted Mikels's documentary *Alex Joseph and His Wives* describes how Alex, a former policeman, became a polygamist in the Allred Group, eventually taking on twelve wives (ironically, from non-Mormon families). He and his wives started their own town in Big Water and introduced libertarian ideals to all new citizens (Mikels 1976).

In addition to seeing polygamy as a viable alternative to monogamy, many fundamentalist women are empowered in their roles as mothers of Zion. This concept is related to the notion of republican motherhood used widely in the Mormon movement for women's suffrage in the late nineteenth and early twentieth centuries, which was directed by outspoken polygamous women such as state senator and doctor Martha

Hughes Cannon (Hanks 1992). The ideas of republican motherhood benefited pioneer women in the private and public realms of life. For example, in the early days of the LDS church, Brigham Young encouraged women not only to become "mothers in Zion" but also to advance their careers in business and politics: "Women are useful, not only to sweep houses . . . but they should stand behind the counter, study law or physics, or become good bookkeepers. . . . All this enlarges their sphere of usefulness for the benefit of society at large" (Young 1869). Elizabeth Joseph agrees with Brigham Young. She says that plural marriage is empowering for women. "It provides me the environment and opportunity to maximize my female potential without all the trade-offs and compromises that attend monogamy" (Joseph 1997, 1). Another advocate of legalizing polygamy writes that plural marriage frees women to pursue a career and increases the overall value of women in society.

In these more favorable, well-functioning polygynous families, all the negative features I cataloged earlier are virtually absent. There is no isolation, poverty, male supremacy, or inequality, and the women have tapped into an affirming, supportive network that affords them volition and relative leisure. Examples of such successes are found in the Darger, Josef, and Williams families, associated at one time or another with the Allred group. Most recently exposed to the public eye is the Brady Williams family. Williams, a building contractor from central Utah, came out of the closet as a polygamist in the summer of 2013, parading his lifestyle on the TLC television network in his new show, *My Five Wives*. His goal, he claims, is to try to "try and keep everyone happy" (McCombs, *Huffington Post*, Sept. 16, 2013). Williams's wives make sure he is on a strict rotation schedule that provides each wife with equal access to her husband, and each wife's children equal time with their father. So, that means he sleeps with one wife every five nights. To avoid any one wife feeling left out or lonely, the wives made huge body pillows to sleep with, and they keep busy with housework, taking care of twenty-four children, attending college, and working in salaried jobs. To reduce jealousy problems, they train Williams not to show too much public affection to any one wife and to make sure he treats them all with respect. This family represents a new type of polygamy that benefits women and children more than it benefits the patriarchy. Williams must appease the demands of his five wives or face their severe unified wrath. The Williamses were members of the Apostolic United Brethren (the Allreds) but claim it was too restrictive and rigidly patriarchal for their tastes. The family lives in an Allred community called Rocky Ridge but faces expulsion because they left the group and now practice a mixture of Mormonism and Buddhism as "independents," who now comprise approximately 15,000 individuals in the Intermountain West (Wilde 2010, 1). They wish to teach good moral values of charity and love in their home with no fear of hell or punishment. In spite of their apostasy, all six spouses grew up in fundamentalism, Williams coming into it when his father and mother joined from the mainstream LDS church. This socialization no doubt helps condition the family to adapt well to plural life. Williams's family lives in two large homes he built on a hillside with a view of Mount Nebo. One looks much like a two-level motel for three wives and the other is a fourplex for two wives. Though the family fears prosecution, they are sure the future is bright for modern-day polygamists like themselves whose only crime is polygamy, not underage marriage, money laundering, welfare fraud, abuse, or illegal arms ownership.

A further example of success is that of Brady's father, Rod Williams, and his three wives, "Ann," "Rosa," and "Emily," whom I visited the summer of 2008 in Washington. Rod Williams's home is located in the middle of a huge cedar forest near the coast on the Olympic Peninsula. They live comfortably on a five-acre property with a large 5,000-square-foot home. Williams renovated the garage to be a full apartment for his second wife, Rosa, and her five children, installing a kitchen, three bedrooms, a bathroom, and a living room with a woodstove. Rosa's style is simple, clean, and earthy. The second floor of the home belongs to Emily, the third wife, and her three children. It has a kitchen with a wraparound counter, a living room, two bathrooms, a laundry room, and three bedrooms. Her style, which is more luxurious, features cranberry-colored walls and exotic furniture. The top floor belongs to Ann, the first wife. It is decorated in a traditional Mormon style of soft pastel colors and Victorian furniture. It has a master bedroom, a living room, a kitchen, a bathroom, and one spare bedroom for Ann's crafts and sewing. Ann is in her sixties and has less need for extra bedrooms as all her children are grown. Outside is a large vegetable garden, a chicken coop, and a woodshop. In all, the house has nine bedrooms, five bathrooms, and three kitchens and living rooms. Williams figured it would have been less expensive for him to build a brand-new home than to spend so much money to renovate each floor to adapt to the decorating styles of each wife. Since the wives did not want a common living room and kitchen, the contractors had to tear down walls to provide for new kitchens, each of which has its own style of cupboards and fixtures. Interestingly, it is Emily who runs the family business and is outspoken and "in charge," just as in the case of Elizabeth Joseph of Big Water, who is a breadwinner and spokesperson to the media instead of her husband, Alex, who does not like to be in the public eye.

According to Anne Wilde of *Principle Voices* (Wilde 2010, 1), watching polygamists like Rod and Brady Williams helps to dispel the negative myths about plural life. Brady said that he wished to do the TLC show to illustrate how polygamy can be healthy and stable. "There is nothing wrong with consenting adults living and loving how they choose" (McCombs, *Huffington Post*, Sept. 16, 2013, 1).

In short, polygamy is clearly the next marriage-rights frontier. The First Amendment and due process clause of the Fourteenth Amendment should allow us to define the contours of our sexuality and express our religious beliefs freely as long as we do not harm the state or other people. Law and policy approaches to plural marriage must be guided by the goal of facilitating meaningful choices for women. As long as polygynous marriage continues to be illegal, these choices will be scrutinized, stigmatized, and threatened with arrest. Polygamy is hard enough without these legal restrictions. That being the case, there is certainly no fear that it will "take over" and threaten democracy, as Maura Irene Strassberg states in this volume. Because the law criminalizes consensual, fully adult sexuality, the United States and Canada fail to fulfill the spirit of a liberal democratic state that promises that consenting adults will be free to define love and marriage without fear of arrest.

Note
1.   One out-of-print book about the reign of terror of Ervil LeBaron—who was the prophet of the Church of the Lamb of God—is Ben Bradlee Jr. and Dale Van Atta's *Prophet of Blood: The Untold Story of Ervil Lebaron and the Lambs of God* (New York: Putnam Pub Group, 1981). Anyone who crossed Ervil LeBaron was slated to be killed, including some people very close to him, such as Verlan, his brother, and the AUB prophet, Rulon C. Allred.
2.   The Proclamation is a document of revelation that affirms the standards, doctrines, and practices relative to the family, as commanded by the living prophets of the LDS Church.

References
Achebe, Chinua. 1959. *Things Fall Apart*. New York: Doubleday.
Altman, Irwin, and Joseph Ginat. 1996. *Polygamous Families in Contemporary Society*. Cambridge, MA: Cambridge University Press. http://dx.doi.org/10.1017/CBO978 0511663987.
Bennion, Janet. 1998. *Women of Principle: Female Networking in Contemporary Mormon Polygamy*. Oxford: Oxford University Press.
Bennion, Janet. 2004. *Desert Patriarchy: Gender Dynamics in the Chihuahua Valley*. Tucson: University of Arizona Press.

Bennion, Janet. 2006. "Abbas Raptus: Exploring Factors Contributing to the Sexual Abuse of Females in Rural Mormon Fundamentalist Communities." *Forum on Public Policy* 1 (Fall): 24.

Bennion, Janet. 2012. *Polygamy in Primetime.* Waltham, MA: Brandeis University Press.

Blake, Adriana. 1996. *Women Can Win the Marriage Lottery: Share Your Man with Another Wife.* Newport Beach, CA: Orange County University Press.

Bradley, Martha. 1990. "The Women of Fundamentalism: Short Creek, 1953." *Dialogue: A Journal of Mormon Thought* 23 (2): 15–37.

Cairncross, John. 1974. *After Polygamy Was Made a Sin: The Social History of Christian Polygamy.* London: Rutledge and Kegan Paul.

Carneiro, Robert. 1988. "The Circumscription Theory: Challenge and Response." *American Behavioral Scientist* 31 (4): 497–511. http://dx.doi.org/10.1177/000276488 031004010.

Chamberlain, Linda. 2002. "Domestic Violence: A Primary Care Issue for Rural Women." *National Women's Health Network.* https://nwhn.org/domestic-violence-primary-care -issue-rural-women.

Cooper, Rex. 1990. *Promises Made to Fathers.* Salt Lake City: University of Utah Press.

Diamond, Jared. 1999. *Guns, Germs, and Steel: The Fate of Human Societies.* New York: Norton.

Gray, Christen. 2001. "Got One Wife? Have Another." *The Tech,* May 17. http://tech.mit .edu/V121/N37/col37gray.37c.html.

Hales, Brian C. 2006. *Modern Polygamy and Mormon Fundamentalism: The Generations after the Manifesto.* Salt Lake City: Greg Kofford Books.

Hanks, Maxine. 1992. *Women and Authority: Re-emerging Mormon Feminism.* Salt Lake City: Signature Books.

Hassouneh-Phillips, Dena. 2001. "Polygamy and Wife Abuse: A Qualitative Study of Muslim Women in America." *Health Care for Women International* 22 (8): 735–48. http://dx.doi.org/10.1080/073993301753339951.

Hinckley, Gordon B. 1995. "The Family: A Proclamation to the World." *The Church of Jesus Christ of Latter-Day Saints.* https://www.lds.org/topics/family-proclamation?lang= eng&cid=PA0414-02.

Hunt, Dave, and Ed Decker. 1980. *The God Makers.* Videocassette. Produced by R.J.M. Productions. Los Angeles: Jeremiah Films.

Joseph, Elizabeth. 1997. "Polygamy—the Ultimate Feminist Lifestyle." *Islam for Today,* May. www.islamfortoday.com/polygamy3.

Mikels, Ted. 1976. *Alex Joseph and His Wives.* DVD. Directed by Ted V. Mikels. Distributed by Ted V. Mikels.

Kilbride, Phil. 1994. *Plural Marriage for Our Times: A Reinvented Option?* Westport, CT: Bergin and Garvey.

Kimmel, Michael S. 2008. *The Gendered Society.* New York: Oxford University Press.

LeBaron, Verlan. 1981. *The LeBaron Story.* El Paso, TX: Keels and Co.

Leis, Nancy B. 1974. "Women in Groups." In *Woman, Culture and Society,* edited by Michelle Z. Rosaldo and Louise Lamphere, 223–42. Stanford, CA: Stanford University Press.

Llewellyn, J. 2004. *Polygamy Under Attack: From Tom Green to Brian David Mitchell.* Salt Lake City: Agreka Books.

Maudsley, Randy. 1997. "Man and Wives: A Look at Polygamous Marriages in the U.S." Episode of *20/20,* ABC, October 17.

Musser, Joseph. 1948. *Celestial or Plural Marriage.* Salt Lake City: Truth.

Myers, Wade C., and Steve J. Brasington. 2002. "A Father Marries His Daughters: A Case of Incestuous Polygamy." *Journal of Forensic Sciences* 47 (5): 1112–16.

Nakanike, Musisi. 1991. "Women, Elite Polygyny, and Buganda State Formation." *Signs (Chicago, Ill.)* 16 (41): 757–77.

Netting, Robert. 1969. "Women's Weapons: The Politics of Domesticity among the Kofyar." *American Anthropologist* 71 (6): 1037–46. http://dx.doi.org/10.1525/aa.1969 .71.6.02a00020.

Parker, Seymour. 1976. "The Precultural Basis of the Incest Taboo: Toward a Biosocial Theory." *American Anthropologist* 78 (2): 285–305. http://dx.doi.org/10.1525/aa.1976 .78.2.02a00030.

Renteln, Alison. 2004. *The Cultural Defense.* New York: Oxford University Press.

Saitoti, Tepilit. 1988. *The World of a Maasai Warrior.* Berkeley: University of California Press.

Slonim-Nevo, Vered, and Alean Al-Krenawi 2006. "Success and Failure among Polygamous Families: The Experience of Wives, Husbands, and Children." *Family Process* 45 (3): 311–30. http://dx.doi.org/10.1111/j.1545-5300.2006.00173.x.

Stacey, Judith, and Tey Meadow. 2009. "New Slants on the Slippery Slope: The Politics of Polygamy and Gay Family Rights in South Africa and the United States." *Politics & Society* 37 (2): 167–202. http://dx.doi.org/10.1177/0032329209333924.

Thornhill, Randy, and Craig Palmer. 2000. *A Natural History of Rape.* Boston: MIT Press.

Wilde, Anne. 2010. *Census.* Principle Voices.

Young, Bringham. 1856. *Journal of Discourses* 4: 53–4.

Young, Brigham. 1869. *Journal of Discourses* 13: 1–4. Liverpool: LDS Church.

4

ETHICS OF SISTERHOOD
African American Muslim Women and Polygyny

Debra Majeed

Walladah sits before her computer, excitedly reflecting upon the results that her next key strokes could bring.[1] This African American Muslim woman in her fifties is self-confident, happily married, and the mother of five. When a PhD was her goal, Walladah's husband of four years took the lead with housework, cooking, parenting their children, and removing roadblocks so that she could have quiet time to think and write. In many ways, partnership has defined their union, her third marriage. With the successful defense of her doctoral dissertation behind her, Walladah has embarked upon another arduous road. This time, she's taking the lead in her husband's search for a second wife. You see, in this marriage, as with the pursuit of an advanced degree, personal goals have a way of becoming family matters.

Family matters take shape in starkly different ways for another female midwesterner also in her fifties. An accomplished executive, Karimah spends quiet evenings in her suburban home, alone and without heat. Months into a marital arrangement in which her husband took a second wife, Karimah's standard of living has plummeted so low that "the only thing that has not been interrupted is the lights because I just could not stay there without any lights." In contrast to the power Walladah exerts, the impact of multiple-wife marriage for this African American Muslim female reinforces the dynamics of male privilege associated with such unions and the devastating effects they can have on the well-being of women.

Are plural marriages in the United States solely the extension of male desire? Do they exploit women? How do Americans make meaning of some family structures and disavow others? How do African American Muslims explain what they're doing and why when they establish multiple-wife households? What form(s) of agency do Walladah, Karimah, and other Muslim women exert when they share their husbands? And, finally,

DOI: 10.7330/9780874219975.c004

"What ethic of solidarity or sisterhood exists among African American Muslim women *living polygyny?*"[2] These and other questions have tugged at my consciousness since 2002, much as I once clung to the hem of my mother's skirt until I captured her attention. They are the foundational queries that drive a larger project, one that explores the practice of polygyny in more than fifteen mosques in the United States.[3] I draw my informants largely from those associated with the leadership of Imam W. D. Mohammed. Though he maintains an international following, Mohammed's "community" represents the single largest group of indigenous African American Muslims.[4] The project also considers the extent to which women living on the periphery of society—as women married to husbands contemplating or practicing polygyny often are—can assert some form of agency or power by redefining plural marriage and socializing polygyny.[5] I assert that commitment to cultural survival and communal exegesis compel some American Muslim women to share their husbands. For them, multiple-wife marriage is one remedy for, and a demographic challenge to, the absence of marriageable African American men and/or the high number of female-led households.

In this essay, I draw particular attention to what for me was an even more startling discovery, wives who single out potential mates for their husbands. To such women, their efforts represent a form of personal authority and a way to rearticulate multiple-wife marriage as a liberating rather than abusive structure. I contrast the experiences of women like Walladah with women like Karimah, for whom polygyny is an imposition at best; at worst, it creates toxic situations. The possibility of sisterhood, or the solidarity among African American Muslim women who are "related"—not by biology, but by the husband they share—is largely determined by the multiple connections among them and the material bonds that position women differently. Ultimately, the divergent experiences explored here symbolize the urgent need for critical exegetical studies in local mosques and an expansion of accessible resources to support healthy Muslim family life in America. They vividly contradict representations that universalize the particularities these women live.

Plural marriage in Islam is described as the practice of a husband being married to up to four wives at the same time.[6] Unlike *polygamy*, which refers to more than one spouse—husband or wife—and, thus, is un-Islamic, polygyny in the form practiced by Muslims is mentioned in the Qur'an, the authority of the fast-growing religion—one with a global population projected to reach 2.8 billion by 2050.[7] In other words, similar to what occurs around the globe, plural marriage in Islam is the exclusive prerogative of men. Cultural wars directed at same-sex marriage, the visibility of multiple-partner families as exhibited by the television series *Sister Wives*,[8] and recent prosecutions of the leaders of the Fundamentalist Church of Jesus Christ of Latter-Day Saints (FLDS) have introduced new images and discourses about marriage and partnering in the sociopolitical landscape of the United States. Noteworthy, too, is the presence of other forms of religiously inspired polygyny that lead to monolithic characterizations of several separate and very diverse groups.[9] For instance, communities such as the FLDS church sanction a husband marrying as many wives as he chooses, who become his partners for eternity.

In contrast to generations of women before them who were afforded little input in their own marriage possibilities, African American and other Muslim women do have a choice in whom and how they marry. By *choice* I do not mean to suggest that saying "I do" somehow steers Muslim women in the direction of more egalitarian decision making between themselves and their husbands. After all, gender roles remain clear-cut for the majority of Muslim wives, beginning with the marriage proposal extended by the male and accepted by the female, and inclusive of the husband possessing ultimate power in regards to the number of wives (up to a maximum of four) that he has at any one time.[10] In other words, the experiences of African American Muslim women living polygyny reinforce what scholars have determined about motherhood and reproduction among women in general: patriarchal values and structures "set the limits" of women's choice (Rowland 1992). As I intend to make clear, to reduce *choice* to binary oppositions for African American Muslim women who desire marriage to African American Muslim men disguises the complexity of the issue at many levels.

The historic practice of a husband living with multiple wives is *not* the preferred form of marriage for the estimated 1 to 2 million African American Muslims who reside in the United States. When the majority of African American Muslims marry, they enter into heterosexual monogamous unions—as do most other Muslim Americans.[11] In fact, I estimate that there are fewer than 1,000 African American Muslim polygynous households in the United States. This figure represents about 0.07 percent of all African American Muslims according to the 2010 study "Muslim American Outreach" (Allied Media Cooperation 2010)—a small segment of the estimated 30,000 to 100,000 people living polygyny in the United States.[12] Nevertheless, ethnographic research from 2003 to 2013 among more than fifteen distinct African American Muslim communities in which current and/

or former polygynists and their families reside confirms that the practice of polygyny is becoming more visible, if not growing. For example, A Refreshing Look at Polygyny with Qur'anic Insights and a Focus on Justice & Freedom in an Adverse Environment, a 2009 marriage conference, was well publicized, with posters visible in the downtown Atlanta area where the conference was held.

With such visibility comes whispered speculation about the legality of such unions, the agency and financial protection of the women involved, communal responsibility for the health and maintenance of polygynous families, and the unwanted governmental attention these households attract. Attention to polygyny among African Americans also occurs at a time when Western discourses about Islam concentrate on what are perceived to be the abnormalities of Muslim life, especially after the events of September 11, 2001, and on the agency available to Muslim women to structure their public and private spheres. It is not my intent to contribute to any perceived malaise about Muslims or Islam. Indeed, I am unapologetically and unashamedly Muslim. Yet, I have come to realize that by living polygyny, African American and other Muslims often live splintered lives. Moreover, the impact of their "difficult reality," the description of multiple-wife marriage offered by one religious leader who cautioned me against pursuing this study, easily extends beyond the polygynous household. In other words, when women like Karimah internalize an ethic of self-denial and are socialized into demeaning forms of dependency regardless of their personal successes, perhaps wider chasms other than time and image exist.

Ten years ago, I was a divorced Muslim woman hoping to remarry an African American Muslim man. Though I realized I could consider potential mates from any cultural group, I believed—as do most of my informants—that I resonated most with Muslim men who share my cultural heritage. Intellectually, I was also drawn to consider the influence of religion and ideology in the organization of African American Muslim family life. By then I had read and heard enough about the strains on Muslim women who share their husbands to be wary of people who spoke highly about the benefits of multiple-wife unions. Like many of you, I thought such relationships were merely about sex, male privilege, and female submission. What's more, it is commonplace for husbands to take additional wives without the awareness or approval of their current spouses and without being financially, psychologically, or spiritually prepared to handle the conflicts that arise between their wives and within their individual households. Many women who share their husbands encounter a different lifestyle than the one they had expected in marriage. Even with the growing number of women-only online forums specifically designed to support and facilitate discussion among Muslim women considering or currently engaged in a multiple-wife marriage, many Muslim women are not prepared to become wives whose primary obligations include getting along with their husband's other spouses.[13] As I struggled to support Karimah, a good friend whose husband was about to take another wife, I discovered that in the world of African American Muslims, this form of plural marriage is more complex than most literature would suggest.

KARIMAH'S STORY

For fifteen years, Karimah and Abdul Aziz lived monogamously, raised children from former marriages, and built a prosperous business together. People in their local religious community, of which Karima and her husband were long-time members, revered them as an ideal married couple. I did, too. While I was acquainted with the husband, I loved and adored his wife. Never during their marriage, according to Karimah, did Abdul Aziz give any indication that he desired a second wife until thirty days before he was about to say "I do."

"I can't even think [about] what triggered me to even kind of . . . pay attention to him," she said, recalling the time in 2003 when she began to suspect that her husband was involved with another woman. "Maybe it was something simple . . . because normally he calls me throughout the day and maybe he was not calling me as much. Something triggered my thinking that something's up with [him]." Out of anger, confusion, and frustration, Karimah began to exhibit behavior more commonly associated with jealous women or the partners of cheating husbands. She started reading his phone bills and using business contacts to locate the residence of his frequent calls. She even confronted Abdul Aziz at the home of the other woman. Months later her husband declared his intentions. Karimah described the exchange this way:

> He said, "I met a sister, and we're going to get married." And I said, "Oh, really?" I said, "Call her up." So he called and said, "I just told Karimah that we plan to get married." She gets on the phone and says, "I'm so glad to meet you and so happy to work with you. This is going to be wonderful and you don't know about polygamy but it's really uplifting and you should see how the sisters do it," and—because she's Hebrew Israelite—"you should see how the sisters handle polygamy in the Israelite community." And I'm just listening. And I told her, "No. I do not care to be involved in a polygymist situation."

But Karimah did remain in the marriage—for two more years. She and I knew that the Qur'an, the single highest authority in Islam, permits men to marry, under certain circumstances and contexts, up to four women simultaneously. Neither she nor I believed the necessary qualifications were present in her situation, however. Nor did we believe that polygyny would benefit the women involved in a marriage that could not legally be recognized in the United States. At the time, most supporters of Imam Mohammed were publicly silent on the issue of multiple-wife marriage, considering family formation to be a private matter. Many still are today. Then, Karimah was convinced that she fully understood Islam's perspectives on marriage. Yet, her "knowledge" reflected unquestioned assumptions taught to her by her husband, in her local mosques, and/or by earlier generations that rendered conditional *permission* as unconditional *approval*. Hers was a stance also taken by nearly all of our Muslim friends and associates. Thus, within months of her husband's marriage, she had grudgingly accepted a role consistent with her self-imposed label: *co-wife*.[14]

WALLADAH'S STORY

By the time Walladah began her Internet search for another wife for her husband of four years, her experience with polygyny showed evidence of a beneficial situation, the type of loving, empowering, and satisfying union all married women crave. One of her previous two marriages was a multiple-wife union, and its end had nothing to do with its form. Rather, like her first marriage, the second was the result of poor mate selection, she says, coupled with the pressure Walladah felt to be married. Like Karimah, Walladah spent years as her former husband's only wife before he expanded their family. Unlike Karimah, however, Walladah says she gained a "sister" in both instances, a co-wife with whom she communicated several times a day. She characterized her former and current husbands as Muslim men of principal—just and fair individuals who financially support their children. Indeed, their approach to living polygyny, Walladah asserts, frees her to want to help other women become part of a family.

> My rights have never been in question or lessened. I have the power that is given me through being a Muslimah, which means I am fully taken care of and protected, that I am treated with respect, given attention and affection and am not left in doubt at all about how my husband feels about me and our relationship.[15] Polygyny does not impact my rights or power in any way.

By 2011, Walladah felt her third marriage was sufficiently grounded to invite into her family a sister who was "striving to be a good, practicing Muslimah, accepting of polygyny and interested in being a part of our overall family structure." When asked what indicated that her husband was spiritually, financially, emotionally, and sexually healthy enough and able to support more than one wife, she was quick to declare, "Everything."

While Walladah and Karimah chose to approach the idea of living polygyny differently, the choices for these women involved both personal issues and situational ethics that can challenge any potential sisterhood among co-wives. What they and other African American Muslim women who share their husbands say, do, and believe symbolizes the wide and complex terrain that is the ideological and experiential practice of polygyny, particularly in a Muslim-minority environment. I will briefly consider speech, action, and belief in the experiences of both women as a means to consider the commonality and diversity among African American women's experience with multiple-wife marriage. Through these lenses we can better understand how the conditions of these women's lives are connected to, made possible by, and influence the conditions of the lives of other American Muslim women who share their husbands.[16] In other words, we have an opportunity to explore the ethics of sisterhood.

When first introduced to the possibility of multiple-wife marriage, Karimah articulated her strong opposition. She knew the practice existed in Muslim-majority countries and that some African American and other Muslims engaged in multiple-wife marriage in the United States. But she felt confident that taking on the responsibility of another wife was something Abdul Aziz would never consider. After all, he seemed to Karimah to be "really easy going, so willing to bend" to her wishes. She saw herself as "on the dominant side," a mother who earned the wrath of her daughter when Karimah appeared to take advantage of her husband: "My daughter . . . she wouldn't tell me in front of him, but she would later say, 'Ma, why you talk to him like that? You just doin' that 'cause he's a nice guy,'" Karimah explained. "It's like, okay. Let me be more considerate of this nice guy . . . I really thought we had an excellent marriage."

Karimah enjoyed a sisterhood of Muslim friends, including me, with whom she could share her pain, frustration, and confusion. We were disappointed that Abdul Aziz chose to go beyond the Muslim community in search of a second wife. While the Qur'an conditionally permits men to marry non-Muslim women and to marry up to four wives, the "stock" of Abdul Aziz decreased further in the view of Karimah's sisterhood because he chose a road he could not afford *and* bypassed single Muslim women with children. Moreover, while he began to live with his new bride, Abdul Aziz began to neglect his responsibilities to Karimah. Soon, Karimah discontinued their marital intimacy. She explained the material condition of her household this way:

> I was like, okay, if you're still telling people I'm your wife, then you have to take the full responsibility. And my charity is not going to be a part of it.[17] So, things were in disarray. Cut off. And sometimes I would have the money to pay [bills], but I would say uh uh, no, I'm not payin' nothing. . . . You know I would tell him that the bill is still here and he would say, "Okay, I'll get it." But then he wouldn't get it and just pass it off. And I would say, "Hey, well it's gonna have to go off," so I would show him that [his approach to polygyny] is not acceptable. This does not meet the criteria that I think Allah gave the guidelines for.

Her sisterhood encouraged Karimah to divorce her husband. We reminded her that in their attempts to "show" their husbands, she and women like her become complicit in their own oppression. But none of us were living polygyny.

Eventually, Karimah consulted friends who were—a woman who "had been in polygamy for a while" and her husband, who agreed to speak with Abdul Aziz. Karimah was pleasantly surprised by the conversation.

> Even though he was in a polygamist situation, he did not advocate polygamy. He was really questioning Abdul Aziz. "What are your motives?" And I was really, really surprised that he would do that because when Abdul Aziz got on the phone I was saying, "Oh my God, now here's somebody who's practicing. I do NOT need Abdul Aziz to talk to *him*." But it was totally the opposite. Other than those two friends, I did not have anybody to really go to where Abdul Aziz would listen to them.

According to Karimah, Abdul Aziz refused to discuss the issue with their local imam, saying instead that "the imam cannot tell him" about plural marriage.[18] Karimah avoided the imam, too; she said, "Every time someone brought polygamy up, in my mind, the imam just blew it off. It was like, there's more things to be concerned about than polygamy. Or, he was really, to me, cavalier about it." Karimah remained in the marriage three months after our initial interview, clinging to the hope that Abdul Aziz would "come to his senses and realize this ain't workin'."

Apparently polygyny *is* working for Walladah. In fact, her online advertisement highlights the collaborative nature of her marriage and her interest in a devout and fertile Muslimah. In the ad she writes,

> My husband is interested in taking another wife and has asked me to assist him in the process. I am 38 and he is 40 years old. We are African

American. He is a professional with a corporate career, attends, prays and studies at the Masjid, *Mashallah*. We live in Texas and are interested in a practicing *Muslimah*, ethnicity is not important. *Inshallah* we want to grow our family not just through marriage but through future children as well, *Inshallah*. If you are interested in any further information, please feel free to email me privately.[19]

While Walladah's example lacks the commitment of my other informants to the continuity of African American culture, it does offer yet another rationale for the exploration of female experience. Like other informants married to polygynist men, Walladah is adamant in her belief that the Qur'an supports the practice of polygyny even where it is illegal. More importantly, perhaps, she views her involvement in the selection process as emotional insurance against the drama typically associated with polygyny, like overt jealousy, second wives attempting to displace first wives, and inadequate distribution of a husband's time, attention, and resources.

Walladah also wants to draw further attention to the particularity of female experience as a necessary component to any exploration of polygyny and Muslim family life. Her concern about the male-centered way many Muslims and others perceive and approach multiple-wife marriage reflects the question, How can we speak of an issue as complex as marriage but base our guidelines only on the opinions and perspectives of half the people involved? In this regard, she echoes the views of Islamic scholar Amina Wadud, who does not support polygyny as practiced today but does maintain that women's participation in and experience of multiple-wife marriage is a source of reliable information, or authority, on multiple-wife marriage.

EXPERIENCE AS AUTHORITY

Amina Wadud (2008) has persuasively argued that "multiple, contested, and coexisting meanings of Islam are integral to struggles for justice." In her published works and public lectures, both nationally and internationally, this gender justice advocate offers a cogent thesis of experience as authority. Key to my work is her acknowledgment of different types of authority including, most important, the *authority of experience* in order to move toward a more nuanced consideration of how and why Muslims organize their households and what is needed to safeguard the rights of women. When Wadud highlights the role women share with men as *khalifah* on earth, or "moral agent of Allah," she draws attention to the rights and responsibilities of Muslim women to be among the "authoritative voices" that establish the canon, so to speak, for determining the proper practice of polygyny or whether it is a viable example of justice today.

To be clear, the apparently egalitarian household dynamics of Walladah's family are shared by few of the African American Muslims I have encountered. That is, the possibility or likelihood that additional wives might join their family is a subject that this couple discusses openly and often. But such a decision is one into which few male polygynists invite their spouses as full participants. Not only is Walladah convinced that the Qur'an sanctions multiple-wife marriage for contemporary Muslims who live in the United States, she is equally certain that wives who share their husbands can and should exert authority over the emotional and concrete ethos of their family. She believes, too, that women who share their husbands have "all the benefits minus any of the stress and pressure" that confront women in one-husband-one-wife unions. Thus, posting an advertisement on an Internet listserv for *Muslimah* eyes is consistent with Walladah's polygyny paradigm, one that upholds patriarchy almost as much as it is fueled by a conviction that multiple-wife marriage works, and that it works best when women design the selection process.

Similar to debates about gender relationships that are becoming more common in women-only online discussions for English-speaking Muslim women in the United States and the United Kingdom, Walladah and Karimah tailored interpretations of the Qur'an and Hadith that provide answers to day-to-day issues (Piela 2010).[20] Walladah understands the Qur'an to permit multiple-wife marriage at any time, in any context, as long as the husband can meet his obligations. The illegality of polygyny in the United States is not a formidable obstacle for Walladah, especially when it meets individual and communal needs. That is, polygyny extends marriage to women who might not legitimately marry and raise children otherwise. So, for women like Walladah, the spiritual law that permits polygyny supersedes the civil law that forbids its practice. Most of my informants take this position and often equate the seventh-century Arabian context of women left widowed due to warfare with the contemporary state of black America and its low percentage of marriageable African American men. That is, in the words of one imam from the East Coast,

> We are at war. With the high incarceration of our men and other social challenges, we have to find some solution to save our community. When polygyny is practiced correctly and honestly, it has tremendous results for everyone involved. When it is not practiced correctly and honestly, the suffering and hurt can be devastating.

The reality that some African Americans might want to define marriage for themselves even if such a definition is contrary to US law is not surprising given the frequency with which black people have found themselves on the "back side" of "bad laws." Also, many African Americans who came to Islam through the doorway of the teachings of the Honorable Elijah Muhammad, whom some contend was himself a polygynist, are accustomed to responding subversively to government intervention into their domestic affairs.

Karimah's views reflect the contradictions that can reflect the experience of women living polygyny. On one hand, she agrees with the majority of American Muslims who contend that Muslims should adhere to the governing ordinances where they reside as long as such laws do not force Muslims to sin. She and they base their argument on a Hadith in which the Prophet directed his followers to be mindful of local authorities.[21] Still, she recognizes that polygyny *can* work for *some* women. Like Walladah and the rest of my informants, Karimah is deeply troubled by the lack of marriageable men for African American Muslim women. They contend that polygyny responds to an unjust law that limits the ability of African Americans to build and maintain healthy families.

On the other hand, living polygyny has led Karimah to join opponents of polygyny in their insistence that few African American Muslim men are able to care for multiple wives and do justice to them at the same time. That is, most men are unable to fulfill their financial obligations *and* care for the spiritual, emotional, and physical needs of multiple wives in a just manner. Moreover, as Karimah learned, few subsequent marriages involve widows or orphans—but they contend that the importance of taking widows and orphans as subsequent wives is clearly articulated in the single most quoted Qur'anic statement on polygyny. Indeed, the revelation given to the prophet *regulated* rather than authorized the practice of polygyny, with gender justice as its goal.[22] According to Jamal Badawi (2012), the atmosphere of seventh-century Arabia necessitated compassion for widows and orphans, not male satisfaction, and the liberation of women was foremost among the values Islam is designed to cement. Those who ascribe to this reading view the permissibility of polygyny through the narrowest of doors—one through which a husband may consider additional marriages only to female orphans in his care, mothers with children whose fathers have died, or women who have lost their husbands. My findings support Wadud's observation that "most proponents of polygamy seldom discuss it within the context of just treatment of orphans" (Wadud 1999).

For women like Walladah and other female proponents of multiple-wife marriage, the status of women selected as second, third, or fourth wives is not an overriding concern. They are more focused on ensuring that as many women as possible have access to the core expression of a family as divinely inspired institution; they are more concerned about the quality of the relationship, the ethics of the sisterhood. In fact, the women in the sisterhood of Walladah do not focus on legitimizing their marriages outside of Islam. As Walladah explains,

> The marriage license for me, and for [my co-wives] is not an essential component to feeling married or having a real relationship. I have never known anyone who obtained two marriage licenses. I do know people who choose not to have a "legal" marriage, but just an Islamic marriage because what is important is being in a *halal* relationship.

Even opponents of polygyny oppose governmental interference in marriage and other issues they consider to be private matters. Clearly, the vast majority of American Muslims register their marriages with the appropriate civil authorities. Still, given the history of neglect and exclusion that has been the experience of generations of African Americans with the US government, it was not surprising to meet African American Muslims who chose not to obtain marriage licenses even for single-wife unions.

Interestingly, perceptions about the importance of marriage and its role in community life as well as about the nature of sisterhood are issues that hold the attention of women living polygyny regardless of their position on the practice. In reference to the nature of marriage, Islam teaches that husbands and wives are garments for each other and that marriage provides the sole legitimate and secure environment for Muslims to conceive and raise children. Understandably then, Muslims approach marriage as a vehicle through which they may gain and provide warmth, comfort, and protection (Dhami and Sheikh 2000). According to Imam Mohammed, Muslim men interested in polygynous marriages should concern themselves with protecting children, protecting the honor of the children's mothers, and securing the status of both in the community. He counsels such Muslims to approach the idea "with a clean heart, clean mind, clean and pure intentions." In his view, "responsible" men live polygyny because they desire to "help the social situation" (Mohammed 2003a; 2003b; 2003c).

Supporters of multiple-wife marriage recognize that sharing a husband can be difficult and that their private arrangements may have public consequences. They concede that many men living polygyny are neither role models nor valid representations of the teachings of Islam. Like opponents of the practice, they affirm the Qur'an and the lifestyle of the prophet as the clearest directives for Islam's position and are quick to remind observers and potential participants of the cautionary spirit of these sources. Specifically, members of both groups turn to Al Nisa 129, which stipulates that Muslim men "have it not in your power to do justice between wives." Their exegesis of this passage lends them to the conclusion that marital justice is illusive even to those who might strive for it. Supporters and opponents also differ in their views of how these sources say polygyny can or should be practiced in a Muslim-minority state.

Without a doubt, I have only begun to touch the surface in an exploration of the daily living of African American Muslim women in polygynous households, particularly those like Walladah who voluntarily identify potential wives for their husbands. I assert that commitment to cultural survival and communal exegesis compel some American Muslim women to share their husbands. For them, multiple-wife marriage is one remedy for and a demographic challenge to the absence of marriageable African American men and/or the high number of female-led households. Walladah's story draws attention to what for me was an even more startling discovery: wives who single out potential mates for their husbands. To such women, their efforts represent a form of personal authority and a way to rearticulate multiple-wife marriage as a liberating rather than abusive structure. Still other women seek multiple-wife marriage rather than assume full responsibility for their husbands. Yes, contradictions and paradoxes abound, and Walladah's success with and promotion of polygyny is rare. Still, what is problematic about the practice should not prevent conscious consideration of the significance of the realities of women who can, and sometimes do, "orchestrate the rules of their own realities."[23] Their experiences suggest that a link exists between the absence of justice and the absence of women in decisions about their role in family life.

THE SISTERHOOD OF POLYGYNY

Polygyny challenges the possibility of sisterhood and the ethics that define it. Sometimes the sisterhood is evident within a single family. Walladah's pursuit of a wife for her husband demonstrates her desire for and expectation of a real connection between the wives of her husband. I can draw parallels between her story and that of Sawdah, the youngest wife I interviewed and a Michigan mother of five, or Amaya, a midwestern administrator. Though Sawdah did not search for a spouse for her husband but expanded another woman's family, her propolygyny stance and the ease with which she engaged her two co-wives aided all of them following the sudden death of their husband. Tiring of her husband's higher level of sexual desire, Amaya engaged in conversations with a woman seeking marriage advice about the possibility of joining their family. Her potential co-wife was neither an orphan nor a widow but she was someone Amaya knew and respected. Her initial attempts to address her husband's sexual needs aside, nine years later Amaya would veto (by threatening divorce) her husband's wedding plans to a much younger woman. Without a doubt, the lived reality of Walladah, Sawdah, and Amaya represents the minority experience of women living polygyny who told me their stories. These propolygyny women believe some level of solidarity is possible between co-wives, even to the point of their considering each other as sisters and their relationships as one of "bonding-in-solidarity."[24]

This notion of shared personal experience among wives or the support women living polygyny receive from other women can set the tone for multiple-wife households. The key, according to Walladah, is for the husband to establish individual dwellings for each wife and for each wife to be a "good practicing *Muslimah*, accepting of polygyny and interested in being a part of our overall family structure." And when issues of jealousy manifest, she adds, "seek refuge in Allah and remember the benefits." It took years before women like Nissa, a mother of eleven, and Salimah, a widow with adult children, were able to consciously consider their relationship as anything close to a bond. Though not best friends, their progress in solidarity is especially evident today in the collaborative workshops they facilitate on multiple-wife marriage and their presentations on the language of Arabic and the Qur'an. Nearly fifteen years ago, however, anything beyond forced collaboration was inconceivable. It was then that Salimah accepted their husband's proposal of marriage while Nissa was about to give birth.

At other times, sisterhood is evident between women whose solidarity is fueled by the empowerment they receive from other women living polygyny. Two Texas women, who watched their families expand as their husbands took additional wives, supported each other by exchanging food and other material resources and offering a shoulder to cry on and a listening ear. Jamillah was to her friend what neither could be with her co-wives; such comforting support was especially beneficial when one of the women discovered that her husband was weeks away from taking another wife. Jamillah's changing family dynamics almost caused her to commit a criminal act. She later described as further insult a conversation she had with her new co-wife. When Jamillah confronted the young woman about why she couldn't get her own husband, the latter replied, "I did, he just happens to be yours."

What it means to live polygyny is often constructed upon divisions along a spectrum that includes women who affirm the practice, those who acquiesce to what they read as a "right" Muslim men have been given by Allah, and those who gladly accept the marginality of polygyny as a site of resistance.[25] The fears, self-awareness, expectations, exegetical processes, and avenues of support of these women intersect in ways that locate them differently and influence the ethics of sisterhood they experience. Obviously, some women living polygyny would prefer to retain exclusivity in terms of physical and emotional access to their husbands, even if they never divorce their husbands. Others initiate their own introductions with potential co-wives in an effort to ensure/ maintain a role in their husbands' spousal decisions. Still, all women in multiple-wife marriages knowingly or unknowingly acknowledge the legitimate interference of other women in their own personal liberty and identity. Naturally, it is the secrecy that often accompanies polygyny that continues to limit thoughtful consideration of this form of marriage. And while Walladah continues to await a response to her ad, a newly single Karimah has removed all conscious thoughts of marrying again. Regardless of outcome, their experiences represent family matters that speak to the distinct perspectives of women living polygyny and the accommodations they choose to make.

Notes

1. Regardless of permission granted, I use pseudonyms for and alter the personal characteristics of all informants who live in polygynous households.

2. I use the phrase *living polygyny* to refer to the diverse and sometimes contradictory experiences of Muslim women who share their husbands and Muslim men who head multiple-wife households. My intellectual focus is on what African American Muslim women say, do, and believe as they encounter multiple-wife marriage, particularly within a Muslim-minority context. An Internet search revealed that the phrase is also the title of a 2012 Youtube video, http://www.youtube.com/watch?v=OeSxEJEmUns. Interestingly, the single subject of the eight-minute video is male.

3. See Debra Majeed 2015.

4. Until his death in 2008, Imam Wallace Deen (W. D.) Mohammed was considered the foremost American Muslim leader in the United States. The seventh son of Clara and Elijah Muhammad, Mohammed succeeded his father as leader of the Nation of Islam in 1975 and quickly guided his father's movement onto the path of mainstream Islam. At the time of his death, court documents revealed that he was married to two women, though he only lived a married life with one. I use the term *community* as a linguistic way to reference the students, followers, and supporters of Imam Mohammed—of which I am one. I recognize, however, that some of his leaders say that Mohammed preferred the term *association*, believing that only

one *ummah* (the Arabic term used for community of or body of believers in Islam) exists—the global community of Muslims.

5. I am grateful to Sonja van Wichlen for introducing me to the idea of "socializing polygyny." While her discussion focuses on polygynous men and their "masculinist desires," a different construction of socializing polygyny can lead to an apt lens for consideration of the sister-to-sister encounters some Muslim women initiate to ensure that they have a role in their husbands' spousal decisions. See Sonja van Wichelen (2009).

6. This type of plural marriage is also referred to as *multiparty unions* or *de facto polygamy* because of its illegal status. For example, see Michele Alexandre (1987) and Mark Holzer Henry (1987).

7. Population figures derived from Pew Research Center report, April 23, 2015, http://www.pewresearch.org/fact-tank/2015/04/23/why-muslims-are-the-worlds -fastest-growing-religious-group/. By associating polygyny with the context for plural marriage identified in the Qur'an, I am not endorsing the practice of my subjects nor asserting that their arrangements are validated by revelation.

8. In July 2011, the series's adult stars—Kody Brown and his four wives—filed suit in federal court to avoid criminal prosecution on the grounds that Utah's antibigamy law goes too far when it declares polygamy to be unconstitutional, especially in the midst of changing social attitudes about homosexuality and marriage rights for gays and lesbians. See Daniel B. Wood (2011). A 2007 documentary titled *Sister Wife* depicts the experiences of a group of black Hebrew Israelites. In 2014, a US District Court judge ruled that the Utah law banning cohabitation was unconstitutional.

9. One exception is Joseph Bozzuti's research on plural marriage and the Constitution. In at least one journal essay, Bozzuti makes clear the dependence of his thesis on "fundamentalist Mormon activity in Utah" and that "Muslim polygamy does not wholly equate with Mormon polygamy" See Joseph Bozzuti (2004, 435, 438).

10. The permissibility for multiple wives carries conditions that most Muslim men are unable to meet.

11. Heterosexual monogamy and polygyny are the two most prevalent forms of family structure among Muslims. Though a minority, some Muslim families are headed by LGBT parents, a reality indicative of diverse gender and sexual identities in the global Muslim community.

12. African Americans account for at least 24 percent of the estimated 6 to 8 million American Muslims, according to the 2010 study "Muslim American Outreach." Granted, not all African Americans associate with Imam Mohammed's community, but given the location of the largest "polygynous" regions inhabited by his supporters, 1,000 households seemed to be a reasonable estimate. http://www.allied-media.com/AM/.

13. One such forum is muslimsinpolygyny@yahoogroups.com, created to "help educate and support sisters who are interested in polygyny, living in polygynous marriages or preparing themselves for an extension to their family." The Female Discussion and Support Group offers grassroots commentaries on the practice of polygyny in the United States and around the globe in light of the participants' interpretation of/engagement with Islamic sources. It encourages honesty and expressions of personal, private feelings and experiences by limiting the use of postings to members of the online group. These postings on polygyny represent a "bank of answers" about multiple-wife marriage in Islam. Any forum conversations used here were obtained with permission from the authors. For a fuller discussion of such Internet conversations, see Anna Piela (2013). I highlight women-only forums because they are organized and moderated by female Muslims and privilege the voices and experiences of those women.

14. African American Muslim women who share their husbands rarely play the game of feminine hierarchy. Rather than assign numbers to each other based on years of marriage, they attempt to relate to each other as "coequals"—at least in theory. At least two of my female informants characterizes themselves as a "polygynist." A second referred to her status and that of her husband's other wife as simple: "wife." Most others, however, generally use the term *co-wife*.

15. *Muslimah* is the Arabic term for a Muslim woman.

16. I am appreciative of the work of Ann Russo, quoted in Pamela K. Brubaker (1993, 59).

17. Muslim men are expected to assume financial responsibility for their families. Any contribution wives make to their household expenses is considered a gift to the husband. Ideally, any income a wife makes is hers to control. African American (and many other) Muslim wives routinely contribute to their family budgets.

18. An imam is one who leads the congregation in *salat* (the five required prayers) and is typically male. Depending upon the size and needs of individual American mosques, the role of an imam may expand to parallel the responsibilities of American rabbis, pastors, and other clergy. That is, imams serve as prayer leaders, religious teachers, marital counselors, conflict mediators, and so forth. Too often, the teachings and/or opinions expressed by their imams are imbued with such authority by some African American Muslims that the latter confuse aspects of an "imam's Islam" with the religion revealed in seventh-century Arabia.

19. *Masha'Allah* and *InshaAllah* are Arabic phrases whose English translations mean "to express appreciation, thankfulness, or praise to Allah" for an event, and "G'd so wills," respectively.

20. Hadith are collections of the sayings and actions of the prophet recorded by his companions or those to whom they told about the lifestyle of the Prophet.

21. "It is necessary upon a Muslim to listen to and obey the ruler in things he likes and dislikes, as long as he is not ordered to carry out a sin. If he is commanded to commit a sin, then there is no adherence and obedience" (al-Bukhārī 1993, 6:2612).

22. "If you fear that you shall not be able to deal justly with the orphans, Marry women of your choice, Two or three or four; but if you fear that you shall not be able to deal justly (with them), then only one, or (a captive) that your right hands possess, that will be more suitable, to prevent you from doing injustice" (Holy Qur'an 4:3). This verse was revealed following the deaths of at least seventy Muslim men. Before this revelation, no limit was set on the number of wives an Arab could have at any one time.

23. Wadud, "Human Civilization Is the Fruit of the Effort of both Women and Men," *Muslim Women News*, http://www.muslimwomennews.com/n.php?nid=6462.

24. Walladah and Sawdah were the only female informants who unashamedly celebrate the term *polygynist* as a descriptive of women who share their husbands. My other female subjects who live polygyny preferred the labels *co-wife* or *sister wife*. To these women, they are monogamously married to one man and it's their husbands' multiple spousal relationships that define the men as polygynists. I first encountered the concept of "bonding-in-solidarity" as a means of eradicating structural oppression in the feminist work of Mary Grey (1991). I use it here as a way to signify the potential for mutual enrichment, with the realization that it may also hold the seeds of conflict. For a discussion of the latter, see Gordon Sammut (2011).

25. In this regard, I compare women living polygyny to third-world women engaged in feminist discourse. See Pamela K. Brubaker (1993). Brubaker's essay was especially illuminating for the concept of sisterhood I explore here.

References

al-Bukhārī, Muḥammad Ibn Ismāʿīl. 1993. *Ṣaḥīḥ al-Bukhārī*. Damascus: Dār Ibn Kathīr.

Alexandre, Michele. 1987. "Lessons from Islamic Polygamy: A Case for Expanding the American Concept of Surviving Spouse so as to Include de Facto Polygamous Spouses." *64 Washington and Lee Law Review* 4: 1461–1484.

Allied Media Corporation. 2010. "Muslim American Outreach." http://www.allied-media .com/muslim_americans/muslim_american_demographics.html (accessed May 23, 2011).

Badawi, Jamal. 2012. "Polygamy in Islamic Law." *Islamic Research Foundation International.* http://www.irfi.org/articles/articles_251_300/polygamy_in_islamic_law.htm.

Bozzuti, Joseph. 2004. "The Constitutionality of Polygamy Prohibitions after Lawrence v. Texas: Is Scalia a Punchline or a Prophet?" *The Catholic Lawyer* 43 (2): 409–42.

Brubaker, Pamela K. 1993. "Sisterhood, Solidarity, and Feminist Ethics." *Journal of Feminist Studies in Religion* 9 (1/2): 53–66.

Dhami, Sangeeta, and Aziz Sheikh. 2000. "The Muslim family: Predicament and Promise." *Western Journal of Medicine* 173 (5): 352. http://dx.doi.org/10.1136/ewjm .173.5.352.

Grey, Mary. 1991. "Claiming Power-in-Relation: Exploring the Ethics of Connection." *Journal of Feminist Studies in Religion* 7 (1): 8.

Holzer Henry, Mark. 1987. "The True Reynolds v. United States." *Harvard Journal of Law and Public Policy* 10 (1): 43–46.

Majeed, Debra. 2015. *Polygyny: What It Means When African American Muslim Women Share Their Husbands.* Gainesville: University Press of Florida.

Mohammed, Imam W. D. 2003a. "Brother's Meeting, Atlanta, GA." Speech to the Men and Women of the American Society of Muslims, May 12.

Mohammed, Imam W. D. 2003b. "Sister's Meeting, Chicago, IL." Speech to the Men and Women of the American Society of Muslims, March 8.

Mohammed, Imam W. D. 2003c. "Sister's Meeting, San Francisco, CA." Speech to the Men and Women of the American Society of Muslims, June 7.

Piela, Anna. 2010. "Muslim Women's Online Discussions of Gender Relations in Islam." *Journal of Muslim Minority Affairs* 30 (3): 425–35. http://dx.doi.org/10.1080/1360200 4.2010.515827.

Piela, Anna. 2013. "Claiming Religious Authority: Muslim Women and New Media." In *Media, Religion, and Gender: Key Issues and New Challenges,* edited by Mia Lovheim, 125–40. London: Routledge.

Rowland, Robyn. 1992. *Living Laboratories: Women and Reproductive Technologies.* London: Pan Macmillan.

Sammut, Gordon. 2011. "Civic Solidarity: The Negotiation of Identity in Modern Societies." *Papers on Social Representations* 20: 4.1–4.24. *Academia.edu.* http://www .academia.edu/574144/Civic_solidarity_the_negotiation_of_identity_in_modern _societies.

Wadud, Amina. 1999. *Qur'an and Woman: Rereading the Sacred Text from a Woman's Perspective.* Oxford: Oxford University Press.

Wadud, Amina. 2008. "Islamic Authority." Presentation to the 2008 International Congress on Islamic Feminism, September 24, Barcelona, Spain.

van Wichelen, Sonja. 2009. "Polygamy and the Politics of Feminism: Contestations over Masculinity in a New Muslim Indonesia." *Journal of International Women's Studies* 11 (1): 181–82.

Wood, Daniel B. 2011. "'Sister Wives' Family Sues to Prevent Prosecution for Polygamy." *Christian Science Monitor,* July 13. http://www.csmonitor.com/USA/Justice/2011 /0713/Sister-Wives-family-sues-to-prevent-prosecution-for-polygamy.

5

AN ECONOMIST'S PERSPECTIVE ON POLYGYNY

Shoshana Grossbard

INTRODUCTION

This article is based on a report prepared for the Supreme Court of British Columbia, Canada, when it was considering whether to eliminate Canada's antipolygamy law (Bramham 2009). It analyzes polygyny (many wives), not polyandry (many husbands), and relies on two assumptions often used since Gary Becker's (1973) path-breaking economic analyses of marriage: (1) marriage is an institution that organizes household production, such production including giving birth, raising children, homemaking, and many more activities, and (2) marriage markets exist.

The economic analysis presented here starts with a demand-and-supply analysis of marriage pioneered by University of Chicago economist Gary Becker. From this analysis Becker (1973, 1981, 2006) concludes that polygyny adds to women's value based on a third assumption: marriage markets are free in the sense that the participants are free to choose and equilibrium prices are allowed to be established where markets clear. The results of a marriage-market analysis depend strongly on whether all participants in marriage markets are free to maximize their own well-being. However, cultures allowing polygamy invariably also have laws and customs that prevent women from capturing the gains from marriage that could have accrued to them had they been free to choose their husbands. This paper lists and discusses some of these institutions. It then documents some of the harmful effects of polygyny for women and briefly discusses institutions aimed at alleviating this harm.

From the perspective of political economy, institutions are created and maintained due to the interests and influences of various groups in society. This also holds for marital institutions such as monogamy laws and bride price. The men who have an interest in establishing and maintaining polygyny also have an interest in establishing institutions that

DOI: 10.7330/9780874219975.c005

prevent women from capturing the gains from marriage that polygyny could have generated in free marriage markets.

GARY BECKER'S ARGUMENT

When awarding him the Nobel Prize in economics, the Swedish academy mentioned Becker's contributions to the economics of the family, which include his economic analyses of polygamy. Becker's (1973, 1981) demand-and-supply analysis of marriage markets is based on more detailed assumptions also found in other applications of demand-and-supply analysis, including that (1) brides and grooms can potentially substitute for each other (or be substituted for each other, if others decide who marries whom and when), and (2) there is competition in the market. In this case, men compete among each other to obtain a wife, while women compete among each other to obtain a husband.

Becker considers a marriage market for brides in which the supply is by women. The existence of polygyny does not change the number of women and therefore the supply of brides. In this market the demand is by men who would possibly marry these women. Demand is based on the marginal productivity of women in household production and the number of men. Polygyny allows men to enter the market multiple times, adding to the demand. As a result, assuming that markets for wives are competitive and allowed to clear at the intersection of demand and supply, the higher demand will cause higher market values. Becker concludes that women's market value as brides will rise if polygamy is permitted.

While writing my doctoral dissertation under Becker's supervision, I supported Becker's conclusion with evidence from cross-cultural comparisons (Grossbard-Shechtman 1978a; 1978b; 1980). First, I found that societies with polygyny are more likely to have a bride-price (sometimes called *bride-wealth*) system than monogamous societies and interpreted that association as evidence of the higher value of women in marriage markets with polygamy. Becker liked it and cited that part of my dissertation (Grossbard-Shechtman 1978a) in the following context in his *Treatise on the Family*:

"My analysis of efficient, competitive marriage markets indicates . . . that the income of women and the competition by men for wives would be greater when polygyny is greater if the incidence of polygyny had been determined mainly by the relative marginal contribution of women to output. This view is supported by the fact that bride prices are more common and generally higher in societies with a greater incidence of polygyny" (Becker 1981, 56).

Second, I argued at the time that women's lower age at marriage in polygynous societies also serves as evidence that women have a higher value in these societies than in monogamy. Another student of Becker in the 1970s, Michael Keeley, associated early age at marriage with higher value in marriage markets in the context of the United States. Based on a Beckerian demand-and-supply analysis, Keeley (1977) predicted that the more individual Americans were to gain from being married, the younger they married. His econometric analysis confirmed some of his predictions. For instance, he found that in the 1960s, two groups with higher expected gains from marriage married younger: men with higher wages and women with lower wages. I thought of applying Keeley's insights to polygyny:

> When women gain more from marriage, they are also likely to marry younger. This seems indeed to be the case: women's average age at marriage is 13 or 14 among the Hausa and the Kanuri of Eastern Nigeria, societies with widespread polygyny. The Tallensi, another West Africa tribe, are slightly less polygynous and their daughters marry somewhat later. Here the average female age at marriage is 16 and 17. On the whole, women marry considerably earlier in polygynous areas like Africa and the Moslem world than in monogamous Europe and America. Polygyny also raises the difference in mean age at marriage of men and women. (Grossbard-Shechtman 1978b, 36; 1978a)

To his credit, Becker did not cite this piece of "evidence."

WHEN MARRIAGE MARKETS ARE NOT FREE

Marriage markets may never be free. They certainly are far from free in polygynous societies. The following institutions that undermine women's freedom to choose their partners tend to be correlated with the existence of polygyny.

Child Brides

Limitations on women's freedom start with these societies' marrying off their daughters when they are close to the onset of puberty. Could women marrying at age thirteen possibly be better off than women who have a chance to wait until they are closer to age twenty? Anthropological evidence indicates that in Maiduguri, Nigeria, thirteen-year-old girls have very little choice about when they marry and whom (Cohen 1971). Elsewhere, in my own econometric study of individuals living in either polygamous or monogamous Nigerian households (Grossbard 1976; Grossbard-Shechtman 1980), I had assumed that women prefer monogamy and found that they are more able to achieve their monogamy goal when they are in their early twenties than when they are teenagers.

If women are forced to marry, that coercion prevents them from taking advantage of the increased competition among potential grooms created by the possibility of polygynous marriages. Becker's argument about the value of polygyny to women will hold in a society where the average age at marriage is fourteen only if parents are perfectly capable of representing their young daughters' best long-run interests.

There is evidence that women in polygynous households in North America also marry at particularly young ages and are substantially younger than their husbands (see the evidence brought to the court of British Columbia in 2010 and 2011 [Henrich 2010]). Not only are young girls forced too young into marriage likely to suffer, but such a system increases the likelihood of early widowhood and financial hardship for women later in life.

Bride Price

The existence of a bride-price system is likely to add to women's inability to take advantage of their market value in a polygynous society. Becker (1981) and my early work (Grossbard-Shechtman 1978a; 1978b) assumed that women benefit from a *bride-price* payment, a payment men make for getting married. In reality this is rarely the case. Where bride price is exchanged, it typically consists of men paying fathers for the right to marry their daughters. If forced arranged marriages are the standard, the possibility of earning bride price by marrying a daughter off often places the father's need for income above the daughter's best interest.

Bride-price systems go hand in hand with *child marriages*. It is easier for relatives to marry women off against their will if they are very young. Furthermore, fathers often can't afford to feed their adolescent daughters and sell them as brides as a means of raising income.

A bride-price system is likely to be particularly harmful to women if a society allows bride price to be refundable, as is the case in Uganda. It has been found that when bride price is refundable, there are stricter standards of fidelity imposed on women than on men (Bishai and Grossbard 2010). This inequality creates a sense of unfairness in marriage.

Polygamy and bride price also go hand in hand with *arranged marriage*. If we compare monogamous countries with countries where polygamy is legal, we observe a much higher frequency of arranged marriage in polygamous societies. In particular, large proportions of young couples in Africa and the Indian subcontinent have arranged marriages, and most of the countries in which they live have legalized polygamy. To impose arranged marriages on their children, societies typically use violence or the threat of violence.

We do not know whether the existence of polygamy caused these three other institutions (bride price, child marriage, and arranged marriage), or if causality runs the other way. The association between polygamy and these three institutions could be spurious in the sense that a fifth factor could be responsible for polygyny as well as bride price, child marriage, and forced marriage. Regardless, it is revealing that cross-culturally, polygamy is associated with these three features that are unequivocally undesirable from the perspective of young women wanting to reach maximum happiness in their lifetimes.

Seclusion of Women

Many societies, including Saudi Arabia and the Kanuris of Nigeria, practice both *purdah* and polygamy (Cohen 1971). The institution of *purdah* limits women's freedom of movement and typically means that women don't participate in the labor force, which makes them more dependent on their husbands financially. The Canadian polygamous society of Bountiful does not have *purdah*, but its geographic isolation creates a distance from the rest of Canadian society and makes it difficult for women to get jobs (Campbell 2005) and finance themselves out of unwanted marriages.

Deemphasis on Romantic Love

Cultures such as the Kanuris that adopt polygyny also tend to discourage romantic love. (Cohen 1971). In the case of the Fundamentalist Church of Jesus Christ of Latter-Day Saints (FLDS) of Canada or the United States, the young are taught to marry out of religious duty and not to expect much personal satisfaction (Bramham 2009). This deemphasis of romantic love is likely to hurt women more than men to the extent that women seem to place more emphasis on romantic love than do men. Some consumption preferences in democratic industrialized societies reveal more of a taste for romance among women than among men. For example, most readers of Harlequin romance novels are women, and what are commonly called *chick flicks* tend to be romantic movies ("Chick Flick" 2011).

Female Genital Mutilation

Many of the same societies that have polygamy also practice female genital mutilation, an institution that reduces women's potential for a happy married life. In communities where polygyny is prominent, female genital mutilation is partially intended as a tool to curb women's sex drive. This limits women's ability to optimize their lifestyle and satisfaction in life. In the case of married women, it also eases the pressure on the husband to satisfy all of his wives sexually (Rahman and Toubia 2000). In polygynous societies, women have been found to justify the custom of female genital mutilation based on the belief that it increases the sexual pleasure of men and therefore reduces the chance that their husband will take another wife (Gruenbaum 2001).

Easy Divorce

Divorce also tends to be directly associated with polygyny and tends to place married and divorced women in a position of vulnerability, thereby limiting their freedom to choose the best possible partner. For example, the Kanuris of Nigeria have very easy divorce and high rates of polygamy. Divorce tends to be relatively easy to perform in Muslim societies, and these societies are also typically accepting of polygamy. In the case of Judaism, the rabbis who outlawed polygamy in the eleventh century also gave more protection to women at divorce (Grossbard-Shechtman 1986). However, easy divorce could also be detrimental to women (Grossbard-Shechtman 1993). For example, after the introduction of no-fault divorce in California, divorce became easier and women's property settlements went down (Becker 1981). Also, when laws regulating the division of property in the case of divorce offer less protection to women, women have more of a tendency to have children out-of-couple (Ekert-Jaffe and Grossbard 2008).

THE POLITICAL ECONOMY OF POLYGYNY

The high value of women in marriage markets in polygynous societies is expected to increase men's incentives to control women by way of political and religious institutions, such as early arranged marriages (Grossbard-Shechtman 1993; Guttentag and Secord 1983). Asymmetric polygyny is clearly instituted by men. Would any society where both men and women influence the legal process equally approve laws that allow men to take plural wives but do not give this option to women? This asymmetric form of polygamy reflects men's control of the political/cultural system that also establishes and maintains marriage institutions.

If men design their society's rules, they will not institute polygyny unless they find ways to prevent women from capturing the high market value that would accrue to them if marriage-market participants were free to marry whom they want. They would then also allow child marriages, bride price, female genital mutilation, and other institutions mentioned in the previous section.

It is very possible that bride price originated when polygyny was allowed as a means to help marriage markets clear without allowing women to capture a high market value. With women's access to the gain from marriage set at a maximum level (the equivalent of a price ceiling), shortages of women would occur as women (and their families) would be reluctant to enter marriage. As argued by Becker (1981), bride price gives further incentives for families to supply their daughters as brides. Using the analogy between marriage markets and housing markets, bride price is the equivalent of lump sums that new tenants pay to either other tenants or to landlords in order to access scarce and coveted rent-controlled housing. In the case of housing, landlords control access to housing. In the case of most polygynous societies, men control other men's access to the women they can marry.

The men who control the political economy and the economy of a polygynous society will also limit women's ability to earn income, as having their own money would increase their freedom to achieve personal happiness. This helps explain why these societies have *purdah* and why members of the FLDS live in isolated communities with few employment opportunities for women. The main industry in Bountiful is logging, a male-dominated industry. When African immigrants practice polygyny in France, it is also frequently the case that women are limited in their freedom of choice, be it as a result of early forced marriage, illegal status, or lack of employment opportunities (Conseil du statut de la femme 2010).

If men institute polygyny and prevent women from having an equal voice in the political economy, it follows that detrimental consequences of polygyny are likely to be the result for women.

HARMFUL EFFECTS OF POLYGYNY

Jealousy

Within polygamous societies, it has been observed that polygyny is associated with high levels of jealousy among co-wives (Al-Krenawi, Graham, and Al-Krenawi 1997; Al-Krenawi, Graham, and Izzeldin 2001). This makes sense to the extent that men in polygamous households divide their attention among more than one wife. Women seem to be concerned about the constant threat of being reduced to the second-wife position (M'Salha 2001).

Women's Psychological Health Problems

Polygamy has been associated with psychological distress. It has been reported that senior wives expressed great distress when their husbands took another wife (Al-Krenawi, Graham, and Izzeldin 2001).

Early Widowhood

By contributing to a lower age of marriage for women and a larger age disparity between husband and wife, polygyny increases the likelihood that women become widows at an early age.

Women are not the only ones likely to suffer from polygyny. Children and men unable to find wives are also likely to suffer.

Detrimental Impact on Children

Polygyny also tends to be associated with health problems in children. For example, a positive cross-sectional association between polygyny and child mortality has been documented (Amey 2002; Gyimah 2009). It has also been documented that polygamist men tend to spend their money on having more children and investing little in their education, as opposed to having fewer children with higher levels of human capital (Gould, Moav, and Simhon 2008).

Detrimental Impact on Single Men

In polygynous societies, some men remain unmarried and are likely to suffer. As long as the population grows fast and life expectancy is low, young men can hope that they will be able to marry by the time they reach a certain age. Young men also seem to suffer because of polygyny in the FLDS of Bountiful (Bramham 2009).

Expressed Opinions

In light of these arguments, it is not surprising that when interviewed, very few women in either Mali or South Africa—countries where polygyny is prevalent—said they look favorably upon polygamy (Dangor 2001; Madhavan 2004). Some political actions are also consistent with the adverse effects for women. For example, educated African women are often actively fighting for bans on polygamy. A recent survey of South Africans found that 64 percent of men disagreed with having more than one wife and 83 percent of women disagreed ("Most South Africans against Polygamy, Survey Shows," *Mail and Guardian*, Jan. 11, 2010).

INSTITUTIONS THAT INDIRECTLY POINT TO PROBLEMS CAUSED BY POLYGYNY

A number of the institutions found in polygynous societies can be interpreted as alleviating some of the problematic features of polygyny mentioned above.

Limits on Number of Wives

Most societies allowing polygamy limit the number of wives allowed per husband. Following Islamic law, many of them limit the number of wives to four. Implicitly, this limitation recognizes that polygamy can be detrimental and must be restricted. The harm caused by polygamy does not necessarily fall only on women. It could also fall on men who may find it difficult to secure a wife when they have to compete with potential polygamists.

Rotation

It is the custom among the Kanuris of Nigeria that a husband rotates among his wives: he takes turns sleeping in each wife's home following a fixed schedule that allocates equal time to each wife (Cohen 1971). Such regulation appears to be the result of the wives' suffering from their husband's attention being divided among multiple wives.

Encouragement of Cooperation

Cooperation in household production should be encouraged among the various wives. Giving authority to the senior wife is one way conflicts among co-wives are reduced (Gage-Brandon 1992).

Separate Dwellings

It is important for each wife to have a separate dwelling, possibly meaning that one wife is in the countryside and one in the city (Clignet and Sween 1974).

Sororal Polygyny

Sisters may be less likely to fight with each other than unrelated co-wives are. Murdock (1949) found that 70 of the 193 polygynous societies he surveyed had sororal polygyny.

The existence of these "remedial" institutions indicates that there are problems with polygyny from the point of view of women's well-being.

CONCLUDING ASSESSMENT

If marriage markets were free and all agents were free to choose and follow their best interests, the natural economic consequence of polygyny would be that women's market value and well-being would increase. However, women in polygynous societies do not realize the economic benefit of their greater value. Rather, women's freedom to manage their own economic circumstances and destinies tends to be reduced in polygynous civilizations. This disadvantage is, to a large extent, the result of early arranged marriages, which are so prevalent in these societies, along with the practice of bride price, limited job opportunities for women, and deemphasis on sexual fulfillment. Lack of protection in case of divorce adds to women's undesirable circumstances observed in these societies. Worldwide, in the cultures and societies that have embraced it, polygyny is associated with undesirable economic, societal, physical, and emotional factors related to women's well-being. Many of the societies that have tolerated the practice of polygamy simultaneously recognize its harm and have created institutions that limit the extent to which polygyny can hurt women.

The undesirable outcomes associated with the institution of polygyny don't contradict the value of a marriage-market analysis. Instead, they indicate that marriage markets are not free. From a political-economy perspective, it makes sense that men would institute polygyny as a means to prevent women from capturing the gains they would obtain if they were free to choose their marriage partners. There is no single example of a society that allows polygyny, an asymmetric form of polygamy, and simultaneously gives women the freedom to choose their marriage partners, as is commonly practiced by most people living in the West.

In terms of how they treat women, small polygynist groups such as the FLDS seem to be closer to the Kanuri of Nigeria than to most others living in Western democracies.

The British Columbia Superior Court judge who ruled in 2011 that the ban on polygamy should not be lifted found some of the arguments presented here convincing. I hope his decision prevails for many decades; I don't think polygyny should be legalized. However, social experiments should be allowed. If entire communities of men and women voluntarily choose to practice polygyny, allow their sons and daughters to marry when they want and whom they want, and encourage them to obtain the skills needed for personal success, and this goes on for at least three generations, then the ban on polygyny should be reexamined. However, given that all existing polygynous societies— including those in North America—are characterized by multiple institutions that limit women's freedom and well-being, I am skeptical that such hypothetical free polygynous communities will ever be created, and if they are, I doubt that the third generation will continue to give complete freedom of choice to its members.

References

Al-Krenawi, Alean, John Graham, and Salem Al-Krenawi. 1997. "Social Work Practice with Polygamous Families." *Child & Adolescent Social Work Journal* 14 (6): 445–58. http://dx.doi.org/10.1023/A:1024571031073.

Al-Krenawi, Alean, John Graham, and Abuelaish Izzeldin. 2001. "The Psychosocial Impact of Polygamous Marriages on Palestinian Women." *Women & Health* 34 (1): 1–16. http://dx.doi.org/10.1300/J013v34n01_01.

Amey, F. K. 2002. "Polygyny and Child Survival in West Africa." *Social Biology* 49(1–2): 74–89.

Becker, Gary S. 1973. "A Theory of Marriage: Part I." *Journal of Political Economy* 81 (4): 813–46. http://dx.doi.org/10.1086/260084.

Becker, Gary S. 1981. *A Treatise on the Family*. Cambridge: Harvard University Press.

Becker, Gary S. 2006. "Is There a Case for Legalizing Polygamy?" *Becker-Posner Blog* (blog), October 22. http://www.becker-posner-blog.com/2006/10/is-there-a-case-for-legalizing-polygamy-becker.html.

Bishai, David, and Shoshana Grossbard. 2010. "Far Above Rubies: The Association between Bride Price and Extramarital Sexual Relations in Uganda." *Journal of Population Economics* 23 (4): 1177–88. http://dx.doi.org/10.1007/s00148-008-0226-3.

Bramham, Daphne. 2009. *The Secret Lives of Saints: Child Brides and Lost Boys in Canada's Polygamous Mormon Sect*. Toronto: Vintage.

Campbell, Angela. 2005. "How Have Policy Approaches to Polygyny Responded to Women's Experiences and Rights?" Final Report, Status of Women in Canada.

Clignet, Remy, and Joyce Sween. 1974. "Urbanization, Plural Marriage, and Family Size in Two African Cities." *American Ethnologist* 1 (2): 221–42. http://dx.doi.org/10.1525/ae.1974.1.2.02a00010.

Cohen, Ronald. 1971. *Dominance and Defiance*. Washington, DC: American Anthropological Association.

Conseil du statut de la femme. 2010. *La polygamie au regard du droit des femmes* [Polygamy and the Rights of Women]. Avis, Gouvernement du Quebec.

Dangor, Suleman. 2001. "Historical Perspective, Current Literature and an Opinion Survey among Muslim Women in Contemporary South Africa: A Case Study." *Journal of Muslim Minority Affairs* 21 (1): 109–29. http://dx.doi.org/10.1080/13602000120050578.

Ekert-Jaffe, Olivia, and Shoshana Grossbard. 2008. "Does Community Property Discourage Unpartnered Births?" *European Journal of Political Economy* 24 (1): 25–40. http://dx.doi.org/10.1016/j.ejpoleco.2007.06.006.

Gage-Brandon, Anastasia. 1992. "The Polygyny-Divorce Relationship: A Case Study of Nigeria." *Journal of Marriage and the Family* 54 (2): 285–92. http://dx.doi.org/10.2307/353060.

Gould, Eric D., Omer Moav, and Avi Simhon. 2008. "The Mystery of Monogamy." *American Economic Review* 98 (1): 333–57. http://dx.doi.org/10.1257/aer.98.1.333.

Grossbard, Amyra. 1976. "An Economic Analysis of Polygamy: The Case of Maiduguri." *Current Anthropology* 17 (4): 701–7. http://dx.doi.org/10.1086/201804.

Grossbard-Shechtman, Amyra. 1978a. "The Economics of Polygamy." PhD diss., University of Chicago.

Grossbard-Shechtman, Amyra. 1978b. "Towards a Marriage Between Economics and Anthropology and a General Theory of Marriage." *Papers and Proceedings, American Economic Review* 68 (2): 33–7.

Grossbard-Shechtman, Amyra. 1980. "The Economics of Polygamy." In *Research in Population Economics*. Vol. 2. Edited by Julie DaVanzo and Julian Simon, 321–50. Greenwich, CT: JAI.

Grossbard-Shechtman, Amyra. 1986. *Economics, Judaism, and Marriage. Dinei Israel: A Journal of Science and Jewish Law* [in Hebrew].

Grossbard-Shechtman, Shoshana Amyra. 1993. *On the Economics of Marriage: A Theory of Marriage, Labor and Divorce.* Boulder, CO: Westview.

Gruenbaum, Ellen. 2001. *The Female Circumcision Controversy: An Anthropological Perspective.* Philadelphia: University of Pennsylvania Press.

Guttentag, Marcia, and Paul F. Secord. 1983. *Too Many Women: The Sex Ratio Question.* Beverly Hills, CA: Sage.

Gyimah, Stephen Obeng. 2009. "Polygynous Marital Structure and Child Survivorship in Sub-Saharan Africa: Some Empirical Evidence from Ghana." *Social Science & Medicine* 68 (2): 334–42. http://dx.doi.org/10.1016/j.socscimed.2008.09.067.

Henrich, Joseph. 2010. "Polygyny in Cross-Cultural Perspective: Theory and Implications." Affidavit submitted to the Supreme Court of British Columbia in the matter of the constitutionality of s. 293 of the Criminal Code of Canada, R.S.C. 1985, c. C-46, July 15.

Keeley, Michael C. 1977. "The Economics of Family Formation." *Economic Inquiry* 15 (2): 238–50. http://dx.doi.org/10.1111/j.1465-7295.1977.tb00468.x http://www.vancouversun.com/pdf/affidavit.pdf.

Madhavan, Sangeetha. 2004. "Best of Friends and Worst of Enemies: Competition and Collaboration in Polygyny." *Ethnology* 41 (1): 69–84.

M'Salha, Mohammed. 2001. "Qu'en est-il aujourd'hui de la polygamie et de la répudiation en Droit Marocain?" *Revue internationale de droit compare* 53 (1): 171–82. http://dx.doi.org/10.3406/ridc.2001.18017.

Murdock, George P. 1949. *Social Structure.* New York: Macmillan.

Rahman, Anika, and Nahid Toubia. 2000. *Female Genital Mutilation: A Guide to Laws and Policies Worldwide.* London: Zed Books.

6

THE EFFECT OF POLYGYNY ON WOMEN, CHILDREN, AND THE STATE

Rose McDermott and Jonathan Cowden

INTRODUCTION

Recent state action against polygynous sects in the United States and Canada for sex trafficking and child abuse raises questions about the causal relationship between polygyny and violence, particularly violence against women and children. Here we seek to examine the effects of such marital structures—and the economic, political and social practices that often accompany them—on violence toward women and children, as well as civil rights, political freedoms, and weapons procurement.

To begin, a few definitions are in order. Polygamy includes both polygyny, in which one man has many wives, as well as polyandry, in which one woman has many husbands. Polyandry is rare, and the consequences we document here do not extend to such cases of polygamy. Rather, here we examine the effects of polygynous practices in which one man has more than one wife simultaneously. The sequelae documented here do not extend to conditions when one man has more than one wife sequentially over the course of a lifetime, whereby each independent relationship remains monogamous at any given moment in time, separated by formal and legal divorce proceedings between single wives. We focus on polygyny because it holds important implications for reproductive success and control, and having children with more than one wife at a time affects the allocation of time and resources in ways that differ significantly from having children sequentially with different mates over time. In our analysis, the critical concern revolves around the sources and consequences of violence by men toward women and children and how polygyny affects the tendency toward violence and suppression of civil rights and political liberties within states.

In addition, we are not concerned with simultaneous sexual relationships that do not involve childbearing or prospects for the intergenerational transfer of wealth as a result of the shared economic

DOI: 10.7330/9780874219975.c006

circumstances that remain intrinsic to legal marriages. We are not concerned with these kinds of relationships because there can be two potential uses of the meaning of polygyny, the first as a social bonding system and the second as a breeding one. Most mammals, including gorillas for example, have both polygynous social and polygynous breeding systems, while there are no species who exhibit a polygynous social system in concert with a monogamous mating structure. By contrast, most birds have monogamous social bonding in the context of polygynous breeding, while a few, including the black vulture (and some humans), demonstrate both monogamous bonding and breeding preferences.

Religious and cultural practices often exacerbate the political issues surrounding laws about polygyny. Polygyny remains a common practice around the world, existing in more than 83 percent of 849 cultures worldwide; in about 35 percent of cases such practices are sororal, meaning men marry women who are sisters to each other. Such a practice may be undertaken to help reduce the risk of intermarital tension and hostility among wives. Everywhere it exists, the practice is more widespread among high-status, high-wealth men. By contrast, polyandry is found in only 4 of 849 cultures worldwide and always co-occurs with polygyny, such that high-status men in such cultures take multiple wives, while wealthy women may take multiple husbands (Coult and Habenstein 1965; Gray 1998). In such cultures, polyandry tends to occur only briefly, and among low-status men, although it is often fraternal in nature as well. While many Westerners argue that it is inappropriate to make value judgments about other cultures, we see the issue of polygyny in terms of basic human rights, and we demonstrate here that such rights in women and children are fiercely abrogated in societies and cultures where polygyny is present. We argue that female financial and social independence in polygynous areas are feared not merely because of their material effects but also because of their threat to the cultural values and personal power of many men in patriarchal societies, particularly in underdeveloped and developing regions of the world. Specifically, the emancipation of women erodes men's control over their own families in culturally humiliating and emotionally painful ways. In addition, it may also threaten the position of senior women in these societies, who often dominate junior women, such as daughters and daughters-in-law, as well as junior men, including sons. Additionally, poor or low-status men are often left without wives because of the enforced shortage of women when one man can control many women. Female equality therefore provides a potent source of male—and sometimes even female—support for anti-Western movements, particularly in more patriarchal societies.

We argue that violence and suppression of basic rights can be potentiated by a number of factors, including patriarchy, pastoralism, patrilocality, and polygyny. These cultural features and social structures often go hand in hand and, in common, enhance male control over women and children in ways that allow, and often encourage, violence and suppression of political rights and liberties. Here we look more specifically at the role played by polygyny in potentiating violence against women and children and within nation-states. We demonstrate, using extensive and detailed empirical data, that polygyny is strongly correlated with a wide array of different kinds of violence against women and children, as well as suppression of political rights and liberties and increased spending on weapons.

One of the overwhelming findings from our analysis is the incredible consistency of the effect of polygynous structures on a wide variety of negative outcomes, with not a single documented positive outcome occurring as a result in the aggregate. This does not mean, of course, that individuals do not claim or actually benefit from such structures; indeed, polygynously married men may like having more than one wife. However, when examined in comparison with states that largely prohibit polygyny, and in the aggregate, there is not a single positive outcome we have been able to find that is statistically correlated with high rates on polygyny. On the contrary, we have been able to document at least eighteen discrete negative consequences that are all statistically significantly correlated with increases in polygyny rates. While it might be possible to get rid of many of these negative outcomes by instituting laws unrelated to polygyny, at least eighteen separate laws would need to be put in place, whereas the prohibition of polygyny can eradicate or ameliorate all these ills in one fell stroke. It is like the consequences that follow from obesity; doctors can give medications for high blood pressure and high cholesterol and diabetes and other sequelae of obesity, or they can encourage a patient to lose weight. The only reason the former is more common than the latter is because patients prove largely incapable of losing the amount of weight they need to in order to gain the many health benefits that might result. Similarly, a state can pass any number of laws to increase the consequences for perpetrators of violence against women, and those strategies can be effective and should be undertaken as well. However, states can make major progress toward the prevention of many of the social ills and harms documented here by prohibiting polygyny.

THE PERSISTENCE OF PATRIARCHAL VALUES
IN POLYGYNOUS CULTURES

According to Islamic Holy Law, a father or guardian can prevent a woman from marrying without his permission and can annul her marriage if it occurs without his permission (Lewis 1995). This male expectation of control over a daughter's marriage is critical in many Islamic societies because a man's social status is affected by his kinswomen's alliances. Arranged marriages are therefore traditionally preferred to love matches. In the service of maximizing the benefits from a marriage, a woman's value is enhanced by various practices that restrict her own romantic choices and promote her chastity, including cloistering, genital mutilation, and veiling (Weisfeld 1993). Control is supported by stringent punishments for women who flout cultural norms.

While the degree to which men exert literal physical control over women in any society remains contingent on a whole host of sociological and economic factors, men retain control over the vast majority of physical resources needed to survive in much of the world, including money and property. For example, Lawrence Rosen (1978) notes that while men's lives exist in the public sphere in Middle Eastern societies such as the one he studied in Morocco, women's lives remain largely confined to the household. Ironically, this segregation of sexes can lead to a remarkable degree of female independence over their own social lives and worlds (Fallers and Fallers 1976). Nevertheless, women continue to be restricted in their public movements from the time of puberty in many parts of the world.

A woman's position in polygynous societies is largely determined by her marriage. Because divorce is so common and can be granted by male fiat, and men retain control over most important resources, women's positions remain insecure at best (Rosen 1978). Whatever security a woman enjoys results from the formal nature of her marriage contract, the strength of her family of origin in the particular area and, sometimes, her sons. Any man can be dishonored by threats to the chastity and virtue of his female relatives. However, fathers tend to blame daughters for such behavior, and therefore honor killing on behalf of these women may be committed by brothers or husbands (Fallers and Fallers 1976). Mothers-in-law even participate, often structuring so-called honor suicides by which a daughter-in-law is left in a locked room to drink poison or slowly die of hunger and thirst.

Men use their control over daughters to ensure that a woman marries not just to her advantage (as he perceives it) but, more important, to the advantage of himself and his male kin as well. A woman marrying below her social status dishonors her family, whereas her marriage into a large and high-status kin group creates or cements a relationship of social importance for her entire family. By contrast, there has traditionally been "no objection to a man marrying a woman of lower status, since the woman, in the view of the jurists, is in any case inferior, and no social damage could therefore result from such a marriage" (Lewis 1995, 180). He might benefit in other ways, also. For example, by exchanging his daughter for a wife for himself or a male relative, a man might use his control over a daughter to get an extra bride. Equally, he could resolve a feud by giving a woman in marriage. Or by obtaining as high a bride price as possible, he increases his wealth (and his own future marriage prospects).

Pastoralist societies are characterized as "cultures of honor" because of their central concern with the acquisition of male status. The high value placed on male status derives, in turn, from the value of herds and the ease with which herded animals can be stolen because high status deters rustlers through fear of retaliatory vengeance. This potential for theft means that the maintenance of herds requires a powerful kin group of male warriors and a reputation for ruthless revenge. It encourages societies that are strongly patriarchal and patrilineal and that engage in honor raiding (Cohen and Nisbett 1997; Mace and Holden 1999; Weisfeld 1993). These circumstances make it profoundly important for men to develop alliances of the highest possible quality with other families so that defense against raiders is as strong as possible. Giving a kinswoman in marriage is one important mechanism for alliance formation. In these circumstances, the high value a man places on his control of women is no whim. Rather, male control over women is thus a key part of male family life. Since women increase in value with their modesty and chastity, it is vital for men to control their female relatives' behavior around men. This control remains central not only to his ability to function effectively as a husband and father but also to economic survival (Weisfeld 1993).

The strong resistance many men have shown to monogamy suggests that patriarchal control is not merely the arbitrary remnant of a temporary historical culture. Instead, it is intimately associated with the prevailing economic system. For example, Michele Tertilt (2005, 1341) finds that "banning polygyny decreases fertility by 40 percent, increases savings by 70 percent, and increases output per capita by 170 percent." Ironically, it is often the case in the developing world that societies, including agricultural ones, where women possess more productive value and are thus more independent produce higher rates of polygyny

(Lesthaeghe et al. 1994). This seems to be the case because women in these societies must balance their productive and reproductive responsibilities wisely. In areas that lack access to modern birth control, long periods of postpartum abstinence (over a year) accomplish this goal while encouraging male polygyny.

POLYGYNY AND MALE VIOLENCE

The potential for conflict engendered by patriarchal rejection of female prospects for independence among pastoralists is intensified by polygyny. Wealth-based polygyny (one man having several wives) is widespread in pastoralists. Polygyny has other sources as well, including the uneven accumulation of wealth. The results are in some cases extreme. The Crown Princes of Saudi Arabia, defined as the male descendants of Ibn Saud (who founded the country and died in 1953), are estimated to number between 6,000 and 7,000. Polygyny is concentrated everywhere in the wealthier families and, as noted above, leads to an accumulation of unmarried men in poorer classes.

Thus, one of the biggest problems potentiated by polygyny lies in the large number of poor men left without prospects of finding a wife and having a family. The basic definitional demographics of polygyny make this very clear. In investigating eighteen African countries from 1921 to 1951, Bixler et al. (1981) found that while 61 percent of wives were in polygynous unions, 61 percent of husbands were in monogamous unions. In some cases, monogamous practices may be socially imposed, as in large, complex industrial societies such as predominate in modern Western industrialized democracies. In other cases, they may be ecologically imposed, as in foraging societies where polygyny may be allowed but is rare because it is difficult for men to accumulate sufficient wealth to provide for more than one wife. According to the polygyny threshold model, women can do better as the second wife of a rich man than as the only wife of a poor one; rich women have slightly more children, but rich men have many more children (Irons 1979). Such a model predicts polygyny as partially the result of female preferences when large inequality in wealth among males exists. However, this model also demonstrates the importance of male control over resources for sustaining polygyny since there is little reproductive inequality among women based on how many husbands they have (i.e., it takes long enough for a women to carry and give birth to a baby that she does not tend to have significantly more children in polygynous unions), so women will always prefer monogamy where there is no economic inequality among males. This is because the health of women and their children always benefits from a pair bond; in hunter-gatherer cultures, divorce or a father's death increases children's death rates by 50 percent (Hurtado and Hill 1992). In twenty-two sub-Saharan African countries, children of polygynous unions are 24 percent more likely to die than are children of monogamous unions.

But polygyny does lead to increased reproductive success for men (Irons 1979). Especially in stratified societies with accumulation of wealth at the top, women tend to marry up as wealthy men try to buy as many women as they can. In such dynamics, women compete to be attractive, hoping to garner the best economic deal they can through marriage, and men prefer women who are easily guarded so they do not have to fear straying by bored mates (Dickeman 1979). It thus becomes easy to understand the development of practices that secure these outcomes, such as sequestration, modesty, prizes on virginity, and high punishments for adultery (Betzig 1993).

Polygyny therefore has the unfortunate consequence of generating a class of young, unmarried men, which is statistically more inclined toward violence. To take two examples, most homicides in Canada and the United States result from the actions of males aged fifteen to thirty-five. Among those, the majority are committed by men between the ages of twenty and twenty-nine; and of those, the majority are committed by unmarried men (Daly and Wilson 1999). In his study of the relationship between single men and social violence in American history, David Courtwright (1996) argues that "where married men have been scarce or parental supervision wanting, violence and disorder have flourished, as in the mining camps, cattle towns, Chinatowns, black ghettos, and the small hours of the morning. But when stable family life has been the norm for men and boys, violence and disorder have diminished. . . . What we should not doubt is the social utility of the family, the institution best suited to shape, control and sublimate the energies of young men" (280). Similarly, in India, districts with higher ratios of men to women have higher rates of homicide (Dreze and Khera 2000).

The presence of large numbers of young, unmarried men can arise not only from polygyny but also from distorted overall sex ratios (which can occur from other sources, including sex-selected abortion, female infanticide, and poor healthcare for women). High sex ratios of men to women occur in highly pastoralist areas such as Afghanistan and Pakistan, as well as in other countries such as India and China, where pastoralist economies are less important. High sex ratios have historically been associated with intrasociety violence, aggressive foreign policy initiatives, and governments that, being aware of the threat posed by organizations of unmarried men, tended to be repressive and authoritarian (Hudson and Den Boer 2002).

Even terrorist groups understand the threat posed by large numbers of unmarried men. One of the most notorious terrorist groups ever, the Black September movement, conducted the seizure of Israeli athletes at the Munich Olympics in 1972. When Arafat's organization sought to dismantle this group for fear that their violence would undermine broader political objectives, military leaders decided their best bet to get members of the movement to cease and desist from such activities was to marry them off. Through a system of financial incentives and structured "mixers," members of Black September married attractive young Palestinian women. When such men were later asked to leave the country on legitimate business with legal passports, not a single one agreed to go for fear of losing his family (Hoffman 2001). The Northern Ireland Prison Service used similar strategies when they offered early release to former IRA and loyalist terrorists. None of the men offered early parole through a system designed to reaffirm family ties ever returned to prison (Hoffman 2001). The larger point remains that unmarried men simply have less to lose and may seek the dominance and wealth that might attract a mate through less conventional and potentially more dangerous means.

This phenomenon has both social and physiological bases. Allan Mazur (Mazur and Booth 1998) reports that men with high levels of testosterone, including unmarried men, are more likely to exhibit violent and antisocial behaviors, including getting into trouble with the law, substance abuse, and other forms of aggressive behavior. In addition, he shows that age-adjusted testosterone is not constant over time. Rather, male testosterone increases in the years surrounding divorce and decreases in the years surrounding marriage, independent of age. Mazur and Michalek (1998) argue that this phenomenon helps explain both the low criminality found among married men and the high rates of domestic abuse seen in cases of divorce. This greater propensity toward violence in young men is likely supported, at least in part, by the higher levels of testosterone found within these age ranges. Male testosterone also drops in the time surrounding courtship and marriage and drops further with the birth of each child (Gray et al. 2002). Thus, men married to women show suppressed rates of violence and aggression relative to unmarried men of the same age.

Polygyny not only increases the number of unmarried men but also exacerbates the uneven wealth distribution that accompanies polygyny, further increasing another independent risk factor for violence. Evidence for this risk can be found in data showing that the Gini coefficient of inequality across household incomes accounts for most of the difference between homicide rates among ten Canadian provinces and fifty US states (Daly and Wilson 1999). As noted above, polygyny can be simultaneous or sequential. The analysis here focuses on simultaneous polygyny because it reduces young men's options for marriage and reproduction and has therefore been hypothesized to lead to increased competition among men and intensified efforts by men to control women.

DATA AND METHODS

Here we use a unique data source, the WomanStats project, to provide the first substantial cross-cultural analysis of (1) the impact of polygamous relationships on women's equality; (2) the impact of polygamous relationships on children, including child brides and the children of polygamous unions; and (3) the impact of polygamous relationships on the nation-state.

We examine the link between polygyny and the physical security of women and children. Controlling for the independent effects of gross domestic product and sex ratio, we find statistically significant relationships between polygyny and the following: discrepancy between law and practice concerning women's equality; birth rate; rates of primary and secondary education for male and female children; differences between males and females in HIV infection; age of marriage; maternal mortality; life expectancy; sex trafficking; female genital mutilation; domestic violence; inequity in the treatment of males and females before the law; defense expenditures; and political rights and civil liberties. The elevated frequency of polygynous marriage thus tends to be associated with increases in behavioral constraints and physical costs experienced by women and children in particular. Since our results control for relative wealth (GDP), these costs appear to be due, at least in part, to structural and institutional attempts to control female sexuality and reproduction independent of economic constraints.

The WomanStats project (www.WomanStats.org) provides national data on polygyny and most of the effects we study here. Data used in this paper are sampled from 171 countries for the period 2000 to 2007. We used year-matched data when available. Our maximum gap between data samples was five years, a short period compared to rates of societal change (Eckstein 1988). The WomanStats database provides the largest compilation of information on the status of women in the world, coding over 260 variables for 174 countries. Because we limited our observations to countries with populations over 200,000, we restricted our analysis to 171 of these countries. The preponderance of data in WomanStats comes from scholarly research, NGO and IGO reports, governmental reports, and national statistical bureaus, with each piece of information being fully indexed as to source. The WomanStats project constitutes a unique data set that provides extensive information about women's issues around the world. No other data set on women's issues in the world ranks as its equal, whether in terms of the breadth and depth of its coverage, the degree of its reliability checks, or the time spent in its creation. It literally is the best of its kind and permits a comprehensive, comparative statistical analysis unlike any other data set.

The data on the nation-state comes from two well-respected international organizations whose main goal is to collect the information we examine. The data on arms expenditures comes from the Stockholm International Peace Research Institute (SIPRI). SIPRI describes itself as "an independent international institute dedicated to research into conflict, armaments, arms control and disarmament," although it is supported, in part, by the Swedish government. Its data exists free on the web at www.sipri.org. SIPRI is widely considered to be an unbiased and world-class resource for this material. The information regarding political freedoms and civil liberties comes from Freedom House, an independent, nongovernmental organization widely considered to provide the most accurate and comprehensive data on social and political freedoms for countries around the globe. Its information can be accessed at www.freedomhouse.org.

A total of seventeen outcome variables are considered here, comprising a rich variety of dimensions of women's lives, children's lives, and the influence on the nation-state, aggregated to the level of the state. Taken together, these variables show a systematic and negative influence of polygyny on women's health and equality, children's welfare, and the nation-state.

Naturally, the state is not the only sort of unit of analysis: ethnic enclaves are one alternative, for instance. But states constitute the basic unit of analysis in the international system and add comparative context to unique or anecdotal case material, particularly so when measures of the variables, such as polygyny, are arguably and reasonably homogenous across the subunits a state encompasses.

Because it is not possible to test every variable in the WomanStats database for its relationship to polygyny, we test here those that appear most theoretically plausible and empirically tractable. For instance, we can hypothesize that polygyny is likely to lead to higher rates of prostitution, but we cannot test for this relationship because not enough data exist to make it possible to examine this variable statistically. This does not mean that a significant relationship does not exist or might not be uncovered in the future when more comprehensive data might become available; it just means we cannot know now whether or not a statistically significant relationship exists because we are currently lacking the data to test it. So we must remain agnostic, barring additional data, on whether or not such a relationship exists. In addition, there may be other factors affected by polygyny that exist but that we did not know or think to test or report here. However, every relationship we examined below fell within the conventional accepted standard for a statistically significant effect given a prior hypothesis. This means that the likelihood that such relationships occurred by chance and are actually unrelated to polygyny, while not impossible, remains very, very low.

In this analysis, it is important that we control for variables that might directly cause the outcomes we examine. In particular, we must control for the effect of gross domestic product (GDP), measured in US dollars, on the relationship between polygyny as the cause and the other issues we examine as potential effects. This is because other streams of literature have long indicated a strong relationship between economic development and other aspects of women's rights. If poor outcomes for women are entirely attributable to poverty, then naturally polygyny does not exert an impact, though such a conclusion might be erroneous if attention were paid to polygyny in the quantitative analysis without also controlling for income. But controlling for gross domestic product allows for an *independent* analysis of the influence of polygyny on the outcome variables concerning equity that comprise our concern. Combined, these two characteristics constitute an incredibly powerful tool for the study of polygyny. We thus deductively assess the hypothesized relationship between cause (polygyny) and effect (say, domestic violence), and we do so all other things, including the wealth of a country as measured by GDP, being equal.

RESULTS OF ANALYSIS

The polygyny variable categorizes countries according to its prevalence. Countries were divided into five categories, ranging from places where polygyny is illegal and uncommon to places where it is legal and common, meaning more than 25 percent of women exist in such unions.

We begin with the variable called *discrepancy*. Discrepancy is a variable that taps (1) whether a country's laws are in concordance with the United Nations Convention on Elimination of Discrimination against Women (CEDAW) and (2) whether the country enforces these laws. We use the 2007 coding of this variable in this analysis. In the lowest category are those countries where CEDAW-consonant laws exist and are enforced, while the highest category refers to countries in which CEDAW-consonant laws are not present or are not enforced. Intrastate conduct not consonant with CEDAW does occur more often in more polygynous societies.

Figure 6.1 displays (1) the "scatter" of the data displaying the actual values of discrepancy and polygyny; (2) the line of best fit, which indicates a strong positive relationship between polygyny and discrepancy, as expected; and (3) the CI portraying the accuracy of prediction.

Further evidence of the effect of polygyny comes in the form of a multiple regression controlling for GDP. The fit statistic here used is distributed $F(2, 129) = 75.62$, and this is of the magnitude that indicates that the variables are not jointly 0, at a high level of significance ($p < 0.0005$). There is more evidence of an association, namely, $R^2 = 0.54$. Polygyny retains an effect in the context of a multiple regression. The multiple regression coefficient for polygyny is positive ($\beta = 0.240888$), and the two-tailed significance test of the null hypothesis can be rejected far beyond the conventional standard ($p < 0.0005$). Thus, there is strong confirmation of the role of polygyny. As polygyny goes up, discrepancy rises.

Data is displayed in a series of figures and tables in the appendix to this chapter. Women in polygynous countries have more children, on average, than women in less polygynous states, as shown in figure 6.1 and table 6.1. Figure 6.2 presents the same visuals as figure 6.1 and with the same punch line: polygyny substantially shapes the number of births per 1,000 women per year in a state. The fit statistic with $F(2, 167) = 109.23$, $p < 0.0005$. It is extremely unlikely that the variables are simultaneously 0. To this it may be added $R^2 = 0.57$. What then of the effect of polygyny controlling for GDP? Births per 1,000 go up, as per the regression coefficient ($\beta = 4.690576$) and the apparent rejection of the two-tailed statistical test ($p < 0.0005$).

The scatter of points in figure 6.3 suggest that births for women aged fifteen to nineteen in countries with higher degrees of polygyny are also on average more substantial, and this too is what is to be expected of the line of best fit and also from the relative tightness of the CI.

To compile multivariate evidence of the effect of polygyny, a multiple regression controlling for GDP was performed. The fit statistic with $F(2,$

134) = 41.57 indicates that the variables are not jointly 0, at a high level of significance ($p < 0.0005$). There is more evidence of an association in the form of the squared correlation coefficient, namely, $R^2 = 0.38$.

This regression indicates the separate effect of polygyny, what with a large and positive coefficient estimated as $\beta = 16.885980$, with estimated standard error of 2.724238 and a p-value beyond what is conventionally required for rejection of the null hypothesis ($p < 0.0005$).

Polygyny also exerts an effect on children's welfare, as shown in table 6.2. Girls are less likely to receive an education in primary or secondary school as polygyny become more frequent. The same holds true for boys as well. Boys are less likely to receive either primary or secondary school education in polygynous societies than in those raised by their monogomous counterparts.

The rates of primary enrollment of girls in school are shown in table 6.3 and figure 6.4. Figure 6.4 suggests that in countries that have lower primary enrollments of girls, polygyny is more frequent, on average, this returned by the scatter of data and the line of best fit. The CI suggests confidence in the predictions.

A two-variable multiple regression fits the outcome variable reasonably well, as shown in figure 6.4. Indeed, $F(2, 156) = 11.11$, $p < 0.0005$, and $R^2 = 0.12$. As evinced by figure 6.4, the coefficient linking polygyny to primary enrollment for girls is negative (β–4.454723) and statistically significant ($p < 0.0005$), as anticipated. This means that in polygynous countries, girls are less likely to attend primary schools.

The fifth outcome variable, secondary enrollment of girls in school, behaves in response to polygyny in the same way as that for primary enrollment. Figure 6.5 displays this, composed as it is with the scatter, the slope estimate, and the CI. The fit is better, however. Table 6.3 contains the results: $F(2, 155) = 102.90$, $p < 0.0005$, and $R^2 = .57$. Moreover, it can be seen that secondary enrollment of girls declines as polygyny becomes more frequent ($\beta = -12.064350$) and in a statistically significant way ($p < 0.0005$).

What then of the sixth outcome variable and the seventh, namely, the degree of primary and secondary enrollment for boys in school? In both cases, seen in figures 6.6 and 6.7, enrollment for boys appears structured at least partially by polygyny. The slope of line of best fit is negative in both cases: lower enrollments of boys in primary or secondary institutions are on average occurring in countries with higher levels of polygyny.

While these figures are suggestive, multiple regression is ultimately necessary to untangle the question of the role of polygyny for these outcome variables, and the technique for both outcome variables confirms how polygyny affects them, controlling for GDP.

To begin with, for primary education, the fit statistics ($F(2, 156)$ = 3.97, $p < 0.0209$; $R^2 = 0.05$) suggest a relationship between GDP and/or polygyny and primary education for boys. Moreover, the slope (β ^ = -2.58122) is statistically significant ($p < 0.005$).

Moving to secondary enrollment, table 6.4 shows a good fitting equation ($F(2, 155)$ = 94.90, $p < 0.0005$; $R^2 = 0.55$), indeed far more so than for primary enrollment.

Moreover, secondary enrollment of boys in more polygynous societies is less common on average, as indicated by the regression coefficient ($\beta = -9.722135$) and the two-tailed statistical test ($p < 0.0005$).

Increased polygyny heightens the difference in the occurrence of HIV infection between women and men; women become more likely relative to men to suffer from HIV as polygyny becomes more common. The differences in HIV rates, as displayed by figure 6.8, are loosely driven by polygyny: the line of best fit to the scatter cloud notes that the difference in HIV rates between women and men becomes larger, on average, in countries more beset by polygyny.

The fit statistics for the multiple regression indicate that a joint or possible one-variable relationship is at stake ($F(2, 91)$ = 4.85, $p < 0.01$; $R^2 = 0.10$); it should be noted that the estimated variance explained is not particularly impressive.

The relationship between the difference in HIV rates and polygyny survives a multiple regression analysis ($\beta = 0.377731$) and the two-tailed statistical test ($p < 0.064$). To be sure, the latter misses the 0.05 level, but it should be added that a one-tailed test is reasonable given the expected direction of the relationship and, this being the case, the multiple-regression coefficient is significant at conventional levels ($p < 0.032$).

Women in polygynous countries are more likely to marry at a younger age than women in countries where polygyny is less frequent. The scatter of points in figure 6.9 shows that female marriage age in countries with higher degrees of polygyny is on average lower, and the line of best fit reinforces this. The CI adheres at a reasonable level about the regression line.

Confirming demonstration of the effect of polygyny comes in the form of a multiple regression controlling for GDP. This has three parts. First, the fit statistic indicates that the variables are not jointly zero ($F(2, 153)$ = 54.84, $p < 0.0005$). Second, there is more evidence of an association, namely, $R^2 = 0.42$, the squared correlation coefficient. Third, the slope coefficient is negative ($\beta = -0.751378$). There can be little statistical doubt the null hypothesis is false ($p < 0.0005$).

In table 6.9, we see that women are more likely to die in childbirth as countries become more polygynous. The scatter of points in figure 6.10 and the accompanying line of best fit and the CI are consistent with the hypothesis that as polygyny gets more extensive, so does maternal mortality, defined as the number of women who die in childbirth per 100,000 live births.

A multiple regression affirms that the coefficients linking polygyny and GDP to maternal mortality are not jointly zero ($F(2, 167) = 42.83$, $p < 0.0005$; $R^2 = 0.34$), meaning that both GDP and polygyny, or one of these, contribute to maternal mortality. Multiple regression with GDP as a control produces results reinforcing what is suggested by the bivariate regression.

Polygyny has a separate role to play. Its corresponding coefficient is estimated as $\beta \wedge = 131.537200$, with an estimated standard error of 19.492820 and a p-value beyond what is conventionally required for rejection of the null hypothesis ($p < 0.0005$).

Longevity is also affected by polygyny. Life expectancy taps the average age at which women in a given country die. Polygyny and female life expectancy are inversely linked: more polygynous countries experience lower life expectancy for females. In other words, women in more polygynous countries die at a younger age on average, likely at least partly because they are more likely to die in childbirth, as noted above. Figure 6.11 portrays in two-space the relationship between female life expectancy and polygyny and the according line of best fit, surrounded on either side by the CI. In polygynous societies, female life expectancy is lower than in societies without it.

It can be seen from table 6.6 that a multiple regression with polygyny and GPD as predictors fares well ($F(2, 153) = 74.28$, $p < 0.0005$; $R^2 = 0.47$). The same may be said for polygyny considered on its own, GDP serving as a control. The coefficient is negative ($\beta = -4.479878$), and a high degree of confidence can be expressed in the rejection of the null hypothesis ($p < 0.0005$).

In table 6.6, we see that ordered logistic regression was used to estimate the relationship between the following dependent variables and polygyny, with GDP used in all analyses as a control: sex trafficking; female genital mutilation (FGM); domestic violence (DVS); and inequity in family law. From a statistical standpoint, this technique has many advantages over ordinary least-squares regression when the dependent variable is comprised of a limited number of ordered, unevenly spaced categories.

Sex trafficking increases in more polygynous countries. This variable divides countries into five categories, based on their degree of compliance with the Trafficking Persons Act of 2000. The lowest signifies that there are laws against sex trafficking, while the highest means sex trafficking is permitted and the country is not in compliance with the law. In the current analysis, the five-point scale in the WomanStats database was collapsed into four categories because there was not a sufficient number of observations in two of the categories. Specifically, we collapsed the lowest two categories since only one country fit into the lowest category. When this happens, the coefficients cannot be properly estimated, so this is standard practice in such cases. Table 6.7 displays the results of a proposed model of predictors consisting of polygyny and GDP. The likelihood ratio test for the model produces χ^2 (3) = 64.96, which yields $p < 0.0005$. Consequently, it is very unlikely that the coefficients linking our independent variables to sex trafficking are both 0. The pseudo-R^2 = 0.17 suggests a relationship, though the degree cannot be quantified statistically.

A two-tailed test for the hypothesis that polygyny has no effect on sex trafficking may be rejected using a standard level of significance ($p < 0.047$). One demonstration of the effect of polygyny is via the odds ratio: a movement from one level of polygyny to one immediately subsequent to it increases the odds of being in the uppermost category of the ordered, discrete sex-trafficking scale versus the other categories by a factor of 1.25 times, GDP controlled.

Envisioning the effect of polygyny on sex trafficking via an odds ratio can be supplemented with a consideration of the effect of polygyny on predicted probability associated with categories of sex trafficking. In calculating the degree of association, though, it must be emphasized that while odds ratios do not turn on the values of polygyny or GDP—where they are fixed, in particular—the predicted probabilities for sex trafficking must be calculated for levels of polygyny and some fixed value for GDP.

This is due to the fact that the probabilities associated with categories of the dependent variables are nonlinear expressions of the independent variables: the interpretation of the effect of polygyny for one (fixed) value of GDP may be somewhat different than that for another, and the odds ratio associated with a shift from one level of polygyny to the one immediately following is the same regardless of whether one starts with, say, polygyny = 2 or polygyny = 3.

However, the same is not true when the matter turns to predicted probabilities for sex trafficking or any of our other ordinal dependent variables. Even so, while caution must be exercised, it is still the case that a portrait of predicted probabilities has a substantive and visual appeal, particularly when accompanied by a figure plotting the effects. Such is the case with figure 6.12. The y-axis ranges from 0 to 1, as expected. The x-axis is polygyny, with graphically represented steps of 1 from 0 to 4, also expected. What do the lines represent and how can they be interpreted? For a particular category, say sex trafficking = 4, the lines trace the effect of polygyny from one level to another, and further, across its range. They show how a change, say, from polygyny = 2 to polygyny = 3 alters the predicted probabilities of sex trafficking when the value of sex trafficking is 4.

Notice also that the slopes linking various categories step by step through the range of polygyny are not identical. For instance, when sex trafficking = 1 (p = 1), its associated predicted probabilities generally go down when polygyny goes down, while the general movement of predicted probabilities when sex trafficking = 4 goes up as polygyny becomes more common.

What this means, in fact, is that as polygyny becomes more frequent, trafficking becomes more prevalent and women more victimized. As signaled by the figure, the leap in predicted probabilities for this value of trafficking is impressive, particularly since GDP is controlled at its median value, a good choice given that this is a measure of central tendency.

Female genital mutilation (FGM), sometimes referred to as female cutting, also increases as countries become more polygynous. This practice exerts a detrimental effect on women's health because it can affect subsequent bladder, bowel, and childbirth processes, particularly if it is badly done or conducted under unsanitary conditions, as often occurs. FGM is often referred to as female circumcision, but this represents a clear misnomer and euphemism. As Nahid Toubia (1994, 712) writes in the *New England Journal of Medicine,* "The mildest form, clitoridectomy, is anatomically equivalent to amputation of the penis. Under the conditions in which most procedures take place, female circumcision constitutes a health hazard with short- and long-term physical complications and psychological effects."

In our analysis, the highest category includes countries where more than 10 percent, and sometimes upwards of 50 percent, of women have sustained such cutting. FGM is divided by countries into five categories and then collapsed into three for purposes of the analysis because of the small number of cases for particular values of the variable.

Figure 6.13 shows that the number of cases here is comparatively small, suggesting perhaps that caution is warranted in interpreting the results. But such results are not written in stone; alternatively, it might be speculated that countries with the highest levels of FGM do not report this practice, perhaps looking away, perhaps encouraging it, the impact being a suppressor effect—the relationship might look even stronger were data available for all countries.

This said, the likelihood ratio test for our model of two variables is distributed χ^2 (3) = 48.53, which yields $p < 0.0005$. So we can reject at conventional levels the hypothesis of a joint, null relationship between FGM and our two independent variables.

The pseudo-R^2 = 0.31 is the highest so far seen. A linkage between polygyny and FGM is confirmed statistically with a very high degree of significance ($p < 0.0005$; F,2156) = 3.97, $p < 0.0209$; R^2 = 0.05), suggesting a relationship between GDP and/or polygyny and FGM. Moreover, the slope ($\beta^\wedge$ = −2.58122) is statistically significant ($p < 0.005$). This magnitude is especially impressive and is confirmed by the shape of the lines in figure 6.13. At its most extreme, FGM has predicted probabilities that move almost in lockstep with polygyny.

Of critical importance is the question of whether polygyny contributes to violence toward women. To answer this question, an omnibus measure of domestic violence was employed, one that incorporates domestic violence, rape, marital rape, and honor killings, as well as the extent and strength of the enforcement of the laws prohibiting these crimes in any given state. And indeed, as confirmed in table 6.8 and figure 6.14, polygynous countries experience more domestic violence against women. Table 6.8 shows the likelihood ratio test for our model of two variables is distributed χ^2 (3) = 76.03, which yields $p < 0.0005$. So I can reject at conventional levels the hypothesis of a joint, null relationship between domestic violence and our two independent variables. A supplementary suggestion of a relationship comes courtesy of the pseudo-R^2 = 0.19.

Our test statistic suggests that one or both of our variables drive domestic violence, so what then of polygyny? A linkage between polygyny and DVS is confirmed statistically with a very high degree of significance ($p < 0.001$). The odds ratio may be interpreted by assessing how moving polygyny by one unit upwards shifts the odds of being in the uppermost category of the ordered, discrete domestic-violence scale versus the other categories of domestic violence. Indeed, the odds increase by 1.47 times, GDP controlled. For the value of GDP we have chosen, it can be seen that domestic violence at its worst expression [p(4)], and as expressed in terms of predicted probabilities, goes up as considered across the range of polygyny (fig. 6.14). There is also a dramatic on-balance shift for the category of domestic violence.

Polygyny also affects the treatment of men and women before the law. Differences in the legal treatment of women versus men become greater, to the detriment of women, in more polygynous societies. I refer to this variable as *inequity*. Inequity measures the degree of equal treatment of men and women before the law. More particularly, inequity is defined as the relative standing of men and women under the law, indexed on an ordinal scale. At the low end are countries where the legal age of marriage is eighteen or higher, where women may choose their spouses, where divorce is possible, where both partners are treated equitably by the law, where abortion is permitted, and where women may inherit property. Countries at the high end permit marriage at younger than eighteen years of age, that is, have laws that permit girls aged twelve or less to be married. Table 6.8 contains the results.

Our two-variable model performs well, as expressed by a likelihood ratio test, with a distribution $\chi^2 (3) = 139.07$, which yields $p < 0.0005$. So I can reject at conventional levels the hypothesis of a joint, null relationship between inequity and our two independent variables. As noted, and absent a distribution, the pseudo-$R^2 = 0.27$ conveys the same information as the likelihood ratio statistic.

More evidence for the hypothesis that polygyny matters with regard to inequity comes in the form of a two-tailed statistical test of the null hypothesis that it does not ($p < 0.0005$). The accompanying information about predicted probabilities, displayed in figure 6.15, is difficult to summarize and is perhaps our most notable manifestation of nonlinearities. We observe what we would expect: dips on balance when inequity manifests in its greatest form as polygyny turns from its lowest to its greatest amount, and the reverse being so when polygyny travels from its greatest to its lowest, driving as it does inequity at its lowest level.

Polygyny also has effects that extend beyond the outcome variables already considered. Polygyny can exert effects on various aspects of domestic and international politics for a given nation-state. First, to the extent that junior boys who have been excised from polygynous communities become wards of the state, the cost of educating, socializing, housing, feeding, and job training for them gets transferred from the family to taxpayers. Second, to the extent that secondary wives can obtain aid from the state under laws designed to help women with dependent children, financial costs for such support can escalate as well.

Moreover, the effects of polygyny on the nation-state can be quantified along certain dimensions. States with higher rates of polygyny spend more money per capita on defense, particularly on arms expenditures for weapons.

More specifically, we test whether defense expenditures have a partial foundation in polygyny. Defense expenditures are surely a crucial foreign-policy stance, an orientation toward the outside world, and perhaps an indication of the inner workings of policy elites. So polygyny is examined here for the extent to which it can exert influential impacts beyond the private and domestic spheres.

We investigate first whether states with high levels of polygyny concurrently have low degrees of freedom, the former being a cause of the latter, and the latter a crucial measure of the internal workings of the state and the quality of life for all citizens.

We begin with defense expenditures. The Stockholm International Peace Research Institute has collected data about defense expenditures per capita. A particular advantage of this measure, aside from its being well respected and widely used, is that the unit of the analysis is the state, permitting what I have already done, particularly a comparison of states with lower versus higher levels of polygyny with states that have lower or higher levels of outcomes negative for women, on average. Our question is whether this variable is related to polygyny.

Figure 6.16, complete with the scatter of data, the line of best fit, and the CI, is consistent with the interpretation that states with higher amounts of per capita defense expenditures are more likely on average to have higher degrees of polygyny. Table 6.9 confirms this. The fit statistic confirms this marginally: $F(2, 91) = 2.73$, $p < 0.0687$, and the squared correlation coefficient $R^2 = 0.22$. The coefficient is 0.228663 and is statistically significant at convention levels ($p < 0.025$). We can conclude from this data that states with higher expenditures are, on average, more likely to have higher degrees of polygyny as well, as anticipated.

Polygyny also influences the degree of rights and freedoms experienced by citizens in a given country. Specifically, states with higher rates of polygyny extend fewer political rights and civil liberties than those that have less polygyny. To be sure, a good deal about the liberties women enjoy and the ones stripped from them because of their gender can easily be inferred using data from the project. But here the consideration is liberties more generally construed within society at large, those experienced by both men and women, and there is no measured analog for that in the WomanStats database project. On the other hand, Freedom House has an excellent, well-thought-of omnibus measure, described as "freedom in world historical rankings." A particular advantage of this measure is that the unit of analysis is the state, permitting what we have already done, particularly a comparison of states with lower versus higher levels of polygyny with states that have lower or higher levels of outcomes negative for citizens, on average.

Summarizing the results of the ordered logistic regression, it can been seen from table 6.9 that χ^2 (2) = 52.28 and p < 0.0005. Thus we can dispense with the null hypothesis that there is jointly no effect of the predictors of the measured level of freedom. It is also the case that polygyny survives as an influence, GDP controlled (p < 0.0005). Though elsewhere not as diagnostic in the same ways as the likelihood ratio statistics, the pseudo-R^2 = 0.1463 is suggestive of relationship between at least one of the variables and freedom.

Table 6.9 shows that the odds ratio is 0.682354 and is statistically significant (p < 0.0005), meaning that moving one category upward in polygyny lowers by 0.682354 times the likelihood that a country will be free as opposed to the two (ordered) alternatives. The final figure visually shows how, when GDP is controlled for at its median, changes in polygyny affect the level of freedom of a state. As an example, look at the predicted probabilities for a state as "not free." These probabilities (fig. 6.17), when looked at when polygyny is absent, are lower than the predicted probabilities when at least 25 percent of women are captured by polygyny.

DISCUSSION AND CONCLUSIONS

Examining over 170 countries around the world, we find that polygynous structures increase violence toward women and children, decrease civil rights and political liberties, and increase the allocation of resources for weapons procurement. Polygyny exerts economic, physical, and political consequences for societies in which such practices remain prevalent. Specifically, Satoshi Kanazawa (2001) shows early menarche in polygynous countries, and unrelated work has shown that early sexual trauma leads to increased morbidity, decline in longevity, and intergenerational transfer of changes in genetic expression. Further, children of young mothers have less education, have worse economic prospects, and remain at higher risk for crime.

Our results could in theory be confounded by the presence of other variables not considered in our analysis such as religious affiliation, inequity in income distribution, or political system. The strengths of statistical association might also be modified by taking into account sociocultural similarities or historical continuities among countries. Controlling for such variables represents an important analytical challenge that has been solved when relationships between sample points are linguistic or cultural, but not for countries as a whole since they include multiple populations. Data are currently not available to analyze by distinct cultural units. Future research may be able to test such hypotheses when further data become available. Furthermore, it is possible that causation can go in both directions. For example, female-biased mortality arising from violence toward women could lead to polygyny being favored. Our conclusions must therefore be preliminary.

Nevertheless, the consistency and strength of our findings across multiple independent measures of violence, together with their conformity to a well-supported anthropological theory about the impact of polygyny on the propensity for male violence, are clearly suggestive. In view of the importance of recognizing sources of violence that can be modified by appropriate legislative action, we believe our results warrant further intense investigation. We conclude that the evidence in favor of the role of polygyny is sufficiently strong that efforts should be made to understand more clearly the contexts in which, and the mechanisms by which, polygyny fosters local and institutional violence toward women and children, as well as its role in undergirding support for the suppression of political rights and civil liberties. In addition, polygyny exerts its effects on violence against women independent of the effects of sex ratio alone, so the social, cultural, and institutional practices that support its existence manifest an impact that goes beyond merely increasing the number of unmarried men in society.

Our data also show that increased gross domestic product is generally associated with women having greater freedom from violence. We suggest that wealthier countries may have more resources, and possibly more willingness to devote such resources, to more accurately collect data on many aspects of society, including the treatment of women and children. We also suspect that as income rises, societies have increased their wherewithal to treat women and children better. Possible explanations include women having more power because they generate a higher percentage of the wealth, allowing them to be less economically dependent on men. In addition, wealthier societies might monitor conformity to the law more accurately, thanks to their greater resources. However, the problem of violence against women is not obviated by increasing wealth alone, as is attested to by the fact that many wealthy countries continue to suffer from high rates of violence against women, including domestic violence, rape, and murder. Poverty, while clearly important, represents only part of the problem that generates violence against women.

More than simply increasing the number of men unable to find mates, polygynous practices also encourage control over women in many areas, which is required in order to maintain control over reproductive access. This analysis demonstrates that such control often devolves into systematic practices of violence against women and children. In this way, polygyny may represent a more sensitive measure than sex ratio since sex ratio includes women at less reproductively important ages. This age structure may be particularly important with regard to older women; it may not matter much if there are a lot of old women compared to old men in terms of the impact of sex ratio on violence against women, but it may matter a great deal if most younger women are engaged in polygynous unions.

Polygyny appears to constitute a sizeable and independent piece of the puzzle explaining the emergence of violence directed at women and children. In addition, the institutions necessary to keep it in place may help explain some of the patterns of repression across the globe. And yet polygyny is a practice that will not necessarily be easily changed. One solution to the problem of polygyny as a source of violence toward women might be to increase female social emancipation through education. Yet Ron Lesthaeghe et al. (1994) found that increasing female literacy did not lead to a decline in polygyny rates, at least in sub-Saharan Africa. The ability to read does not help if the only information one encounters merely reconfirms preexisting beliefs. As long as male control of reading material is maintained, female literacy alone cannot begin to shift patterns of patriarchal control until women begin to possess financial and economic means of independence as well.

An irony emerges from our analysis: conventional attempts to empower women in polygynous culture can be expected to make matters worse—at least in traditional pastoralist economies—because they will increase the hostility felt by many men toward women and the cultural values that advocate for female emancipation. We do not conclude that such efforts, including advocacy of women's rights and education of both sexes, should be discontinued. But the inherent obstacles they face should be appreciated. The cultural and political diversity of polygynous cultures creates many different opportunities for sensitively designed efforts to work, even if the emancipation of women can be predicted to encounter continuing resistance in various regions, especially those culturally dominated by pastoralism.

After all, polygyny does not necessarily stem from women being uneducated. If it is rooted in a local socioeconomic system, economics rather than ideas may need to change in order to alter the incentives sustaining its practice. Empowering women alone is not enough. If the underlying causes of male domination of the rights of reproduction remain unchanged, female emancipation will be limited. Such efforts therefore must be complemented with strategies that address the deep causes of patriarchy, including pastoralist economic practices.

We do not intend here to assume that all practices most Westerners see as repressive of women must be changed, such as the wearing of the veil. But neither do we intend to embrace cultural relativism to the disservice of basic human rights and peaceful coexistence. Rather, we take note of Lila Abu-Lughod's (2002) directive to recognize the historical and economic forces that engendered this reality and work to transform it within the context of a universal responsibility to mitigate injustice and prevent harm and injury to all humans, while respecting genuine cultural preferences that do not impinge on basic human rights. With this in mind, we offer two observations.

First, the system by which marital alliances create powerful kin groups is predicated on the importance of male groups as martial defenders of herds. Improvement in policing in pastoralist regions, therefore, can be expected to reduce the importance of a major source of patriarchal culture, that is, a man's critical dependence on male allies. Although pastoralist economies have been associated with violence throughout the world, there are many peaceful cases to show that this correlation is not inevitable. The shift from the Wild West to modern ranching in the United States, or the eradication of raiding in Scotland, are familiar examples. In the United States, such a transition was precipitated by the widespread installation of barbed wire, making it more difficult to move herds across broad swaths of territory quickly.

Here there may be some room for optimism. As pastoralist regions shift from more rural to more urban demographics, the urban explosion of young, unmarried men could produce great social and political volatility. High-status men may still be able to secure many wives, and low-status men may still not be able to garner any wives, but since there will inevitably be more of the latter than the former, it becomes possible to rally the low-status males to overturn the system through sheer numbers. This possibility, however, depends on the development of a more modern economy in which men have economic incentives that differ from those that exist in more pastoral systems.

A bigger question concerns polygyny. Polygynous cultures in which men control women and their reproduction support and encourage violence both within these societies as well as outside of them. Polygynous cultures leave many young, lower-class men unmarried and prone toward violence. They also provide men who have daughters with a certain amount of wealth and status that result from their control over a scarce resource. Elaborate cultures and hierarchies rest on this control over passive women.

Cultural values that favor female emancipation that threaten to replace passive participants with independent women can frighten and enrage men in areas where control and domination of the productive and reproductive capacities of women embodies an important source of power. In the face of their own poverty and unemployment, men who lose control over women may feel they are left with nothing of value. And such a prospect renders these men particularly dangerous because they have nothing to lose in fighting a force that threatens their only status and prospects for reproduction. As long as polygynous marital practices and pastoralist economic structures offer opportunities for such men to use their control of women for their own personal power, any threat to such a system will spawn rage and violence in response. And such systems will leave large numbers of poor men without women.

History suggests two sets of options for governments confronted with too many men (Hudson and Den Boer 2002). They can try policies that reduce the number of men, either through violence or by exporting them to other countries as missionaries or mercenaries. Or they can try to increase the number of women by importing brides or by reducing processes such as sex-selective abortion, female infanticide, female death in childbirth, and early childhood death of girls. But these are stop-gap measures. As long as polygyny persists, countries run a high risk of violence—which may or may not be exported beyond their borders. Only when these structures no longer present an opportunity for such men to benefit from their dominance of women will women's emancipation no longer present a fundamental threat to these cultures.

It may be time, therefore, for human-rights advocates to consider advocating a shift toward endorsing monogamous reproductive structures. The risk is that this shift would be seen as one more attempt to impose Western values. But just as the developing world might point to the seeds of terrorism in Western economic and political injustice, so can the developed world discover some of the sources of violence and repression in the social injustice inherent in polygyny. The promotion of monogamy and female emancipation is a formula for a safer world. By encouraging monogamy, we reduce social inequities, violence toward women and children, and the proliferation of single men and the violence they perpetuate, as well as increase political rights and civil liberties for all. Or, as Laura Betzig (1993) puts it, "When the despots come down and the harems disperse, the veils will come off and poor men will stop trying to get virgins in heaven by blowing up planes."

Appendix

Table 6.1. Effect of polygyny and GDP on discrepancy and births per 1000

Variable	Discrepancy			Births Per 1000		
	Coefficient	SE.	p-value	Coefficient	SE.	p-value
Polygyny	0.240888	0.045434	< 0.0005	4.690576	0.426328	< 0.0005
GDP	−0.000038	0.000005	< 0.0005	−0.000234	0.000044	< 0.0005
N	132			170		
	$F_{(2, 129)} = 75.62, p < 0.0005$			$F_{(2, 167)} = 109.23, p < 0.0005$		
R^2	0.54			0.57		

Notes: Coefficients, associated standard errors, p-values, and fit statistics from ordinary least-squares (ols) regressions with discrepancy and births per 1,000 respectively as dependent variables and polygyny and GDP in each of the regressions as independent variables. For discrepancy, the effect of polygyny can be interpreted as follows: each unit increase in polygyny increases discrepancy by 0.24 units, GDP controlled. The coefficient for polygyny in births per 1,000 indicates that for each unit increase in polygyny, birth rates go up by 4.69 units, GDP controlled. Interpret other ols coefficients in the same manner.

Table 6.2. Effect of polygyny and GDP on births 15–19 and female enrollment, primary

Variable	Births, Women Aged 15–19			Primary Enrollment for Women		
	Coefficient	SE.	p-value	Coefficient	SE.	p-value
Polygyny	16.885980	2.724238	< 0.0005	−4.454723	1.018081	< 0.0005
GDP	−0.000865	0.000265	< 0.001	0.000001	0.000102	> .992
N	137			159		
	$F_{(2, 134)} = 41.57, p < 0.0005$			$F_{(2, 156)} = 11.11, p < 0.0005$		
R^2	0.38			0.12		

Notes: Coefficients, associated standard errors, p-values, and fit statistics from ols regressions with births (15–19) and female enrollment (primary) as dependent variables and polygyny and GDP in each of the regressions as independent variables.

Table 6.3. Effect of polygyny and GDP on female enrollment, secondary, and male enrollment, primary

Variable	Secondary Enrollment for Women			Primary Enrollment for Men		
	Coefficient	SE.	p-value	Coefficient	SE.	p-value
Polygyny	−12.064350	1.291731	< 0.0005	−7.429632	3.675072	< 0.045
GDP	0.000861	0.000129	< 0.0005	−0.000531	0.000367	> 0.151
N	158			159		
	$F_{(2, 155)} = 102.90$, $p < 0.0005$			$F_{(2, 159)} = 2.32$, $p < 0.1012$		
R2	0.57			0.03		

Notes: Coefficients, associated standard errors, p-values, and fit statistics from ols regressions with female enrollment (secondary) and male enrollment (primary) as dependent variables and polygyny and GDP in each of the regressions as independent variables.

Table 6.4. Effect of polygyny and GDP on male enrollment, secondary, and HIV (difference)

Variable	Secondary Enrollment for Men			HIV		
	Coefficient	SE.	p-value	Coefficient	SE.	p-value
Polygyny	−9.722135	1.165776	< 0.0005	0.377731	0.201288	< 0.064
GDP	0.000829	0.000117	< 0.0005	−0.000021	0.000020	> 0.314
N	158			94		
	$F_{(2, 155)} = 94.90$, $p < 0.0005$			$F_{(2, 91)} = 4.85$, $p < 0.01$		
R2	0.55			0.10		

Notes: Coefficients, associated standard errors, p-values, and fit statistics from ols regressions with male enrollment (secondary) and HIV (difference between women and men) as dependent variables and polygyny and GDP in each of the regressions as independent variables.

Table 6.5. Effect on polygyny and GDP on marriage age (female), secondary and maternal mortality

Variable	Female Marriage Age			Maternal Mortality		
	Coefficient	SE.	p-value	Coefficient	SE.	p-value
Polygyny	−0.751378	0.162937	< 0.0005	131.537200	19.492820	< 0.0005
GDP	0.000114	0.000117	< 0.0005	−0.007075	0.002008	< 0.0005
N	153			170		
	$F_{(2, 153)} = 54.84$, $p < 0.0005$			$F_{(2, 167)} = 42.83$, < 0005		
R2	0.42			0.34		

Notes: Coefficients, associated standard errors, p-values, and fit statistics from ols regressions with age of marriage (female) and maternal mortality as dependent variables, and polygyny and GDP in each of the regressions as independent variables.

Table 6.6. Effect of polygyny and GDP on female life expectancy

Variable	Female Life Expectancy		
	Coefficient	SE.	p-value
Polygyny	−4.479878	0.535178	< 0.0005
GDP	0.000293	0.000055	< 0.0005
N	153		
	F(2, 153) = 74.28, p < 0.0005		
R2	0.47		

Notes: Coefficients, associated standard errors, p-values, and fit statistics with female life expectancy as a dependent variable and polygyny and GDP in the regression as independent variables.

Table 6.7. Effects on polygyny and GDP on trafficking

Variable	Sex Trafficking			FGM		
	Odds Ratio	SE.	p-value	Odds Ratio	SE.	p value
Polygyny	1.251951	0.141874	< 0.047	3.763611	0.944152	< 0.0005
GDP	0.999901	0.000018	< 0.0005	1.000018	0.000019	> .365
N	154			74		
LR X2(3)	64.96, p < 0.0005			48.53, p < 0.0005		
Pseudo R2	0.17			0.31		

Notes: Coefficients, associated standard errors, *p*-values, and fit statistics from two separate ordinal logistic regressions with family law and trafficking, respectively, as dependent variables, and in each ordinal logistic regression, polygyny and GDP as independent variables. Odds ratios indicate how the odds of the dependent variable change in response to shifts in an independent variable. For instance, changing polygyny by 1 unit alters the odds of being in the uppermost category of the ordered, discrete family law scale versus the other categories of domestic violence by 2.16 times, GDP controlled. Examples of the consequences of a change in polygyny on predicted probabilities of family law as well as the other dependent variables are presented in the text.

Table 6.8. Effects of polygyny and GDP on domestic violence and inequity

Variable	DVS			Inequity		
	Odds Ratio	SE.	p value	Odds Ratio	SE.	p value
Polygyny	1.466550	0.163000	< 0.001	3.059176	0.423937	< 0.0005
GDP	0.999916	0.000015	< 0.0005	0.999935	0.000014	< 0.0005
N	168			170		
LR X2(3)	76.03, p < 0.0005			139.07, p < 0.0005		
Pseudo R2	0.19			0.27		

Notes: Coefficients, associated standard errors, p-values, and fit statistics from two separate ordinal logistic regressions with FGM and inequity, respectively, as dependent variables and in each case polygyny and GDP as independent variables.

Table 6.9. Effects of polygyny and GDP on freedom and defense expenditures

Variable	Sipri			Freedom		
	Coefficient	SE.	p-value	Odds Ratio	SE.	p-value
Polygyny	0.228663	0.100777	< 0.025	0.682354	0.076193	< 0.001
GDP	0.000004	0.000010	> 0.68	1.000076	0.000020	< 0.0005
N	137			166		
	F(2, 91) = 2.73, p < 0.0687			LR X2(2) = 52.28, p < 0.0005		
	0.22			Pseudo R2 = 0.1463		

Notes: Coefficients, associated standard errors, p-values, and fit statistics from one ols regression (defense expenditures) and one ordinal logistic regression (freedom). The ordinary least-squares regression and the ordinal least-squares regression both employ the same independent variables, viz., polygyny and GDP. Still, the interpretation of the coefficient for polygyny in the ordinary least-squares regression (as so for GDP) is not the same as that for the odds ratio for polygyny (as so for GDP).

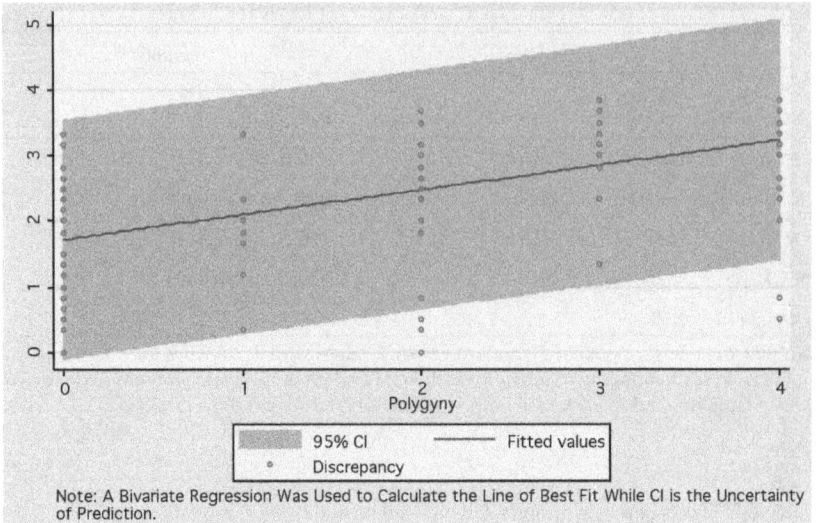

Note: A Bivariate Regression Was Used to Calculate the Line of Best Fit While CI is the Uncertainty of Prediction.

Figure 6.1. Scatterplot, line of best fit, and CIs for discrepancy by polygyny.

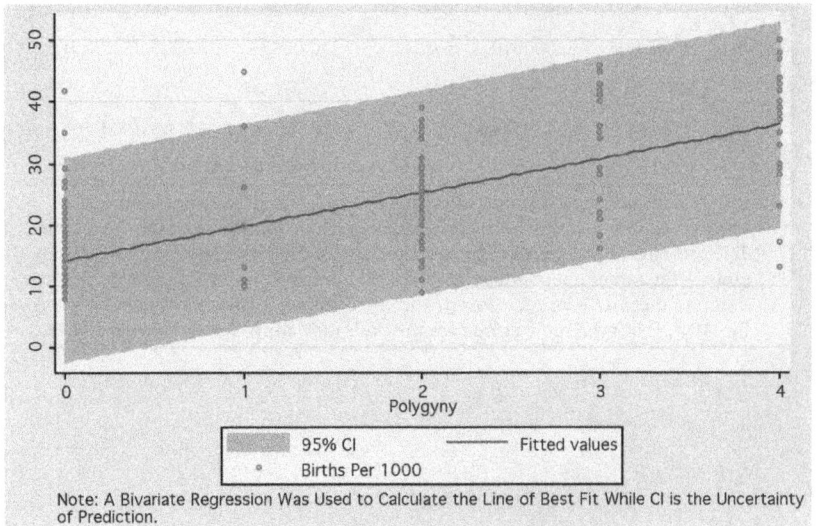

Note: A Bivariate Regression Was Used to Calculate the Line of Best Fit While CI is the Uncertainty of Prediction.

Figure 6.2. Scatterplot, line of best fit, and CIs for births per 1,000 by polygyny.

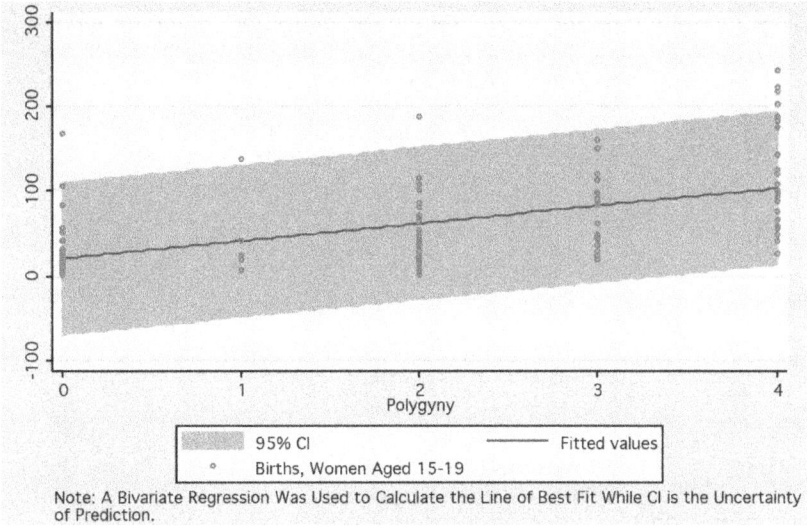

Note: A Bivariate Regression Was Used to Calculate the Line of Best Fit While CI is the Uncertainty of Prediction.

Figure 6.3. Scatterplot, line of best fit, and CIs for births, women aged 15–19 by polygyny.

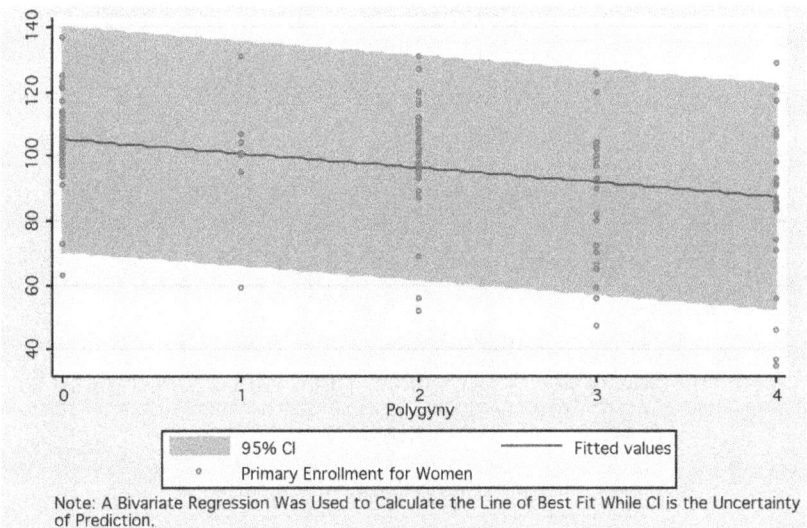

Note: A Bivariate Regression Was Used to Calculate the Line of Best Fit While CI is the Uncertainty of Prediction.

Figure 6.4. Scatterplot, line of best fit, and CIs for primary enrollment for women by polygyny.

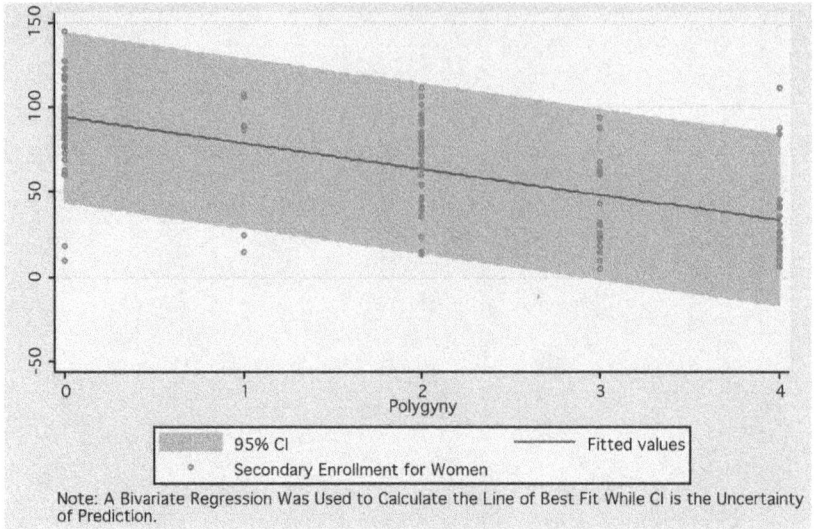

Figure 6.5. Scatterplot, line of best fit, and CIs for secondary enrollment for women by polygyny.

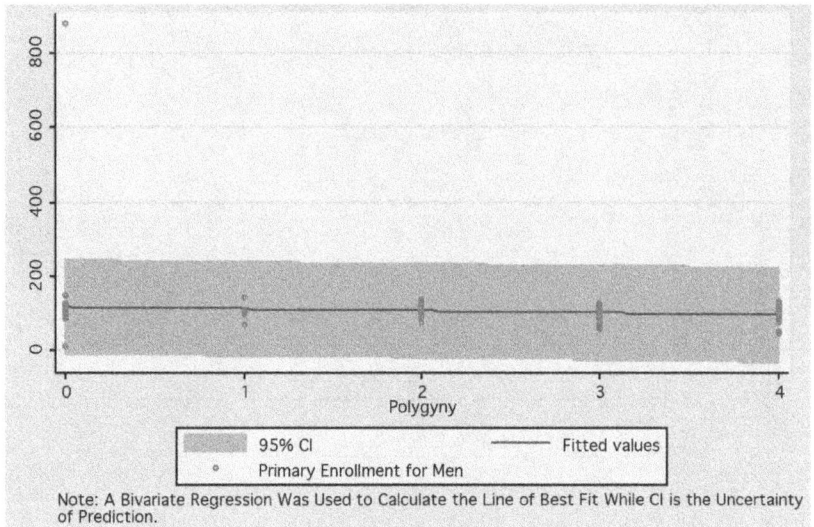

Figure 6.6. Scatterplot, line of best fit, and CIs for primary enrollment for men by polygyny.

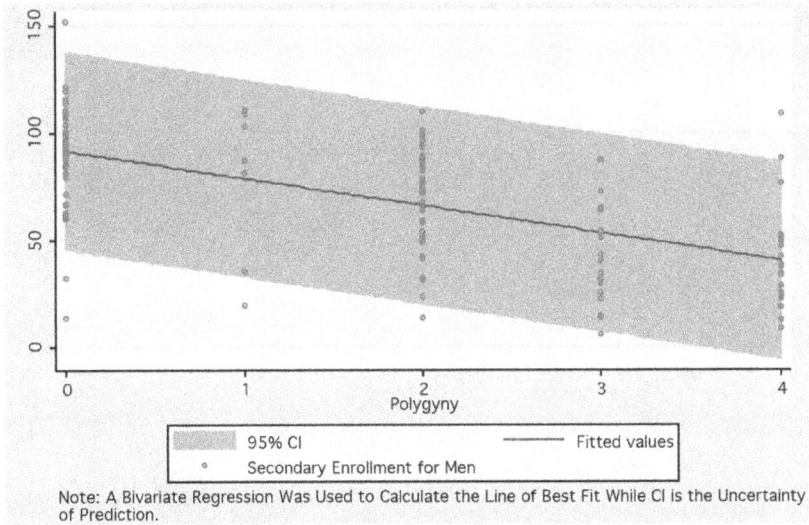

Note: A Bivariate Regression Was Used to Calculate the Line of Best Fit While CI is the Uncertainty of Prediction.

Figure 6.7. Scatterplot, line of best fit, and CIs for secondary enrollment for men by polygyny.

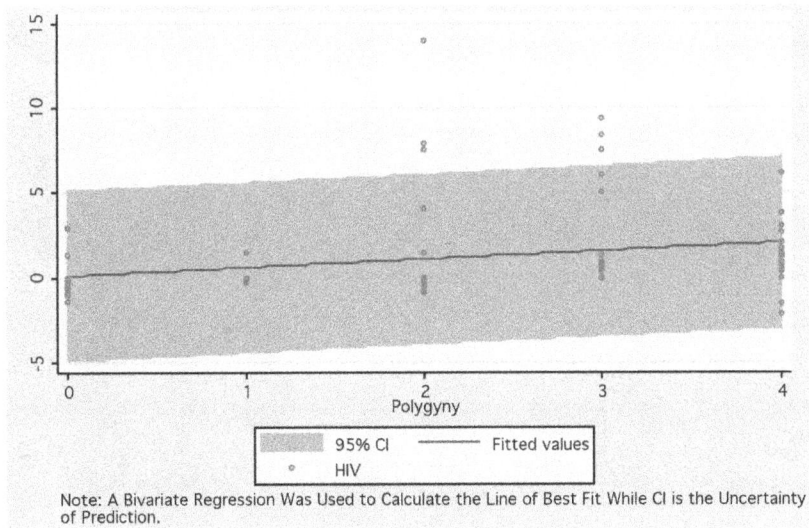

Note: A Bivariate Regression Was Used to Calculate the Line of Best Fit While CI is the Uncertainty of Prediction.

Figure 6.8. Scatterplot, line of best fit, and CIs for HIV by polygyny.

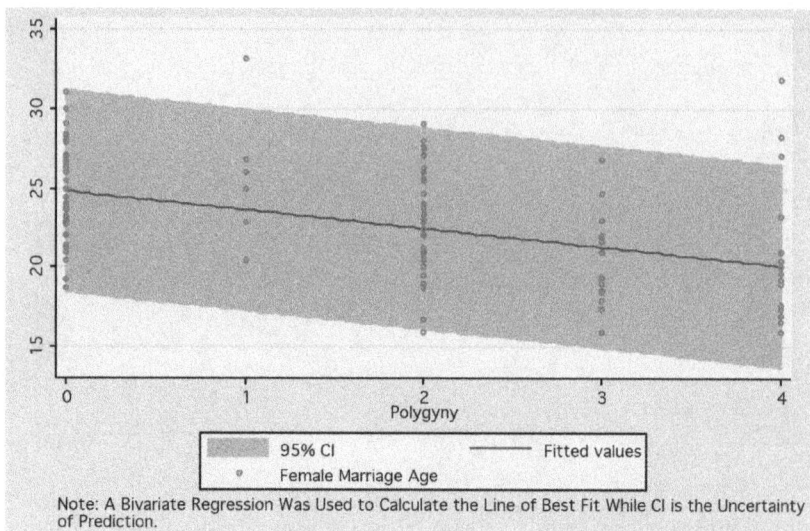

Note: A Bivariate Regression Was Used to Calculate the Line of Best Fit While CI is the Uncertainty of Prediction.

Figure 6.9. Scatterplot, line of best fit, and CIs for female marriage age by polygyny.

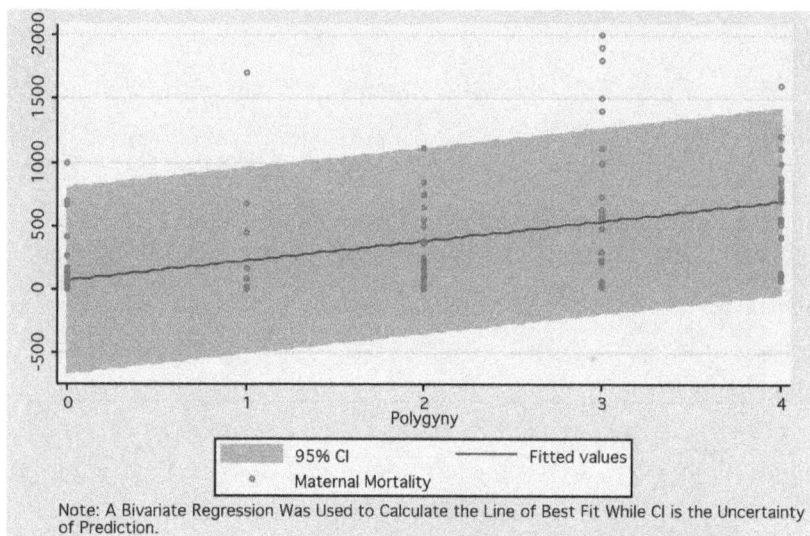

Note: A Bivariate Regression Was Used to Calculate the Line of Best Fit While CI is the Uncertainty of Prediction.

Figure 6.10. Scatterplot, line of best fit, and CIs for maternal mortality by polygyny.

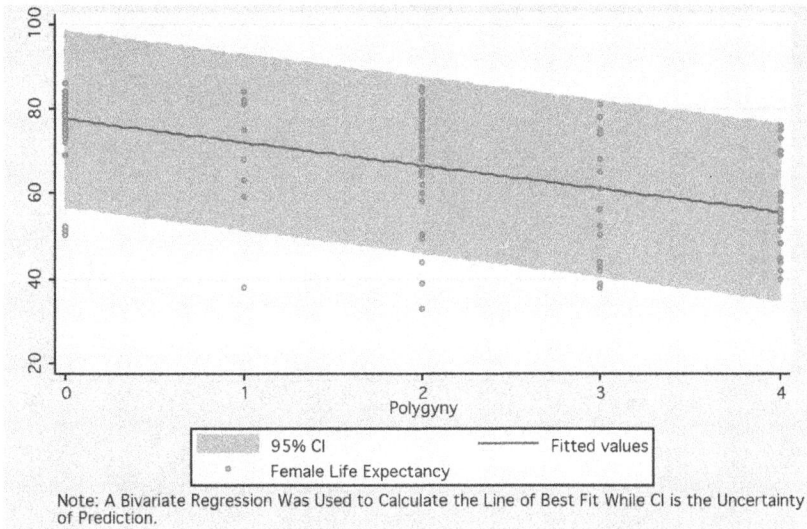

Note: A Bivariate Regression Was Used to Calculate the Line of Best Fit While CI is the Uncertainty of Prediction.

Figure 6.11. Scatterplot, line of best fit, and CIs for female life expectancy by polygyny.

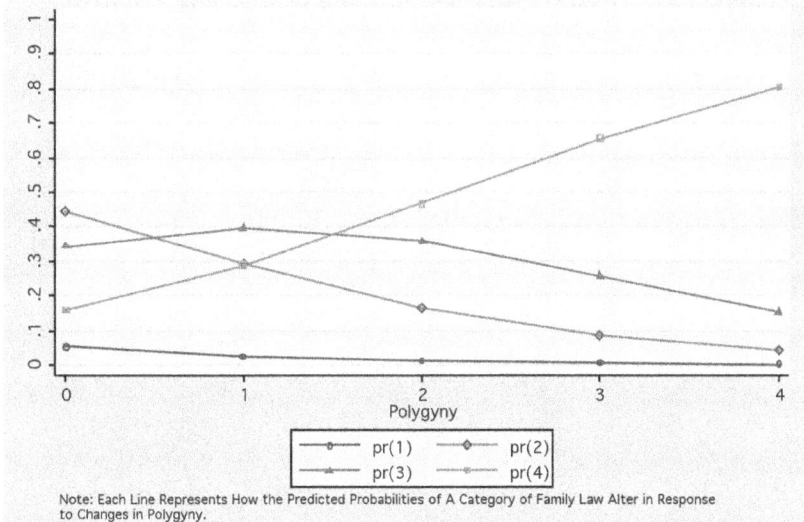

Note: Each Line Represents How the Predicted Probabilities of A Category of Family Law Alter in Response to Changes in Polygyny.

Figure 6.12. Effect of polygyny on the predicted probabilities of categories of family law.

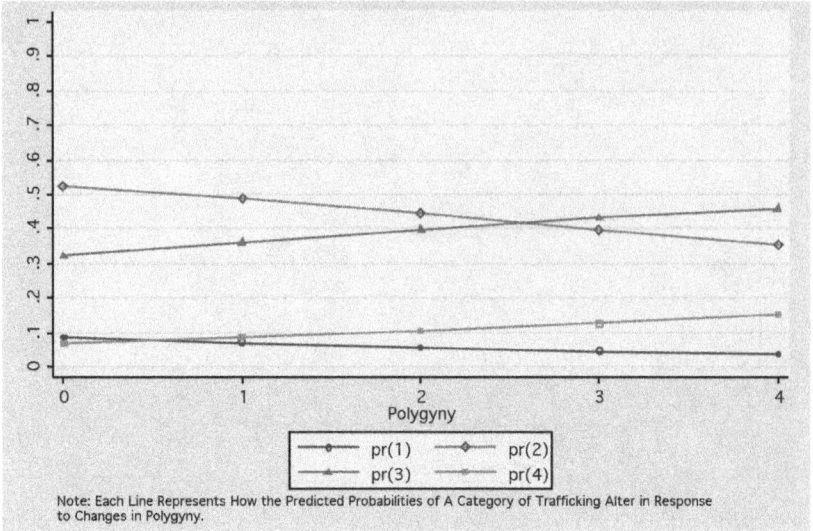

Figure 6.13. Effect of polygyny on the predicted probabilities of categories of sex trafficking.

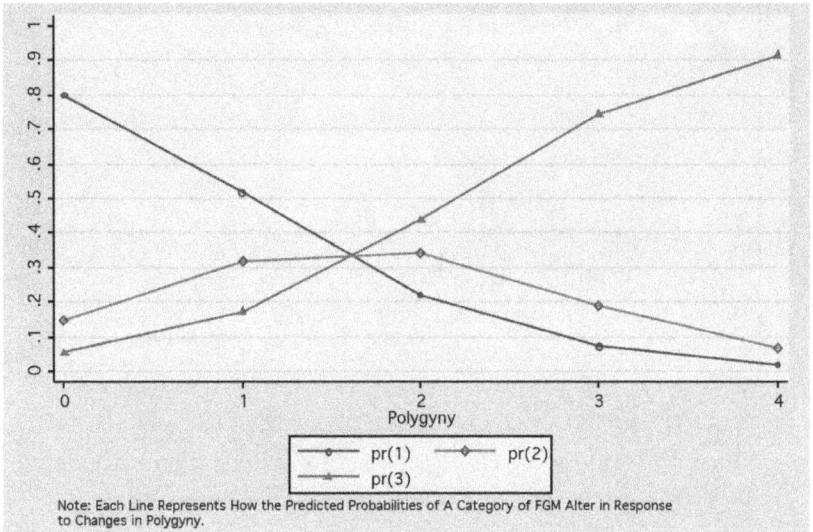

Figure 6.14. Effect of polygyny on the predicted probabilities of categories of FGM.

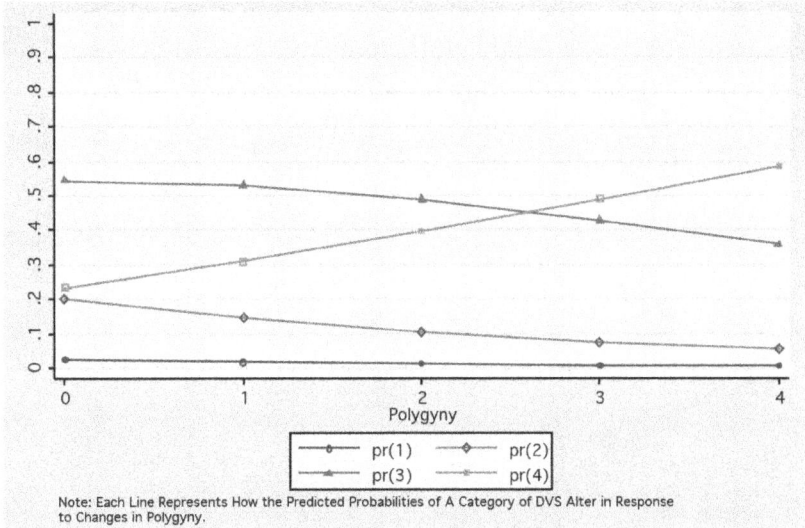

Note: Each Line Represents How the Predicted Probabilities of A Category of DVS Alter in Response to Changes in Polygyny.

Figure 6.15. Effect of polygyny on the predicted probabilities of categories of DVS.

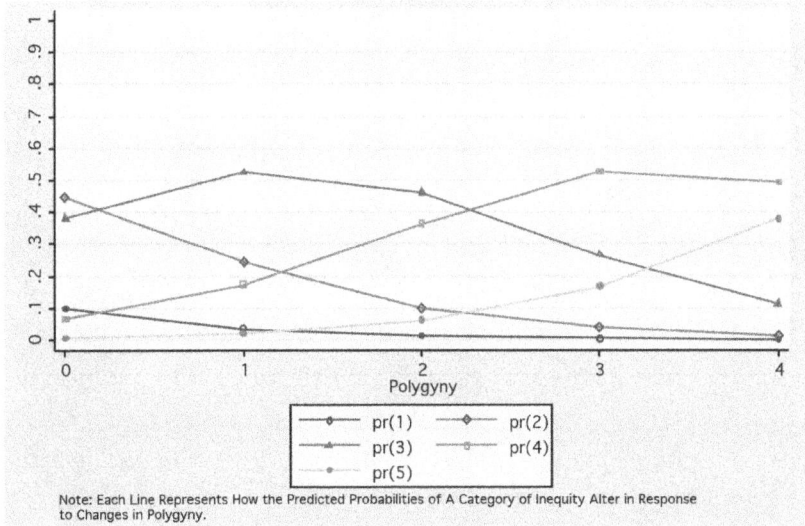

Note: Each Line Represents How the Predicted Probabilities of A Category of Inequity Alter in Response to Changes in Polygyny.

Figure 6.16. Effect of polygyny on the predicted probabilities of categories of inequity.

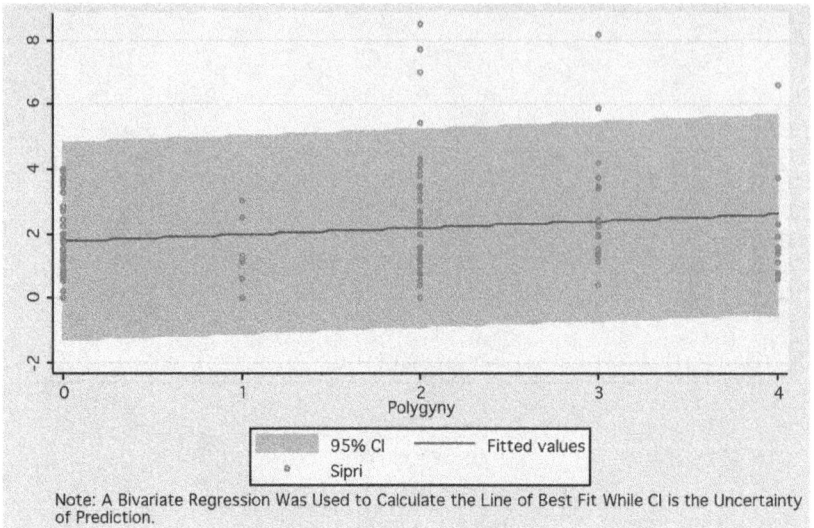

Note: A Bivariate Regression Was Used to Calculate the Line of Best Fit While CI is the Uncertainty of Prediction.

Figure 6.17. Scatterplot, line of best fit, and CIs for SIPRI by polygyny.

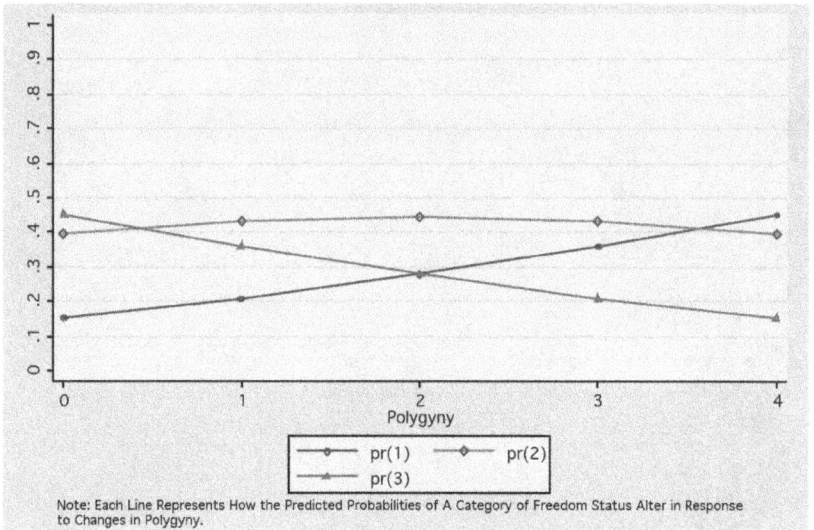

Note: Each Line Represents How the Predicted Probabilities of A Category of Freedom Status Alter in Response to Changes in Polygyny.

Figure 6.18. Effect of polygyny on the predicted probabilities of categories of freedom status.

References

Abu-Lughod, Lila. 2002. "Do Muslim Women Really Need Saving? Anthropological Reflections on Cultural Relativism and Its Others." *American Anthropologist* 104 (3): 783–90. http://dx.doi.org/10.1525/aa.2002.104.3.783.

Betzig, Laura. 1993. "Where Are the Bastards' Daddies?" *Behavioral and Brain Sciences* 16 (2): 284–85.

Bixler, Ray. H., Stuart A. Altmann, David P. Barash, Mary Waterhouse, Brian Charlesworth, Gustavo A. Eskildsen, and Peter L. Van Den Berghe. 1981. "Incest Avoidance as a Function of Environment and Heredity [and Comments and Reply]." *Current Anthropology* 22 (6): 639–54.

Cohen, Dov, and Richard Nisbett. 1997. "Field Experiments Examining the Culture of Honor: The Role of Institutions in Perpetrating Norms about Violence." *Personality and Social Psychology Bulletin* 23 (11): 1188–99. http://dx.doi.org/10.1177/01461672 972311006.

Coult, A., and R. Habenstein. 1965. *Cross Tabulations of Murdock's World Ethnographic Sample.* Columbia: University of Missouri.

Courtwright, David. 1996. *Violent Land: Single Men and Social Disorder from the Frontier to the Inner City.* Cambridge: Harvard University Press.

Daly, Martin, and Margo Wilson. 1999. "Darwinism and the Roots of Machismo." *Scientific American Presents* 10: 8–14.

Dickeman, Mildred. 1979. "Comment on van den Berghe's and Barash's Sociobiology." *American Anthropologist* 81 (2): 351a–57.

Dreze, Jean, and Reetikca Khera. 2000. "Crime, Gender and Society in India: Insights from Homicide Data." *Population and Development Review* 26 (2): 335–52. http://dx.doi.org/10.1111/j.1728-4457.2000.00335.x.

Eckstein, Harry. 1988. "A Culturalist Theory of Political Change." *American Political Science Review* 82 (3): 789–804. http://dx.doi.org/10.2307/1962491.

Fallers, Lloyd, and Margaret Fallers. 1976. "Sex Roles in Edremit." In *Mediterranean Family Structures,* edited by J. Peristiany, 243–60. Cambridge: Cambridge University Press.

Gray, J. Patrick. 1998. "*Ethnographic Atlas Codebook* Derived from George P. Murdock's *Ethnographic Atlas* Recording the Marital Composition of 1231 Societies from 1960 to 1980." *World Cultures* 10 (1): 86–136. http://eclectic.ss.uci.edu/%7Edrwhite /worldcul/Codebook4EthnoAtlas.pdf.

Gray, Peter B., Sonya M. Kahlenberg, Emily S. Barrett, Susan F. Lipson, and Peter T. Ellison. 2002. "Marriage and Fatherhood Are Associated with Lower Testosterone in Males." *Evolution and Human Behavior* 23 (3): 193–201.

Hoffman, Bruce. 2001. "All You Need Is Love: How the Terrorists Stopped Terrorism." *Atlantic Monthly,* December.

Hudson, Valerie M., and Andrea Den Boer. 2002. "A Surplus of Men, a Deficit of Peace: Security and Sex Ratios in Asia's Largest States." *International Security* 26 (4): 5–38. http://dx.doi.org/10.1162/016228802753696753.

Hurtado, A. Magdalena, and Kim R. Hill. 1992. "Paternal Effect on Offspring Survivorship among Ache and Hiwi Hunter-Gatherers: Implications for Modeling Pair-Bond Stability." In *Father-Child Relations: Cultural and Biosocial Contexts,* edited by Barry S. Hewlett, 31–55. Foundations of Human Behavior. Hawthorne, NY: Aldine de Gruyter.

Irons, William. 1979. "Cultural and Biological Success." In *Evolutionary Biology and Human Social Behavior: An Anthropological Perspective,* edited by Napoleon A. Chagnon and William Irons, 257–72. North Scituate, MA: Duxbury Press.

Kanazawa, Satoshi. 2001. "Why Father Absence Might Precipitate Early Menarche: The Role of Polygyny." *Evolution and Human Behavior* 22 (5): 329–34.

Lesthaeghe, Ron, Georgia Kaufmann, Dominique Meekers, and Johan Surkyn. 1994. "Post-Partum Abstinence, Polygyny, and Age at Marriage: A Macro-Level Analysis of Sub-Saharan Societies." In *Nuptuality in Sub-Saharan Africa,* edited by Caroline Bledsoe and Gilles Pisson, 25–56. Oxford: Clarendon.

Lewis, Bernard. 1995. *The Middle East: 2,000 Years of History from the Rise of Christianity to the Present Day.* London: Weidenfeld & Nicolson.

Mace, Ruth, and Clare Holden. 1999. "Evolutionary Ecology and Cross-Cultural Comparison: The Case of Matrilineal Descent in Sub-Saharan Africa." In *Comparative Primate Socioecology,* edited by P. C. Lee, 387–405. New York: Cambridge University Press. http://dx.doi.org/10.1017/CBO9780511542466.019.

Mazur, Allan, and Alan Booth. 1998. "Testosterone and Dominance in Men." *Behavioral and Brain Sciences* 21 (3): 353–97. http://dx.doi.org/10.1017/S0140525X98001228.

Mazur, Allan, and Jack Michalek. 1998. "Marriage, Divorce and Male Testosterone." *Social Forces* 77 (1): 315–30. http://dx.doi.org/10.1093/sf/77.1.315.

Rosen, Lawrence. 1978. "The Negotiation of Reality: Male-Female Relations in Sefrou, Morocco." In *Women in the Muslim World,* edited by Lois Beck and Nikki Keddie, 561–84. Cambridge: Harvard University Press. http://dx.doi.org/10.4159/harvard .9780674733091.c32.

Tertilt, Michele. 2005. "Polygyny, Fertility, and Savings." *Journal of Political Economy* 113 (6): 1341–1371.

Toubia, Nahid. 1994. "Female Circumcision as a Public Health Issue." *New England Journal of Medicine* 331 (11): 712–16. http://dx.doi.org/10.1056/NEJM1994091 53311106.

Weisfeld, Glenn E. 1993. "Social Status and Values in Traditional Arab Culture." In *Social Stratification and Socioeconomic Inequality, Volume I: A Comparative Biosocial Analysis,* edited by Lee Ellis, 75–97. Westport, CT: Praeger.

SECTION II

Regulating Polygamy

7

TESTING THE LIMITS OF RELIGIOUS FREEDOM
The Case of Polygamy's Criminalization in Canada

Melanie Heath

Polygyny was not prohibited because it was a religious belief, or, to turn the coin, because Parliament wanted to impose a Christian religious belief in monogamous marriage. I find that the original prohibition was prompted by largely secular concerns with perceived harms associated with the practice to women, children and society.
Reference re: Section 293 of the Criminal Code of Canada[1]

INTRODUCTION

What are the limits of sexual and familial intimacy in the context of religious belief and its practice? This question was at the heart of the Polygamy Reference trial, the British Columbia Supreme Court constitutional reference concerning the validity of Canada's antipolygamy law (Reference re: Section 293). The central questions focused on whether a family that consists of multiple, conjugal partners is so inherently harmful to individuals and society that it must be criminalized. Does the harm it causes override the right to religious freedom, to liberty, and to freedom of association? Chief Justice Robert Bauman's words above reflect his reasoning that it is constitutional to criminalize polygyny[2] in Canada. The 2012 ruling found that section 293 of the Criminal Code of Canada violates the religious freedom of fundamentalist Mormons, and specifically members of the Fundamentalist Church of Jesus Christ of Latter-Day Saints.[3] However, the justice determined that the harm polygyny brings to women, to children, to society, and to the institution of monogamous marriage outweighs the basic right to religious freedom. Thus, he decided that the current law is justified in criminalizing the practice for anyone eighteen years of age or older, even while recognizing that it impinges on individual religious belief.

The Polygamy Reference put forward the question of how to balance competing rights—predominantly the right to freedom of religion with

DOI: 10.7330/9780874219975.c007

the equality rights of women, both guaranteed by the Canadian Charter of Rights and Freedoms, the bill of rights that forms the first part of the Constitution Act, 1982. Governments and policymakers seek to identify the complexities of competing human-rights claims and to elucidate the best way to balance these to ensure equality of treatment (Hall 2010). The shifting currents of rights clashes, or competing human-rights claims, are intensified in an increasingly globalized and multicultural context. Beverley McLachlin, the chief justice of the Canadian Supreme Court, outlines how competing rights involve the collision of coexisting diverse religious and ethnic practices: "Whether we like it or not, religious, ethnic and cultural diversity is part of our modern world—and increasingly, part of our national and community reality. Human rights and the respect for every individual upon which they rest, offer the best hope for reconciling the conflicts this diversity is bound to generate" (qtd. in Hall 2010, 4).

Concerns over rights and belonging are central to the framework of multiculturalism, and courts must arbitrate how to balance cultural and religious practices that do not reflect a majority perspective in modern societies. Balancing competing rights is particularly challenging in the case of new religious movements (NRMs), often more pejoratively termed *cults* or *sects*. Such minority religions, whether new or old, push the boundaries of social control by promoting beliefs and practices at the margins of acceptable behavior in society (Richardson 2006a). Fundamentalist Mormons who practice polygyny in a remote area of British Columbia offer one such example. *Plural marriage*—the Mormon term for one man having more than one living wife at the same time—is better understood to constitute a practice of "religion as deviance," where a central tenet of religious belief requires participating in an outlawed family form (Hoffmann and Bahr 2006). The cultural and religious practice of polygyny among Muslims and others who live or migrate to Canada has also raised concern. In criminalizing minority religious and/or cultural practices like polygyny, the domain of law provides the state the power to enforce strong moral claims. These conditions put "the constitutional protection of religious conscience and the substantive criminal law . . . on a conceptual collision course" (Berger 2008, 515).

This chapter analyzes the BC Supreme Court decision that determined the criminalization of polygyny to be constitutional in Canada. It considers the consequences of a competing-rights approach to regulating religious and cultural practice. In the following, I examine how the decision, with its insistence on the universal harm of polygyny, actually obscures consideration of important concerns over religious freedom and the right to familial and sexual intimacy. The decision thereby lacks substantive engagement with the rights at stake. First, I outline the sociological and legal literature on competing rights, paying particular attention to the role of religion and law in this balancing act. Next, after explaining the particular context for the criminalization of polygyny in Canada, I offer a content analysis of the decision to argue that its treatment of harm hinders a more robust examination of the importance of religious freedom, gender equality, and family and sexual intimacy in the criminalization of polygamy.

ANTAGONISMS BETWEEN RELIGION AND LAW

The interaction of religion and law raises significant points of contention in modern societies. While legal institutions and the law are important forces in the protection of the free expression of religious belief and practice, these same institutions play a key role in regulating religions and religious groups (Richardson 2009). When law acts as an independent variable with regard to religion, the relationship veers toward social control to regulate religion's boundaries. Majority religions tend to have the power to resist the influence of the state; the law gets involved only in the most conspicuous cases, such as the child sexual abuse scandals within the Catholic church. The case of minority religions, however, is often influenced by their lack of status and a general lack of familiarity that disadvantages newer and smaller religious groups in legal proceedings (Richardson 2006a). The popular imagination, and at times sociological theory (e.g., Hunter 1981), has treated NRMs as involving an antimodern impulse in which individuals seek to bring social order to the increasingly anomic conditions of modern life by turning to archaic rules and practices. An embrace of beliefs and ways of living outside the mainstream perpetuate the outsider status of many minority religions (1998).

While minority religious groups tend to have lower status and may be less tolerated in society, religious freedom—a value pervasive in the modern world—is by definition connected to religious pluralism. As James Richardson (2006b) queries, "If all agreed on religious matters, who would raise the question of rights of religious minorities, and why would it even be raised" (274)? Richardson theorizes that the degree and type of pluralism in a given society influence how openly and freely religious minorities are able to practice their religion. Even in societies where a strong state and an autonomous legal structure promote

religious tolerance, legal systems tend to advance normative understandings of religious and social practice. It is the normative function of the
law that positions religious minorities as the losers in legal contests in
which religious freedom is at stake. Legal sanctions against unpopu-
lar minority religions are often punitive and provide little opportunity
for resolution. For example, government raids on minority faiths have
increased in the past twenty years, often impacting the religious rights of
targeted religious communities (Palmer 1999, 2011; Wright 1995, 2003;
Wright and Richardson 2011).

One approach to studying minority religions has been to examine religion as deviance (Hoffmann and Bahr 2006). Historical and
contemporary manifestations indicate two forms of deviant religious
groups. The more common *sect* is a religious group within a mainstream religious tradition that imposes stricter beliefs and behavioral
requirements. Public attitudes often view sects to be deviant due to their
extreme religiosity. The second type of deviant religious group is the
cult that stands outside mainstream religious traditions. The deviancy
of the cult relates not to strict principles (though these may be relevant) but to its difference from mainstream society (Dawson 1998; Stark
and Bainbridge 1997). One prominent example of behavior labeled as
deviant is the practice of polygyny among Mormons in the nineteenth
century and among fundamentalist Mormons in contemporary North
American society. Sociologists of religion have problematized the term
cult for its negative connotations among the general population and
have advocated abandoning its use in academic circles (Barker 1986,
1989; Olson 2006; Richardson 1993). These scholars argue that the term
provokes adverse, stereotypical images. James Lewis (2003) remarks,
"Minority religions lose their chance at a fair hearing as soon as the label
'cult' is successfully applied to them" (206). Groups in the Anti-Cult
Movement solidified stereotypes in the 1980s and early 1990s through
labeling cult members as victims of brainwashing, totalism, and mind
control (Robbins 2000).

In North America, religion cannot shield one from being charged
for overt criminal acts. Still, the violation of a law assumes special meaning and requires more scrutiny when individuals claim that they act
out of religious motivation. In most cases, special attention is given to
such claims to ensure that individual religious rights are not violated.
Growing religious pluralism in modern societies often leaves the secular state, with its purported neutrality to religion, as the main arbitrator
of competing rights claims, such as clashes between freedom of speech
and religion (An-Na'im 2013). Balancing competing rights claims is also

a challenge for international law, where customary law and international civil and political rights often collide (Perry 2011). The expansive and coercive powers of the state (and international governing powers) to decide whose rights count can lead to the oppression of ethnic, racial, and religious minorities. In response to potential abuse of power by the state, constitutionalists argue that government can/should be limited in its powers and that these limitations define its authority. Yet scholars have pointed to the ways that the ideal of a neutral state or one able to protect the rights of minorities is often unrealized in a judiciary process that adjudicates issues outside the normative dimensions of substantive criminal law (Berger 2008). More generally, there is concern over inadequacies in the ability of judges to protect the rights of women, minority racial and religious groups, sexual minorities, the poor, and others whose interests stand outside mainstream ideologies. Feminists further critique the vestiges of male legal interventions in constitutions that structurally restrict women's full citizenship (MacKinnon 1989).

The recent Polygamy Reference offers an excellent example of the tension between the regulatory aspects of criminal law over family forms, considerations of gender equality, and the freedom connected to the constitutional protection of religion. Polygyny's criminal status facilitates the question of whether it is justifiable to criminalize practices motivated by religious belief. This question becomes particularly fraught by concerns over the apparent harms that polygyny inflicts on women and children. What are the strategies of courts for balancing the competing rights between freedom of religion and women's equality? How do these reflect mainstream ideologies? The polygyny case offers an example that shines light on the interactions between substantive criminal law and the constitutional protection of religion and women's rights.

A CRIME IN THE NAME OF RELIGION

In 2009, the provincial government of British Columbia laid charges against two leaders of Bountiful, a community of about 1,000 people founded in the 1940s by families that broke away from the mainstream Mormon church after it renounced the practice of polygyny. After the charges were dropped for procedural reasons, British Columbia launched a reference case to ask for the courts' direction on the constitutionality of criminalizing polygyny. A reference case allows the government to seek an advisory opinion from the Supreme Court on a constitutional question. In British Columbia, legislation allows the province to initiate a reference case at the trial level to allow the introduction of evidence and witnesses for a more evidentiary-based decision. The Polygamy Reference was unprecedented in the history of Canadian law, putting polygyny on trial and running for over four months. The attorney general of British Columbia referred the following constitutional questions to the BC Supreme Court:

> a) Is section 293 of the Criminal Code of Canada consistent with the Canadian Charter of Rights and Freedoms? If not, in what particular or particulars and to what extent?
>
> b) What are the necessary elements of the offence in section 293 of the Criminal Code of Canada? Without limiting this question, does section 293 require that the polygyny or conjugal union in question involved a minor, or occurred in a context of dependence, exploitation, abuse of authority, a gross imbalance of power, or undue influence? (Reference re: Section 293, at para. 16)

The governments of Canada and British Columbia defended the law's constitutionality and a court-appointed *amicus curiae* challenged it. How did polygyny become an issue leading to an extensive trial-level reference? To answer this question, one must go back to the late nineteenth century.

Polygyny was originally practiced in Western Canada among aboriginal peoples and between White male settlers and aboriginal women (Carter 2008). In two early cases of White settlers who entered successive conjugal relationships with women, descendants fought for succession to large estates. Rather than treat the relationships as wrongfully initiated by the White men, the courts treated the issue of polygyny "as an aboriginal custom that might invalidate the original customary marriages" (Baines 2012, 454). The two cases regarded polygyny as a sideline, and there were no charges under the polygyny criminal law. A third case, however, ended in a conviction for committing the crime of polygyny under its prohibition enacted in 1890 and reenacted in 1892.[4] This case involved Bear's Shin Bone, a member of the Blood nation on the Kaini reserve who had married two women of the Blood nation in accordance with their customs. Sarah Carter (2008) explains that the government singled out this Blood Indian for prosecution due to the immigration of American Mormons who were escaping persecution under antipolygyny laws in Utah. Specifically, authorities did not want Mormon immigrants to think that polygyny was allowed in Canada. Legal scholar Beverly Baines (2012) speculates, "It is more than curious, however, that after criminalizing polygyny in a provision that included explicit reference to prohibiting 'what among the persons commonly called Mormons is known as spiritual or plural union,' Canada launched the test case not against the Mormons in Cardston but rather against Bear's Shin Bone" (456).

Ultimately, the decision to prosecute Bear's Shin Bone discriminated on racial *and* religious grounds.

Eventually the aboriginal populations abandoned the practice of polygyny, and so did the first group of Mormon immigrants. In 1946, however, Harold Blackmore, whose embrace of polygyny was shunned by other local Albertan Mormons, moved his family to Lister, British Columbia, to establish the polygamist community that was renamed Bountiful in 1984. For two decades, the nephew of Harold Blackmore, Winston Blackmore, acted as bishop of the Bountiful group of the Fundamentalist Church of Jesus Christ of Latter-Day Saints (FLDS church), connected to the FLDS in the United States. After Warren Jeffs, the church's prophet, excommunicated Winston Blackmore, the Mormon fundamentalists in Bountiful divided into two groups: about half are members of the FLDS church under the current bishop, James Oler. The other half follows Winston Blackmore.

For nearly fifty years, residents of Bountiful practiced polygyny in seclusion as a central tenet of their faith. Public attention only turned to Bountiful in the 1990s when allegations of polygyny prompted Royal Canadian Mounted Police investigations. No charges were laid, however, due to concerns regarding the constitutionality of the criminal provision. In 2004, Bountiful once again came under scrutiny after allegations of sexual exploitation, child abuse, and forced marriages emerged (Bramham 2008). Investigations culminated in the 2009 arrests of Blackmore and Oler and the subsequent Polygamy Reference in British Columbia in 2010. Eleven groups intervened to provide their opinions for or against criminalization at the trial, including Beyond Borders, the British Columbia Civil Liberties Association, the British Columbia Teachers' Federation, the Canadian Association for Free Expression, the Canadian Coalition for the Rights of Children, the Canadian Polyamory Advocacy Association, the Christian Legal Fellowship, James Marion Oler and the Fundamentalist Church of Jesus Christ of Latter-Day Saints, REAL Women of Canada, Stop Polygyny in Canada, and the West Coast Women's Legal Education and Action Fund. Winston Blackmore did not participate in the case after being denied special status and funding, stating that he could not afford to participate. There were no groups in the list of interveners to represent women living in polygynous relationships, although the trial did include some of these women as witnesses. Likewise, no intervener group was involved to present the interests of some Muslims who believe that the Qur'an permits a man to have up to four wives under certain conditions.

The methods for analyzing the Polygamy Reference involved coding the 265-page opinion issued by Chief Justice Bauman on November 23, 2011. The coding of this opinion is one step in a much larger comparative project of studying familial and sexual intimacy and competing rights claims in the regulation of polygamy. This chapter focuses specifically on the opinion of Chief Justice Bauman to analyze the construction of knowledge concerning competing rights in determining the criminal law's constitutionality. The coding involved the constant comparative method for systematic qualitative content analysis (Lincoln and Guba 1985). All data were coded using a qualitative software program, NVivo 10. Thematic codes were not predetermined but emerged from the data. The following sections examine the ways the treatment of harm in the decision constructs a "vulnerable monogamy" that must be protected as the best means to promote gender equality and the interests of society.

INHERENTLY HARMFUL: THERE IS NO "GOOD" POLYGAMY

In the Polygamy Reference, Chief Justice Bauman thoughtfully acknowledges that the law criminalizes a religiously motivated choice to establish polygynous unions, thereby violating section 2(a) of the charter, which protects the fundamental freedom of conscience and religion. He thus recognizes the case to be one of "competing fundamental rights" (Reference re: Section 293, at para. 1097). At the same time, Justice Bauman argues that the case is at heart about harm: "I have concluded that this case is essentially about harm; more specifically, Parliament's reasoned apprehension of harm arising out of the practice of polygyny. This includes harm to women, to children, to society and to the institution of monogamous marriage" (Reference re: Section 293, at para. 5).

The general content analysis finds that the longest section in the decision deals with the "alleged harms of polygyny." Table 7.1 offers a breakdown of the 717 paragraphs in the evidentiary portion of the opinion. Of the 717, Chief Justice Bauman devotes 13 to the changing family demographics in Canada, 57 to Canada's international obligations, 87 to the historical context, 102 to global polygyny, and 130 to polygyny in Canada. The section on the alleged harms of polygyny is 311 paragraphs, or 44 percent, of the total evidentiary document. A similar pattern holds true for the themes in the opinion. Table 7.1 presents the

Table 7.1 Paragraphs and Themes: Polygamy Reference

Paragraph Topics	Frequency	Percentage/717 Total
Terminology	11	2
Changing Family Demographics	13	2
Canada's International Obligations	57	8
Historical Context	87	12
Global Polygyny	102	14
Polygyny in Canada	130	18
Harms of Polygyny	311	44
Themes: Rights and Harm*	Frequency	Percentage/665 Total
In/equality	64	10
Gender equality	15	2
Religion	216	32
Religious freedom	30	5
Harm	340	51

*There was a total of 35 themes and subthemes.

frequency of themes that were coded for in/equality, gender equality, religion, religious freedom, and harm. By far, harm appears most frequently, at 51 percent. The theme of religion is the next frequent at 32 percent, but a very small portion—5 percent—deals with the issue of religious freedom. Likewise, only 10 percent of the themes deal with in/equality and a mere 2 percent with gender equality. (Please see table 7.1. Paragraphs and themes: Polygamy Reference).

To be sure, this breakdown does not capture the way the important issues were treated in the decision. Specifically, there are good reasons for Bauman's in-depth treatment of harm. An analysis of this topic was not only required by the terms of the reference but also by charter jurisprudence. After the majority opinion in *R. v. Butler* dealing with pornography, the Canadian Supreme Court and the Courts of Appeal have more readily embraced a form of charter analysis linked to preventing harm through legislation as a way to justify infringements of charter rights (Levine 2004). The Supreme Court held that moral corruption and harm to society are inextricably linked. This move contrasts with earlier jurisprudence that more readily accepted moral values as a separate element to assess reasons for infringement. Thus, Bauman notes, "to justify criminalizing an activity, the government must demonstrate a reasoned apprehension of harm. . . . Once it has been established that there is a reasoned apprehension of harm with respect to certain conduct, measures aimed at preventing that harm will almost always be rationally connected to the legislative objective (Reference re: Section 293, at paras. 772, 775). It was also necessary to weigh harm and competing rights in section 1 of the charter, known as the reasonable limits clause or limitations clause in legally permitting the government to limit an individual's charter rights.[5]

The evidence presented in the case also justifies an in-depth engagement with the harms of polygyny to women and children. Substantial testimony was presented throughout the trial as to the kinds of harms women and children, and even polygynous young men, experience. The goal of regulating the negative aspects of polygyny was a point on which all sides agreed. For example, evidence was presented of underage girls (below the age of sixteen years) being forced to marry much older men in both Canada and the United States, and young girls were transported from one country to the other to marry. Young men were also forced out of the tight-knit polygynous communities, ostensibly to reduce the competition for younger brides among older men.

Individuals who had fled polygyny testified in court about the substantial harms they experienced due to living in polygynous families. A few witnesses traveled from the United States to give testimony, and others also gave moving testimony in videos aired during the trial. Rowena Mackert grew up in a polygynous family in the United States. She recounted how her parents woke her up in the middle of the night to inform her that the prophet had a revelation and she was getting married the next day. Chief Justice Bauman quotes her words:

> I was 17. My father—my mother asked don't you want to know who you're supposed to marry, or who you're marrying, and I kind of looked in disbelief, you know, I really didn't want to know. Told me John, and John who, and I'm running down the list of all the Johns that I know and my father said Swaney and it was like a knife was stabbed through my heart. There was no love lost between the two of us. I was really headstrong and he was too. (Reference re: Section 293, at para. 667)

Her experience speaks to the issue of a lack of choice, in this case being forced to marry a boy of similar age. Former wives and children of polygamous families testified about the hardships they experienced within polygamy, including physical and verbal abuse.

However, the idea of universal harm to women and children was not uncontested. A number of witnesses shared their positive experiences of growing up and choosing to live in polygynous families. Chief Justice Bauman quoted several witnesses who countered the stereotype that polygynous women are disempowered. Jennifer Zitting, who was raised in a monogamous family and married a man in a polygamist community, told the court:

> While living in a polygamist community, I met women who had the freedom to pursue high powered careers. Many women in the community held Masters Degrees in teaching and special education. Quite a few women had nursing degrees, the nurse practitioner who ran the clinic was a woman, and there was even a female lawyer. Even the women who stayed home accomplished feats that would amaze the average woman. I know one who raised 24 children, and did it well. I have noticed that these women have freedom that monogamous wives don't have because they are not 100% responsible for the care and feeding of their husbands. (Reference re: Section 293, at para. 691)

If there are, in fact, women and children who are not harmed or who may choose to live in polygynous families, and if these families are polygynous as a fundamental aspect of their religious faith, the rationale of criminalizing polygyny would violate these individual charter rights. Chief Justice Bauman readily admits this.

In his treatment of religious freedom, Justice Bauman recognizes a fundamental breach of religious liberty for fundamentalist Mormons, some Muslims, and Wiccans who sincerely hold plural marriage as a religious belief. It is interesting that he comes to this conclusion without much discussion of the meaning of religious freedom. He cites Chief Justice Dickson (and four colleagues) on freedom of religion in the decision of the Lord's Day Act:

> The essence of the concept of freedom of religion is the right to entertain such religious beliefs as a person chooses, the right to declare religious beliefs openly and without fear of hindrance or reprisal, and the right to manifest religious belief by worship and practice or by teaching and dissemination. But the concept means more than that.
> . . . Freedom in a broad sense embraces both the absence of coercion and constraint, and the right to manifest beliefs and practices. Freedom means that, subject to such limitations as are necessary to protect public safety, order, health, or morals or the fundamental rights and freedoms of others, no one is to be forced to act in a way contrary to his beliefs or his conscience. (Reference re: Section 293, at para. 1086)

In his reasons for why the criminal ban on polygamy offends religious freedom, Justice Bauman turned to the testimonies of individuals from religious faiths to underline the importance of sincerely held belief and the connection of polygamy to religious texts.

Thus, his decision maps out an important space for religious freedom concerning sincerely held religious belief. However, when he turns

to the section 1 analysis, which requires an assessment of whether limiting religious freedom is prescribed by law and justified in a free and
democratic society, Justice Bauman justifies limiting religious freedom
by accepting the claim that polygamy is inherently harmful. He argues:

> When one accepts that there is a reasoned apprehension that polygamy
> is inevitably associated with sundry harms, and that these harms are not
> simply isolated to criminal adherents like Warren Jeffs but *inhere in the
> institution itself,* the Amicus' complaint that there are less sweeping means
> of achieving the government's objective falls away. And it most certainly
> does when one considers the positive objective of the measure, the protec-
> tion and preservation of monogamous marriage. For that, there can be
> no alternative to the outright prohibition of that which is fundamentally
> anathema to the institution. In the context of this objective, there is no
> such thing as so-called "good polygamy." (Reference re: Section 293, at
> para. 1343; my emphasis)

An in-depth analysis of the content of the decision reveals that Justice
Bauman concentrates on evidence to juxtapose polygamy (and particularly polygyny) against monogamy to assert polygamy's inherently harmful nature.

The decision quotes from the voices of women and men in polygamous relationships, highlighting why some choose polygyny; however, it
never considers polygyny as a form of familial and sexual intimacy. The
freedom to practice it is understood only in terms of religious belief,
a belief that is not seen as rational in the face of the substantial harms
Justice Bauman views as intrinsic to polygyny. On the other hand, Justice
Bauman does address the "postmodern" concept of polyamory, or consensual relationships with more than one partner, as offering a new lens
on the idea of polygamy:

> Imaged as a form of commitment which is flexible and responsive to the
> needs and interests of the individuals involved, . . . This new polygamy
> reflects postmodern critiques of patriarchy, gender, heterosexuality and
> genetic parenthood. Such a "postmodern polygamy" might occasion-
> ally look like traditional patriarchal polygamy, but it differs in important
> ways. For example, it could as easily encompass one woman with several
> male partners as it could one man with multiple female partners. It also
> includes the expanded possibilities created by same-sex or bi-sexual
> relationships, neither of which is contemplated by traditional polygamy."
> (Reference re: Section 293, at para. 430)

The decision concludes that section 293 doesn't apply to multiparty,
unmarried relationships or common law cohabitation unless these couples enter "into a 'marriage' with more than one person at the same
time, whether sanctioned by civil, religious or other means, and whether

or not it is by law recognized as a binding form of marriage" (Reference re: Section 293, at para. 1036). However, regarding the religious forms of polygyny, it does not matter that there may be variation in the ways it is practiced (i.e., some women and men may benefit from it). For Justice Bauman, polygyny is a direct threat to monogamous marriage and therefore a threat to the social order. The next section considers the evidence presented that leads to this conclusion.

POLYGYNY, VULNERABLE MONOGAMY, AND THE NATION

Chief Justice Bauman argues that the prohibition of polygyny is essential to sustaining a democratic society. Early in the opinion, he specifies the specific harms that polygyny inflicts on society:

> Polygyny has negative impacts on society flowing from the high fertility rates, large family size and poverty associated with the practice. It generates a class of largely poor, unmarried men who are statistically predisposed to violence and other anti-social behaviour. Polygyny also institutionalizes gender inequality. . . .
>
>   Polygyny's harm to society includes the critical fact that a great many of its individual harms are not specific to any particular religious, cultural or regional context. They can be generalized and expected to occur wherever polygyny exists." (Reference re: Section 293, at paras. 13–14)

To make this statement about the generalizability of the harms of polygyny, Chief Justice Bauman draws on evidence from a commissioned statistical study conducted by Rose McDermott, a professor of political science at Brown University. The study compares countries to demonstrate the generalized negative outcomes of polygyny across a number of indicators, including such diverse factors as sex trafficking, maternal mortality, female genital mutilation, political and civil rights, and even defense expenditures. Controlling for gross domestic product as a possible causal factor, McDermott's analysis found multiple negative outcomes for an increase in the incidence of polygyny: "As polygyny becomes more frequent, female genital mutilation increases; Women sustain greater domestic violence in polygynous societies; Differential legal treatment of women relative to men increases, to the detriment of women, in more polygynous societies" (Reference re: Section 293, at para. 621).

In outlining these negative impacts, Chief Justice Bauman turns to the testimony and research of Joseph Henrich, an associate professor in the psychology and economics departments at the University of British Columbia. Henrich argues that men and women are better able to follow their evolved mating strategies by pursuing polygyny. Males form multiple simultaneous pair bonds, while females have access to high-status males. For Henrich, "Culturally-transmitted social norms that motivate and regulate social behaviour" are the only way to control these basic instincts (Reference re: Section 293, at para. 502). Especially important is the norm of monogamous marriage, which establishes rules about the numbers of and arrangements between partners. Justice Bauman expresses the view that "these marriage norms do not entirely replace or subvert mating psychology, but they can strongly influence behavioural patterns, both because compliance with these norms is intrinsically rewarding and because third parties are willing to punish norm violators" (Reference re: Section 293, at para. 502). With this focus on norms, Chief Justice Bauman does not shy away from embracing justifications for moral coercion in criminalizing polygyny (Berger 2008).

In fact, Chief Justice Bauman spends a substantial amount of space outlining the emergence of what one expert witness calls "socially imposed universal monogamy" (SIUM). He argues against the amicus's contention that the original purpose of the polygyny law was connected to Parliament's desire to impose a Christian religious belief on monogamous marriage. If this were the case, it would be harder to defend the law against a charge of religious animus. He relies on the expert testimony of John Witte, a professor and director of the Center for the Study of Law and Religion at Emory University, to detail how monogamy first appeared in ancient Greece and Rome. Witte is a well-known scholar in the United States who has defended the importance of promoting heterosexual marriage as key to a successful society. He was a signatory on the self-identified marriage movement's statement in 2000 that called for a broad movement to renew a marriage culture and detailed the need to promote marriage and impose restrictions on divorce (see Heath 2012). Witte argues:

> Prohibitions against polygyny are pre-Christian and post-Christian in their formulation in the West. Pre-Christian in that we have these formulations already in Greek philosophical texts and especially in pre-Christian Roman law, and post-Christian in that the architects of modern liberalism and the very formulation of what goes into a just liberal society are making clear that if we want to respect rights, if we want to respect dignity, if we want to respect the needs of all individuals in society and their inalienable and alienable rights, it is critical to maintain an institution of monogamy and prohibit and criminalize the institution of polygyny. (Reference re: Section 293, at para. 271)

Chief Justice Bauman agrees with the idea that SIUM is integral to "the development of ideas of normative egalitarianism" (Reference re: Section 293, at para. 154).

The historical characterization of SIUM offered in the trial fails to take into account feminist critiques of marriage as a primary vehicle for oppressing women (Millett 1969). There was no discussion of feminist critiques of monogamous, heterosexual marriage in the case. Expert testimony did bring evidence of harms that inhere in monogamous marriage, but in his decision, Chief Justice Bauman dismisses this evidence as outside the purpose of the trial, which must assess the criminalization of polygyny and not the question of oppression within monogamous marriage. Perhaps he would have also dismissed evidence in feminist critiques of marriage as outside the scope of the case. However, feminist historical accounts offer a different perspective on marriage in contrast to the focus on the benefits of monogamy. Justice Bauman states, "I speculate that the spread of monogamous marriage, which represents a kind of sexual egalitarianism, may have created the conditions for the emergence of democracy and political equality, including women's equality" (Reference re: Section 293, at para. 167). In contrast, feminist critiques of marriage ranging from liberal (e.g., Bergoffen 1999) to radical (e.g., Ettelbrick 1989) emphasize the patriarchal structure of marriage as problematic for women and its history of oppression that gave married women few independent legal and social rights. *Patriarchy* is a word that appears quite often in the decision but only in connection to polygamy.

The link between polygamy and patriarchy makes it possible to justify Parliament's suppression of it as an "evil" in order to safeguard "a threatened interest—the institution of monogamous marriage" (Reference re: Section 293, at para. 888). Justice Bauman states, "Polygamy leads to the patriarchal principle, and . . . when applied to large communities, fetters the people in stationary despotism, while that principle cannot long exist in connection with monogamy" (Reference re: Section 293, at para. 892). In contrast to monogamous marriage, which discharges "essential goods for the human species and essential goods for human society," polygamy has consistently been linked to "harm against women, against children, against men and against society" (Reference re: Section 293, at para. 229). Chief Justice Bauman links the despotic practice of polygamy to Islam. He notes that it is still legal and practiced in sub-Saharan Africa, the Middle East, and certain regions in Asia where "Islam provides a religious grounding" (Reference re: Section 293, at para. 235). He devotes a very brief discussion to the practice of polygyny in Islam (fourteen paragraphs), detailing competing views on the Islamic legal basis in the Qur'an for permitting polygyny. The decision acknowledges that there was much less testimony concerning the issue of Muslim polygyny. Yet the basis for his judgment relies on generalizable data largely drawn from the practice in Muslim or other African countries where polygyny is part of a cultural tradition.

Thus, the decision focuses attention on the normative practices of monogamy in Western societies and views polygyny as nonnormative without addressing the ways it might be normative in other cultures. Similar to the narrow interpretation of monogamy, the lack of attention to understanding polygyny as normative in some cultures allows Justice Bauman to focus predominantly on harm. Yet the picture is more complex when cultural context is taken into account. According to Mariam Koktvedgaard Zeitzen (2008), polygamy "has always been a statement of beliefs, in that practitioners were following cultural or religious norms that most people in their societies strived towards, but few were able to achieve" (182). Neither is polygamy monolithic: "Like all social institutions, it can be manipulated to fit the needs and purposes of its various practitioners" (182). In the global North, anxiety over its nonnormative aspects has fuelled the creation of laws and legislation to guard against "Oriental" religion, plural marriage, and a despotic type of governance (Carter 2008; Cott 2000; Ertman 2010; Talbot 2006).

Chief Justice Bauman acknowledges that many of the harms he outlines as serious social dangers would only pose a problem if Canada experienced a nontrivial increase in the practice of polygyny. Based on the expert testimony of Joseph Henrich, he finds that, without criminal sanction, polygyny would indeed spread in Canada. Turning to evolutionary psychology, he argues that individuals are naturally inclined toward polygyny, and that if it were decriminalized, there is a likelihood it would grow, especially if high-status individuals who are in the public's eye participate. Chief Justice Bauman also expresses concern that Canada would become a "beacon" for immigrants from around the world: "Polygyny is practiced in many countries from which Canada draws immigrants. This includes states in the Middle East and Africa. It also includes the United States, where as many as 50,000 fundamentalist Mormons reside" (Reference re: Section 293, at para. 558). He recognizes that Parliament could make polygyny a distinct ground of inadmissibility even if it were decriminalized. Nevertheless, he concludes, "I am not satisfied that this completely takes away from the possibility of an increase in immigration-based polygamy" (Reference re: Section 293, at para. 573). Immigrants from underdeveloped countries where polygyny is practiced often have more children, also a concern for a higher incidence of polygyny.

According to historian Nancy Cott (2000), at the time of the founding of the United States, dominant, common-sense knowledge embraced the rightness of monogamous marriage in a model of liberal democracy set against the despotic and unruly practices of other cultures, and specifically of those that practiced polygyny: "Moral and political philosophy (the antecedent of social science) incorporated and purveyed monogamous morality no less than religion did" (9). This common-sense idea of monogamy was set against the "belief systems of Asia, Africa, and Australia, of the Moslems around the Mediterranean, and the natives of North and South America [that] all countenanced polygamy and other complex marriage practices" (10). She explains:

> From the perspective of the American republic, stock [*sic*] contrasts between monogamy and polygamy not only illustrated the superiority of Christian morality over the "heathen" Orient and reassured Christian monogamists in their minority position worldwide, but also staked a political claim. . . . The thematic equivalence between polygamy, despotism, and coercion on the one side and between monogamy, political liberty, and consent on the other resonated through the political culture of the United States all during the subsequent century (Cott 2000, 22).

Chief Justice Bauman quotes legal scholar Martha Ertman, who offers a similar analysis: "Accordingly, in establishing a separatist theocracy, Mormons were regarded as equivalent to 'backward African and Asian races.' This despotic government was primitive, as was their practice of polygamy, thus rendering Mormons unfit to participate in civilized society and politics" (Reference re: Section 293, at para. 299).

In the end, Justice Bauman dismisses this latter evidence in favor of another scholar who denies that the federal polygamy laws were motivated by any kind of animus against the Mormons. In fact, the opinion echoes the concerns of these early American founders over the threat of polygyny, in this case resulting from immigration and its practice among high-status individuals. Bauman embraces an ideal of the Canadian state as one that participates in an enlightened egalitarianism in comparison to the despotism enshrined in the practice of polygyny in other parts of the world. The comparison of the liberal state to the despotism of other places that countenance polygamy is reflected here in the view that polygyny is a threat to civilized society. Thus, Chief Justice Bauman concludes that the coercive powers of the criminal law are needed to curb the possible expansion of this worrying practice.

Finally, a brief section of the opinion deals with the issue of stereotyping religious minority groups (fourteen paragraphs). In this section, Chief Justice Bauman addresses the expert testimony of religious studies scholar Lori Beaman, who has written extensively on the legal rights of religious minorities, and of legal scholar Angela Campbell, the primary scholar to conduct ethnographic research in Bountiful. He states, "Both Professor Campbell and Dr. Beaman properly caution against the acceptance at face value of what may be stereotypical portrayals of life in polygamous communities. As they rightly point out, construing unfamiliar practices as harmful without careful examination can result in the perpetuation of stereotypes and an unjustified curtailing of fundamental freedoms" (Reference re: Section 293, at para. 747).

He follows this with reasons their testimony should be given less weight compared to other credible evidence: "I found the evidence of these two witnesses sincere, but frankly somewhat naive in the context of the great weight of the evidence" (Reference re: Section 293, at para. 752).

Neither does he give credence to the testimony of the anonymous witnesses from the Bountiful FLDS community. In fact, he questions whether they can even be considered victims as long as they continue to live the polygynous lifestyle:

> I question whether the capable consenting spouse is a "victim." To the contrary, she can be seen to be facilitating an arrangement which Parliament views as harmful to society generally.
> It is, in any event, constitutionally permissible for the state to attempt to deter vulnerable people from self-harm by criminalizing the harmful conduct. (Reference re: Section 293, at paras. 1197–98)

While women in polygynous relationships remain criminalized, in his opinion, Chief Justice Bauman does find that, insofar as the criminalization of polygyny applies to persons under the age of eighteen, it violates section 715 of the charter. Thus, by focusing on the inherent and social harms of polygyny, and especially the harms it would cause to the institution of monogamous marriage, Bauman offers an opinion that justifies criminalizing it for everyone in a polygynous union except for those below the age of eighteen.

CONCLUSION

Good justification exists to criminalize practices that are unlawful and harmful to women and children, such as underage and forced marriages and sexual abuse of all kinds, no matter their source. There is also very good reason to examine carefully the context in which polygyny occurs.

The Polygamy Reference uncovered substantial evidence of numerous social problems and harms associated with the practice. There is no doubt that the issue of polygyny in Western societies brings to the foreground essential questions of how best to assess the competing interests and the consequences of restrictions upon individual rights and freedoms. These challenges are difficult in the context of certain fundamentalist religions and sects that appear to limit women's equality rights.

I have analyzed Chief Justice Bauman's opinion to uncover his methodology for undertaking such a balancing act and find it lacking. The opinion examines the evidence concerning the psychological and social harms of polygyny, as well as the health consequences, to individuals and especially to children. Bauman's sweeping opinion, however, does little to shed light on the complex issues surrounding fundamentalism, the people who engage in the stigmatized family form of polygyny, or the cultural variability of its practice. Rather than fully addressing the ways competing interests might engage questions of coercion versus consent, rights versus freedoms, and so forth, Bauman focuses on the *possible* harms of polygyny to mainstream society and to monogamous marriage, as if these are themselves threatened and in need of protection. This conclusion concerning the state of monogamy is quite perplexing given the fact that most social-scientific research demonstrates a trend in the opposite direction. Polygyny is attenuating in Africa and the Middle East, where its practice has been most prevalent, due to globalizing and modernizing forces (Zeitzen 2008). On the other hand, it is unlikely that polygyny will disappear as a practice. There is little doubt that in North America, fundamentalist Mormons and other Christian groups will continue to embrace polygyny as a calling from a higher heavenly order.

In the context of societies that offer a smorgasbord of familial and sexual structures (common-law relationships, open relationships and marriages, same-sex marriage, covenant marriage, blended families, and so forth), can polygyny threaten the institution of monogamous marriage? Many opponents and scholars such as John Witte argue that decriminalizing polygyny would represent another assault on an already weakened institution, and an especially lethal one given the harms associated with its practice. On the other hand, "To more and more people in the Western world who are members of religions that allow (or used to allow) polygamy, becoming [a] member of a plural family represents an individual choice, a lifestyle choice" (Zeitzen 2008, 179). Thus, the issue of polygyny has become politicized as either an inherently harmful institution or one that can be freely chosen when the practice doesn't hurt anyone else. This politicization is evident in the decision, in which Justice Bauman takes a strong stand that polygyny is ultimately a threat to the institution of marriage.

The opinion's 1,367 paragraphs focus predominantly on the *inherent* harms of polygamy and do very little to shed light on the interactions of criminal law and religion and how these relate to competing rights regarding family and sexual intimacy, gender equality, and religious freedom. This discussion is especially important given the growing diversity in Western societies and their hopeful commitment to democratic values. In the North American context, both the constitutional protection of religious freedom and substantive criminal law rely on the state to create and apply normative and moral standards, but they approach these from opposite directions. Legal scholar Benjamin Berger (2008) explains this tension:

> On the one hand, the constitutional protection of religious freedom and equality, a now-orthodox component of any modern constitutional democracy, is, at core, the quintessential reflection of the modern liberal demand that the state remain withdrawn from the domain of moral judgments and claims about the good life . . . On the other hand, the substantive criminal law is precisely a domain of moral judgment. It is a field not only concerned with notions of individual moral blame, but one whose very conceptual foundation is that society can judge certain actions to be so morally repugnant as to warrant state actions with fearsome consequences for the individual. (514–15)

The tension between the normative and coercive aspects of law and the liberal ideal of nurturing diversity reflects profound contemporary uncertainty about imposing values through the legal system. The case of the Polygamy Reference demonstrates the fact that there is no simple solution to these difficult questions. The opinion offers perspective on the consequences of sidestepping the issues at stake to focus on anxieties concerning harm to the social order (via polygyny's threat to monogamous marriage). The moral language that supports arguments in favor of regulating and imposing monogamy is shielded from view but lurks in the background. Many would agree that there is a moral advantage to enforcing monogamy in society, but others would not. Chief Justice Bauman missed an important opportunity to articulate the values being pursued in criminal law and to engage broader social debate that might facilitate a broader vision of social justice concerning familial and sexual intimacy, gender equality, and religious freedom.

Notes

1. *Reference re Section 293 of the Criminal Code of Canada*, BCSC 1588 (2011), at para. 1088.
2. *Polygamy* is a general term referring to relationships involving more than two people, regardless of the ratio between genders. *Polygyny* is a relationship between one man and more than one woman, and *polyandry* involves one woman and more than one man. *Polyamory* is a postmodern type of family that is generally attached to a particular religion where people seek more than one intimate relationship at a time with the knowledge and consent of everyone involved. In this article, *polygamy* is used to denote *polygyny* (and not *polyandry* or *polyamory*).
3. "Canada Criminal Code, R.S.C. 1985, c-46, s. 293 provides: (1) Everyone who
    - (a) practises or enters into or in any manner agrees or consents to practise or enter into
    - (i) any form of polygyny, or
    - (ii) any kind of conjugal union with more than one person at the same time, whether or not it is by law recognized as a binding form of marriage, or
    - (b) celebrates, assists or is a party to a rite, ceremony, contract or consent that purports to sanction a relationship mentioned in subparagraph (a) (i) or (ii),
    is guilty of an indictable offense and liable to imprisonment for a term not exceeding five years.
4. There have been only two convictions entered in Canada for the offence of polygamy, both at the turn of the twentieth century and both resulting from the prosecutions of aboriginal men (*Queen v. Bear Shin's Bone, R v. Harris*) (Campbell 2014).
5. Section 1 of the Canadian Charter of Rights and Freedoms acknowledges the principle that individual rights and freedoms are not absolute and that some circumstances may require limitations on rights by the state in order to protect the interests of the community. Section 1 provides that rights are "subject only to such reasonable limits prescribed by law as can be demonstrably justified in a free and democratic society." In its 1986 decision in *R. v. Oakes*, 1 SCR 103 (1986), the Supreme Court of Canada established a framework to decide whether a law found to violate a charter right can still be justified under section 1. This balancing rights test became known as the *Oakes Test*. Chief Justice Bauman found that the law violates the religious freedom of fundamentalist Mormons, but the harm against women and children outweighs that concern. This is called *passing the Oakes test*.

References

An-Na'im, Ahmed A. 2013. "An Inclusive Approach to the Mediation of Competing Human Rights Claims." *Constellations (Oxford, England)* 20 (1): 7–17. http://dx.doi.org/10.1111/cons.12016.

Baines, Beverley. 2012. "Polygyny and Feminist Constitutionalism." In *Feminist Constitutionalism: Global Perspectives*, edited by Beverley Baines, Daphne Barak-Erez, and Tsvi Kahana, 452–74. Cambridge: Cambridge University Press. http://dx.doi.org/10.1017/CBO9780511980442.032.

Barker, Eileen. 1986. "Religious Movements: Cult and Anticult since Jonestown." *Annual Review of Sociology* 12 (1): 329–46. http://dx.doi.org/10.1146/annurev.so.12.080186.001553.

Barker, Eileen. 1989. *New Religious Movements: A Practical Introduction*. London: Her Majesty's Stationery Office.

Berger, Benjamin L. 2008. "Moral Judgment, Criminal Law and the Constitutional Protection of Religion." *Supreme Court Law Review* 41 (2): 513–52.

Bergoffen, Debra. 1999. "Marriage, Autonomy, and the Feminine Protest." *Hypatia* 14 (4): 18–35. http://dx.doi.org/10.1111/j.1527-2001.1999.tb01250.x.

Bramham, Daphne. 2008. *The Secret Lives of Saints: Child Brides and Lost Boys in a Polygynous Mormon Sect.* Toronto: Random House.

Campbell, Angela. 2014. *Sister Wives, Surrogates and Sex Workers: Outlaws by Choice?* London: Ashgate.

Carter, Sarah. 2008. *The Importance of Being Monogamous: Marriage and Nation Building in Western Canada to 1915.* Edmonton: University of Alberta Press.

Cott, Nancy F. 2000. *Public Vows: A History of Marriage and the Nation.* Cambridge: Harvard University Press.

Dawson, Lome L. 1998. "Anti-Modernism, Modernism, and Postmodernism: Struggling with the Cultural Significance of New Religious Movements." *Sociology of Religion* 59 (2): 131–56. http://dx.doi.org/10.2307/3712077.

Ertman, Martha M. 2010. "Race Treason: The Untold Story of America's Ban on Polygyny." *Columbia Journal of Gender and Law* 19 (2): 287–366.

Ettelbrick, Paula. 1989. "Since When Is Marriage a Path to Liberation?" In *Same-Sex Marriage: Pro and Con*, edited by Andrew Sullivan, 122–28. New York: Vintage Books.

Hall, Barbara. 2010. "Preface to 'Summer.'" *Canadian Diversity* 8 (3): 3–5.

Heath, Melanie. 2012. *One Marriage under God: The Campaign to Promote Marriage in America.* New York: New York University Press.

Hoffmann, John P., and Stephen J. Bahr. 2006. "Crime/Deviance." In *Handbook of Religion and Social Institutions*, edited by Helen Rose Ebaugh, 241–63. New York: Springer.

Hunter, James D. 1981. "The New Religions: Demodernization and the Protest against Modernity." In *The Social Impact of the New Religious Movements*, edited by Bryan R. Wilson, 1–19. New York: Rose of Sharon.

Levine, Roslyn J. 2004. "In Harm's Way: The Limits to Legislating Criminal Law." *Supreme Court Law Review* 24 (2d): 195–216.

Lewis, James R. 2003. *Legitimating New Religions.* New Brunswick, NJ: Rutgers University Press.

Lincoln, Yvonna S., and Egon G. Guba. 1985. *Naturalistic Inquiry.* Beverly Hills, CA: Sage. http://dx.doi.org/10.1016/0147-1767(85)90062-8.

MacKinnon, Catharine. 1989. *Toward a Feminist Theory of the State.* Cambridge: Harvard University Press.

Millett, Kate. 1969. *Sexual Politics.* New York: Avon Books.

Olson, Paul J. 2006. "The Public Perception of 'Cults' and 'New Religious Movements.'" *Journal for the Scientific Study of Religion* 45 (1): 97–106. http://dx.doi.org/10.1111/j.1468-5906.2006.00008.x.

Palmer, Susan. 1999. "Frontiers and Families: The Children of Island Pond." In *Children in New Religions*, edited by Susan Palmer and Charlotte Hardman, 153–71. New Brunswick, NJ: Rutgers University Press.

Palmer, Susan. 2011. *The New Heretics of France.* New York: Oxford University Press.

Perry, Robin. 2011. "Balancing Rights or Building Rights? Reconciling the Right to Use Customary Systems of Law with Competing Human Rights in Pursuit of Indigenous Sovereignty." *Harvard Human Rights Journal* 24: 71–114.

Richardson, James T. 1993. "Definitions of Cult: From Sociological-Technical to Popular-Negative." *Review of Religious Research* 34 (4): 348–56. http://dx.doi.org/10.2307/3511972.

Richardson, James T. 2006a. "Law." In *Handbook of Religion and Social Institutions*, edited by Helen Rose Ebaugh, 227–40. New York: Springer.

Richardson, James T. 2006b. "The Sociology of Religious Freedom: A Structural and Socio-Legal Analysis." *Sociology of Religion* 67 (3): 271–94. http://dx.doi.org/10 .1093/socrel/67.3.271.

Richardson, James T. 2009. "Religion and the Law: An Interactionist View." In *The Oxford Handbook of the Sociology of Religion*, edited by. P. Clarke, 418–31. Oxford: Oxford University Press.

Robbins, Thomas. 2000. "'Quo Vadis' the Scientific Study of New Religious Movements?" *Journal for the Scientific Study of Religion* 39 (4): 515–23. http://dx.doi.org/10.1111 /j.1468-5906.2000.tb00013.x.

Stark, Rodney, and William S. Bainbridge. 1997. *Religion, Deviance, and Social Control*. New York: Routledge.

Talbot, Chris. 2006. "'Turkey Is in Our Midst': Orientalism and Contagion in Nineteenth Century Anti-Mormonism." *Journal of Law and Family Studies* 8 (2): 363–88.

Wright, Stuart A. 1995. "Construction and Escalation of a Cult Threat: Dissecting Moral Panic and Official Reaction to the Branch Davidians." In *Armageddon in Waco: Critical Perspectives on the Branch Davidian Conflict*, edited by Stuart A. Wright, 75–94. Chicago: University of Chicago Press.

Wright, Stuart A. 2003. "A Decade after Waco: Reassessing Crisis Negotiations at Mt. Carmel in Light of New Government Disclosures." *Nova Religio* 7 (2): 101–10. http:// dx.doi.org/10.1525/nr.2003.7.2.101.

Wright, Stuart A., and James T. Richardson, eds. 2011. *Saints under Siege: The Raid on the Fundamentalist Latter Day Saints in Texas*. New York: New York University Press.

Zeitzen, Miriam K. 2008. *Polygamy: A Cross-Cultural Analysis*. Oxford: Berg.

8

DISTINGUISHING POLYGYNY AND POLYFIDELITY UNDER THE CRIMINAL LAW

Maura Irene Strassberg

In North America, criminal polygamy laws date back to the mid- to late nineteenth century, when polygynist Mormons (members of the Church of Jesus Christ of Latter-Day Saints) began to gain political power and, in the case of the United States, threatened to create a state in which polygyny was both legal and widely practiced (Strassberg 1997, 1504–5, n. 5).[1] More recently, polygamy has been defended as an alternative sexual practice and family structure, like same-sex marriage, that is repressed by sexual prejudice and is deserving of legal protection and recognition in a liberal state (Chambers 1997, 81–83). Fundamentalist Mormon polygamy has also been defended as a religious practice that cannot be selectively burdened.[2] Indeed, arguments along these lines were the basis for two of the strongest legal challenges to the criminalization of polygamy in modern times, the unsuccessful reference to the British Columbia Supreme Court on the constitutionality of the Canadian polygamy law under the Canadian Charter of Rights and Freedoms (Reference 2011 re: Section 293, at para. 1) and the successful challenge to the constitutionality of portions of Utah's bigamy law in *Brown v. Buhman*.[3] It should be noted, however, that as both opinions have or will be appealed, the future of the criminalization of polygamy is still to be determined.

Beginning with my 1997 law review article defending same-sex marriage, I have taken a position against decriminalizing polygamy on the grounds that it poses social and ethical concerns that distinguish it from same-sex and opposite-sex monogamous relationships (Strassberg 1997, 1615–18). Later, I sought to distinguish polygyny from polyamory on the grounds that the two practices were inherently different (Strassberg 2003b, 363–431). My focus has largely been on the state interests that might be served by modern polygamy laws rather than

DOI: 10.7330/9780874219975.c008

on the constitutional rights that might or might not be burdened. Certainly it is the case that since I first began writing about polygamy, the legal landscape has shifted considerably. *United States v. Windsor* (2013) and *Obergefell v. Hodges* (2015) in particular opened up the possibility of liberty-based arguments supporting the decriminalization of polygamy.[4] As to religious free-exercise arguments against criminalization of polygamy, I must admit that my own arguments about the dangers of polygamy require an understanding of the religious context that largely shapes the most problematic version of this marital practice. The consequence of this is to make my arguments particularly susceptible to free-exercise attacks. But I am not sure this vulnerability makes my observations about the interaction between religious doctrine and practice either wrong or legally irrelevant. As I will describe below, the coercive power of religious doctrine melded into a polygynous marital practice may be sufficient to justify unusual state burdens on this practice. Whether or not the same state interests can really be served by decriminalizing the overall practice of polygamy and using other criminal laws to prosecute the coercive abuses, as many, including the Utah court in *Brown*, have argued, is essentially an empirical prediction.[5] However, I remain deeply skeptical that the practice of polygamy fully defined by fundamentalist Mormon doctrine can be free of such coercion and abuse.

Some support for the decriminalization of polygamy, especially from the feminist and queer-rights communities (Stacey and Meadow 2009, 192), may be understood as motivated by a confusion between religious polygyny and polyamory. *Polyamory* is a recently invented term denoting a relationship form based on two premises: no one individual can meet all the needs of any other individual, and multiple loving relationships are necessary to allow individuals to realize their full sexual, emotional, intellectual, and spiritual potential (Strassberg 2003a, 455). Polyamory celebrates the individual; therefore, polyamorous relationships arise out of the voluntary and individual choices of partners based on romantic love and sexual attraction (452). Informed by both the women's and queer-rights movements, polyamory values both male and female sexual pleasure and can include multipartner sexual and romantic relationships that are exclusively same sex, exclusively opposite sex, or a mixture of both (453). While *polyamory* is an umbrella term covering everything from individuals with multiple separate partners to open marriages, it is only the group-marriage version of polyamory, called *polyfidelity* (466), that could by any stretch of the imagination be potentially covered by laws criminalizing polygamy. For purposes of this chapter, therefore, references to polyamory in general should be understood as referring to polyfidelity in particular.

It may also be the case that there is a new Mormon polygamy that may be understood as a blend of polyfidelity and fundamentalist Mormon polygyny. The Brown family might be seen as illustrative of this alternative, although the family is too young to know for certain what will develop from it. This polygyny would be characterized by its independence from existing fundamentalist Mormon polygynous communities, although the members of the family continue to identify as Mormons and have some religious understanding of their polygynous marriage. Factors other than religion, such as sexual interest and anticipated relationships between the wives, must emerge as strong determinants of whether additional wives are added to the family, with the wives having considerable power over any such addition. Such a marriage, if it maintains these features and does not seek to become the nucleus of a greater religious community with the husband serving as a new prophet or to control the marriages of the children to promote religious ends, might be described as an emerging Mormon polyfidelity. If this practice were to replace the existing fundamentalist Mormon polygyny, many of the concerns that underlie my support for continued criminalization of polygamy might be addressed.

As I will argue below, understanding polyfidelity and its practice reveals that it is not inherently either coercive or abusive, particularly when the size of the group remains relatively small. Thus, I see no reason to criminalize polyfidelity. Consequently, to the extent that criminalization of polygamy in general results in criminalization of polyfidelity, I view it as unwarranted. The very aspect of the Utah bigamy law struck down by the Utah court in *Brown*, forbidding cohabitation while concurrently married to another, would seem to reach polyfidelity involving one legally married couple and other individuals linked only by cohabitation.[6] In addition, the definition of criminal polygamy found in Canadian law also has a serious likelihood of criminalizing polyfidelity. The current Canadian polygamy statute now in effect prohibits entering into "any kind of conjugal union with more than one person at the same time" (Reference 2011 re: Section 293, at para. 17). Under the Canadian court's interpretation of the statute, most polyfidelitous relationships would be excluded due to an absence of any kind of commitment ceremony or external authority understood as capable of "binding" the parties to each other (Reference 2011 re: Section 293, at paras. 1000, 1016–17, 1094). However, this interpretation may well be an attempt to "rewrite the provision [to exclude polyamory] in order that it pass constitutional muster" (Bailey 2015, 13–14).

At the same time, there are definitions of the criminal offense of polygamy, in particular those adopted by American jurisdictions following the Model Penal Code, that arguably would not reach polyfidelity. Although there is no case law to this effect, it is likely that the Model Penal Code requirement that multiple cohabitation be an "exercise of the purported right of plural marriage" would effectively exclude polyfidelity (Strassberg 2003b, 421). The term *plural marriage* can be understood as a specific reference to Mormon polygyny, as it is the term used by Mormons to describe marriages involving one husband and multiple wives (424). In addition, the "purported right" likely refers to a claim rejected by the United States Supreme Court in 1878 that plural marriage by Mormons is an exercise of religious freedom (*Reynolds v. United States*).[7] Polyfidelitous families certainly do not use the term *plural marriage* and may not even use the term *marriage* at all to describe their relationships (Strassberg 2003b, 425). In addition, they are more likely to view their conduct as an exercise of the right of intimate association rather than either the right to marry or the right to exercise religious freedom (423). As a result, it would be difficult to argue that the Model Penal Code polygamy law gives clear notice, as criminal statutes must, that polyfidelity is covered conduct.

Yet this interpretation of the Model Penal Code to exclude polyfidelity while continuing to cover fundamentalist Mormon polygyny exposes code-based laws to free-exercise constitutional challenges very similar to the successful challenge to Utah's bigamy law in *Brown*.[8] In addition, it is not clear how emerging Mormon polyfidelity would be treated under this interpretation. It may well be impossible to ensure that polyfidelity of either kind is not made criminal without exposing the remaining criminalization of fundamentalist Mormon polygyny to constitutional attack. Thus, it may be that either polyfidelity of any kind must be swept up in criminal laws targeting polygamy to ensure that the laws remain "valid and neutral law[s] of generalized applicability," or polygamy should be decriminalized to protect polyfidelity.[9] Only if it is possible to strongly justify a state interest in continuing to criminalize only fundamentalist Mormon polygyny or similarly coercive practices will it be possible to ensure that polyfidelity is not criminalized while fundamentalist Mormon polygamy is. Given my deep concerns about the way fundamentalist Mormon polygyny may be inherently coercive and abusive, and my lack of similar concerns about polyfidelity and perhaps the emerging Mormon polyfidelity, this latter alternative is my preferred alternative. In what follows, I attempt to set out the justifications for any such differential treatment of fundamentalist Mormon polygyny and polyfidelity, perhaps including the emerging Mormon polyfidelity. Whether these justifications are sufficient to allow such a statute to pass constitutional muster is a matter that will not be addressed below, although it is extremely important. The question here is whether there are good reasons for even trying to defend such a position.

POLYGYNY

Contemporary polygyny seems to have two faces, one that is somewhat attractive to feminists and queer theorists and another that is quite frightening. These two sides of polygyny are illustrated by two articles that appeared in the online version of the *New York Times* within two weeks of each other in January 2010. The first article described a Muslim Malaysian family with four wives, each of whom is a highly educated and successful woman: a medical doctor, a lawyer, a college professor, and a teacher (Gooch, *International Herald Tribune*, Jan. 6, 2010). The article suggested that the doctor, lawyer, and college professor, who were mostly financially independent, had chosen to become the second, third, and fourth wives of their wealthy, industrialist husband because they had put off marriage to further their careers and were unable to find monogamous husbands by the time they wanted to marry. Their polygamous marriage provided them with an opportunity to be in a sexual relationship and have children in a socially conservative society that limited these activities to heterosexual marriage. During the week, the doctor, lawyer, and professor had their own homes near their workplaces while their young children were cared for by the first wife at the family home. On weekends they all converged on the family home, where they cooked together, shared clothes, and enjoyed their sisterhood. From a feminist perspective, what is attractive about this polygynous family is that, although polygyny ultimately allowed these women to take on gender-typical roles as wives and mothers, at least they did so voluntarily and in a way that also allowed them to balance gender-atypical roles as professionals.

In contrast, the second article described a police raid on a Jewish polygynous family in Israel headed by a religious leader who views himself as the savior of the universe (Kershner, *New York Times*, Jan. 15, 2010). A raid by the Israeli police on his apartments in Tel Aviv turned up seventeen wives and forty children. While the women had joined the family willingly at first, they had subsequently been abused and terrorized into what became a state of enslavement. Here polygyny magnifies the worst antifeminist aspects of heterosexual marriage, allowing a single abusive man to dominate and abuse more than one woman.

These two faces of international polygamy are also present in the predominant context for polygamy in the United States, fundamentalist Mormon polygyny. Professor Janet Bennion, an anthropologist who has done extensive field research while living with Mormon polygynous families, observed wives who as mature adults voluntarily left mainstream, monogamous Mormon communities to enter into fundamentalist Mormon polygynous marriages. She describes them as flourishing in a way they were unable to do in the absence of polygyny (Bennion 1998, 9, 65, 96). On the other hand, women who have escaped abusive polygynous marriages in fundamentalist communities have described conditions that more closely resemble the Israeli family (Strassberg 2003b, 395–402). Positive outcomes in polygyny seem to arise when mature women control and use the institution to meet their need for a family in a larger social and religious context that requires heterosexual marriage. In such cases the polygynous family so created may be considerably less patriarchal in its day-to-day operation. However, when men and religious belief control polygyny, it is a very different institution. This, I believe, is most typically the situation in fundamentalist Mormon polygyny, in large part because of the particular religious beliefs that make polygyny a religious practice for such fundamentalists.

Fundamentalist Mormons believe, as did the original historical Mormons, that God himself was once a mortal man who had achieved godhood (Strassberg 1997, 1579). This means that men can also ascend to godhood by creating the right foundation during earthly life. In addition to the initial requirement that a man be righteous, which means faithful and loyal adherence to Mormon church doctrines and institutions, the primary earthly foundation for godhood is the accumulation of power over large numbers of people for whom the man will subsequently be a god in the Kingdom of Heaven (1579). Such power can only be accumulated through the institution of celestial marriage, by which a woman is sealed to a man for all eternity, and by the birth in such a marriage of blood progeny who are also subordinated to their patriarch for all eternity (1579). Since only men can achieve godhood, salvation and eternal life for fundamentalist women requires that they enter into a polygynous union with a righteous man, bear him as many children as possible, and support the further expansion of his progeny by the addition of more wives (1579–80). Rejection of polygyny by women is believed to result in damnation (Strassberg 2003b, 381–82). In addition, to ensure that they marry a righteous man, women must accept marriages approved by church elders and often arranged by them as well (366–37, 391).

Polygyny thus serves two religious purposes. First, it reinforces the hierarchy of men over women by, as the founder of the Mormon religion said, freeing men "from the unnatural sexual influence women hold over men" in monogamous marriage (Foster 1981, 176). Second, it is a crucial instrument in making godhood possible by vastly expanding the progeny of men aspiring to god status. Consequently, the religious significance of procreation and patriarchy must be understood as the driving force behind fundamentalist polygynous marriages. Contrary to the title of the Home Box Office cable television show *Big Love*, fundamentalist Mormon marriages are not meant to be defined by love, although love may arise.

The role of coercion in how women come to be polygynous wives is the most troubling aspect of polygamy and the primary basis for justifying its continued criminalization. However, all fundamentalist Mormon polygynous wives are not coerced. Some join polygynous communities and polygynous marriages as mature adult converts to fundamentalism and are usually divorcees or widows with children, or never-married "thirty-somethings" (Foster 1981, 390–91). They typically come from the mainstream Mormon community which, although it has repudiated polygyny, maintains beliefs about godhood, celestial marriage, and eternal power through blood progeny that make divorced women, widows with children, and older, never-married women disfavored marriage partners (390–91). Such women are often both financially vulnerable and socially disconnected from mainstream church culture due to their unmarried state. They find that polygynous marriage addresses their needs for survival, sex, family, community, and salvation (390–91). Entry into these relationships is no more coercive than entry into many monogamous heterosexual relationships motivated by religious prohibitions on extramarital sex and childbearing. These marriages most closely resemble the Malaysian polygynous marriage profiled in the *New York Times*.

However, given fundamentalist beliefs about the purpose of polygyny being to exponentially grow men's kingdoms through procreation, older women from outside the fundamentalist community make up only a small proportion of polygynous wives. The majority of such wives enter polygynous marriages from within the isolated polygynous community they grew up in (Foster 1981, 393). Many, if not most, enter into arranged marriages as teenagers between the ages of twelve and eighteen (Bramham, *Vancouver Sun*, Feb. 2011; Foster 1981, 366, 386), both because this age range is the time when girls begin to be capable of reproduction, but also because girls in this age range are sexually inexperienced and easily controlled, manipulated, or coerced. Most of these marriages are with middle-aged to older men who already have multiple wives and families (Strassberg 2003b, 366) because older men form the "righteous" religious hierarchy, and they give these teenage wives to themselves and each other (Bramham, *Vancouver Sun*, Feb. 2011; Strassberg 2003b, 391). Many of the younger men who might be natural objects of affection and attraction for these teenage and young adult women are ejected from the fundamentalist community, often as minor teenagers themselves, for the simple reason that polygyny cannot accommodate equal numbers of men and women, and the young men who threaten to undermine polygyny must be removed from the competition for women (Harris 2005, 1–2).

Anecdotal evidence suggests that a number of teenage wives are coerced into polygynous marriages by physical violence and threats of spiritual damnation (Strassberg 2003b, 366–68). These are girls who are raised to obey religious authority in isolated and closed communities, are taught to expect polygynous marriage, and are pulled out of school before high school because they will not need further education. If they don't actively resist marriage, their compliance may only be because they believe that resistance will be met with extreme punishment and that they have no real chance of escape from their community (366–68).

There are, at the same time, teenage girls in these communities who do not seem coerced into these marriages. They embrace their faith and consent to the marriage arranged for them (Strassberg 2003b, 373–74). However, as I have argued in greater detail elsewhere, religiously motivated consent by teenage girls to polygynous marriage should be seen as uninformed, just as we see a teenager's religiously motivated refusal to accept life-saving medical procedures as insufficiently informed to count as consent legally (381–89). Although teenage girls do not risk certain or even likely death by consenting to become polygynous wives, they are consenting to sexual relations that will be designed to get them pregnant both as soon as possible and as many times as possible during the next twenty to thirty years. For young teenagers, any pregnancy is physically risky, and multiple early pregnancies will have debilitating effects over the long term. Beyond the health risks, however, are the life-changing effects of accumulating a large brood of children that she will largely raise on her own or with the help of her similarly burdened sister wives.

Indeed, just at the point at which a polygynous wife might become disenchanted with polygyny, she will find it extremely difficult to leave her marriage. Sarah Song has referred to this as the problem of "exit" (Song 2007, 160–62). Exit is difficult for wives married as teenagers due to their lack of education and exposure to the outside world, their financial dependence on the church and other polygynous wives, and their fear of losing their children and their eternal salvation (Strassberg 2003b, 400–404). These factors serve to make teen-age consent to polygynous marriage both deeply life changing and irreversible. Thus, these marriages should be viewed as coerced.

Many of these same exit difficulties are present for those adult polygynous women who can be presumed to enter into such marriages voluntarily. Their voluntary entrance into polygyny does not ensure voluntary exit (Strassberg 2003b). These coercive realities make me ambivalent at best about the decriminalization of polygynous marriages involving only mature adult women. Furthermore, any attempt to decriminalize polygyny involving only mature adult women must come to grips with the fact that fundamentalist Mormon polygyny, even at its best, is not an individual-focused alternative lifestyle designed to meet the needs of otherwise unmarriageable older Mormon women (410). Rather, Mormon fundamentalist polygyny is largely and most successfully a community-based practice (393) in which the communities are inevitably theocracies that have been created by and around a male prophet (405–6). Polygyny is an essential element of the political success of these theocracies because it allows for the control and concentration of sexual, reproductive, and economic resources in the hands of the prophet and his favored delegates. Given the specific religious significance of fundamentalist Mormon polygyny, decriminalizing mature polygynous marriages would not stop the coercive polygynous marriages of teenage girls. Teenage wives are the mainstay of Mormon fundamentalist polygyny for both practical and religious reasons. Consequently, the entire institution is inevitably tainted by the sexual coercion and reproductive exploitation of young women, not to mention the sexual exclusion and emotional cruelty displayed toward the young men summarily ejected from their families and communities.

This does not mean that I support the criminal prosecution of polygynous wives in general, which is simply a revictimization, although some criminal penalty could be appropriate where polygynous wives become active coercive agents in the marriages of their own young daughters. Maintaining a crime of polygyny on the books is in large part a symbolic rejection of both the specific coercion of teenage and adult polygynous wives and the theocratic communities created by and around polygyny. The rejection has been largely symbolic because the experience of prosecuting polygyny in the context of these theocratic communities, as illustrated most recently by the raid on the Warren Jeffs compound in Texas, has shown that it is impossible to do so without also harming the many innocent victims of the practice: children, mothers, coerced wives, and even coerced men. Essentially, it is an attempt to prosecute an entire community's violation of the law. As I have suggested in more detail elsewhere, a more effective strategy against those most problematic aspects of polygyny might be to try to reassert government control and oversight over the economic and social institutions of polygynous communities while simultaneously working to empower both teenage girls and dissatisfied adult women in these communities (Strassberg 2003b, 430). However, I remain skeptical that such efforts can truly produce a kinder, gentler form of fundamentalist polygyny. They may just be a better band-aid on the problem. I suspect that the religious ideology driving Mormon fundamentalist polygyny is simply inconsistent with our desire to reform the institution.

POLYAMORY

There are a number of crucial distinctions between polygyny and polyamory that justify exclusion of polyfidelity from criminalization. To begin with, polyfidelity is not the developed social institution that polygyny is. Even the relatively new institution of Mormon fundamentalist polygyny, which was founded as a return to the patriarchal polygyny described in the Bible (Strassberg 1997, 1582), has been practiced for more than 150 years (Strassberg 2003b, 353n3). Although there may have been antecedents to polyamory as far back as such nineteenth-century social experiments as the Oneida community (Foster 1997, 257–60), the roots of polyamory are more accurately traced back to the free-love movement of the 1960s, the concurrent development of the women's and queer-rights movements, and the practical experiences of certain utopian communities that existed through the 1970s and 1980s (Strassberg 2003a, 439–42). The term *polyamory* itself only first appeared in print in 1990 (439, n. 4). Around that time a movement was born that has spent the last two decades largely focused on itself: exploring its own theoretical underpinnings, creating a national community through print and Internet media, and giving advice on the practical challenges of polyamorous life (442–43). Whether out of a fear of drawing too much attention to itself, or a lack of energy available for external focus caused by the internal demands of polyamorous relationships, polyamory has not developed the political/activist character of the women's- and queer-rights movements (447).

Because there is no stable social institution of polyfidelity that can be easily studied and characterized (Strassberg 2003a, 447), determining the impact of polyfidelity upon the adult individuals who choose to enter such relationships, upon the children who may be raised by polyfidelitous families, and upon society as a whole is a matter of some speculation. Nonetheless, to the extent that polyfidelity may have been criminalized by the polygamy laws in such countries as Canada, or by bigamy laws in the United States, it is necessary to try to do so. In what follows, I shall use the movement's own writings and anecdotal descriptions to compare polyfidelity to polygyny.

Ideologically, polyamory begins with a focus on the individual and the conditions necessary for individuals to flourish. Its values are "individual choice, voluntary cooperation, a healthy family life and positive romantic love" (Nearing 1992, 59), along with "sexual equality, a non-possession orientation towards relationships, and a widening circle of spousal intimacy and true love" (59). Polyfidelity ensures that each individual has equal value within a multipartner relationship by requiring that each person must be in a loving, although not necessarily sexual, relationship with each other "marriage" partner (10). Adding new partners to the "marriage" thus requires the knowledge and full consent of each other member (69, 26–27). Many couples interested in polyfidelity spend years looking for just one additional partner whom both partners love and who wants to be "married" to both of them (Northrop 1997, 40–42). Adding a fourth or fifth "marriage" partner is even harder. Maintaining this complex web of relationships in the face of the inevitable jealousy that can arise requires a commitment to communication, emotional honesty, negotiation, and trust as well as lots of family meetings. Egalitarian decision-making processes, like consensus or majority democracy, are used (Nearing 1992, 36–37). Thus, while fundamentalist Mormon polygyny is defined by obedience, patriarchy, and hierarchy, polyamory is defined by autonomy, egalitarianism, and democracy.

Another important distinction between polyfidelity and fundamentalist Mormon polygyny is that polyfidelity is not practiced by members of a preexisting community who share religious beliefs, cultural bonds, or difficult economic circumstances, nor is it imposed upon anyone (Strassberg 2003b, 413). Rather, it is a choice that individuals from anywhere in society may come to if they find themselves attracted to and in love with more than one person. This may arise as a combination of temperament and happenstance. As a result, polyfidelity neither arises out of, nor seeks to create, a homogeneous and self-perpetuating community engaged in such group "marriages" (413).

A direct focus on the particular concerns used to justify criminalizing fundamentalist Mormon polygyny also shows that polyfidelity does not cause the same individual or social harms. The primary reason for continuing to criminalize polygyny is to protect the teenage girls who are a significant source of plural wives. Polyfidelity, on the other hand, seeks to maximize the sexual and romantic connections between partners. As a result, these "marriages" are not particularly interested in reproduction, let alone maximizing the number of children born to the family (Strassberg 2003a, 492–94). Consequently, polyfidelity has no reproductive-based need to target teenage or young adult women.

In addition, a polyfidelitous "marriage" seeking to expand is looking for an individual who is comfortable with sharing sexual and emotional intimacy with more than one person. Teenagers and young adults are quite unlikely to already be dissatisfied with monogamy and seeking multiple-party relationships for themselves. Furthermore, teenagers and young adults are not likely to be emotionally mature enough to deal with the jealousy that comes with sharing partners or sufficiently self-aware and skilled at communication to live in a group (Strassberg 2003b, 426). Thus, the teenage girls of polyfidelitous families are presumably not going to be married off to other polyfidelitous families, nor are the teenage boys of polyfidelitous families going to be banished from their families and communities. Polyfidelity's emphasis on individual choice requires allowing any children the family might have to make their own life and relationship choices. In addition, unlike most polygynous families, polyfidelitous families do not live in isolated communities that exert almost total community control over the lives and minds of their children, from education to media exposure (428). As a result, polyfidelitous families are not likely to have the power to coercively marry off their young teenage girls or brainwash them into wishing to enter into such marriages.

Although, unlike polygyny, entry into polyfidelity is limited to adults and is noncoercive, there is a potential "dark side" (Slomiak 1997, 22) to such relationships. To begin with, it is a core principle of polyamory in general that jealousy is an unnecessary emotion we have been socialized to feel but can "unlearn" (Strassberg 2003a, 456–60). Since jealousy makes it impossible for sexual and romantic partners to tolerate the existence of others (456–57), polyamory devotes considerable energy to helping its practitioners unlearn jealousy (West 1996, 110–59). However, if polyamorists are wrong and jealousy is inevitable, then polyamory "itself is coercive because it necessarily provokes jealousy and then demands of its practitioners that they accept what they cannot accept and pretend not to feel what they cannot help but feel" (Strassberg, 2003a, 506). The invisible self-coercion demanded by polyamory may, in turn, generate a need to coerce other existing or potential partners.

Larger polyfidelitous families may be especially at risk for coercive internal dynamics. Although group decision making in polyfidelity is ostensibly democratic, the reality of group dynamics is that individual differences between group members can produce power differentials that turn group decision making from autonomous deliberation to coercive manipulation (Strassberg, 2003a, 496–97). In larger polyfidelitous families, such power differentials can arise if some members of the family are sexually connected to more family members than others (496). Such a differential occurs when, in a particular family, the family members are not sexually fully mutual; that is, all the family members are not in sexual relationships with all other family members. Thus, in a triad, if one person has a sexual relationship with the two other triad members but the two other members do not have a sexual relationship with each other, one person is the "sexual hinge" (496, n. 312). In larger polyfidelitous families, especially those that are purely heterosexual, there are likely to be one or two individuals who are sexual hinges. In addition, even in the context of fully mutual sexual relationships within the family, each relationship is unique, and the level of connection will vary both from relationship to relationship and within relationships over time. Those family members who are in the most relationships, or in the most intense relationships, will likely have more power in the group (496, n. 312). Other factors contributing to power differentials in polyfidelity can include links between particular members created by longer-term relationships, legal marriage, biological and/or legal parenthood, and asset ownership. Family members not linked to others in such ways can be more vulnerable than those who have such links. Finally, personal charisma, verbal fluency, and personal aggressiveness can create and/or exacerbate otherwise existing power differentials (496, n. 312). Thus, with all that goes into the relationships that constitute polyfidelity, a procedural commitment to deliberative and democratic decision making may be subverted by emotional dominance and vulnerability (497).

The Kerista community, a twenty-five-member San Francisco community credited with coining the word *polyfidelity*, suffered from just such coercive and manipulative group decision making (Slomiak 1997, 20–26). This community began as two group marriages that ultimately merged into one marriage over a twenty-year period (18–20). Although ideologically Kerista was committed to "equality, democratic decision-making, and personal freedom" (20), in reality there was a social hierarchy that used highly effective techniques of emotional manipulation and intimidation to force conformity with the desires of powerful family members (22–26). Pressure of this kind extended even to decisions such as the addition of new members to the marriage, which meant that ultimately some family members were coerced into sexual relationships with others to maintain the ideology of equality (23).

Of particular interest in the Kerista community was the use of a threat of banishment to wield control over family members (Slomiak 1997, 24). Because this community was an economic as well as family community, members stood to lose everything if banished: love, friends, home, and livelihood. This threat of banishment successfully kept dissatisfied community members from challenging the family power brokers for many years (24). The example of Kerista, therefore, suggests that individuals in polyfidelity can have exit problems similar to those of polygynous wives.

It is a paradox of polyfidelity that a commitment to individual autonomy ultimately makes "marriages" capable of exercising much greater control over the individual than any single spouse could possibly have exerted (Strassberg 2003a, 500–404). Larger polyfidelitous families have the capacity to take on the coercive and autonomy-depriving characteristics of a cult, as Kerista did. Whether this actually occurs may depend, at least in part, on two interrelated factors: the size of the family and the ideology driving it. Kerista ultimately involved a twenty-five-person marriage but started out as two associated group marriages sharing a vision to create a utopian community (Slomiak 1997, 19–20). Like Kerista, there are many polyfidelitous families with visions of utopian community at their core (Strassberg 2003a, 498). Such a focus on community is likely to drive attempts to expand the marriage to a size at which the coercive potential becomes much greater (498, n. 323). It may well be the case that many polyfidelitous groups larger than four adults have some kind of "compelling communal dynamic" that helps both bring and hold them together (Nearing 1997, 22–23). In contrast, smaller polyfidelitous families may view themselves as merely larger nuclear families with no aspiration to grow bigger than the three or four romantically and sexually connected adults already involved (Northrop 1997, 40–42). This suggests that there may be an important difference between polyfidelity used as an alternative to the nuclear family and polyfidelity used as a basis for the organization of utopian communities. It is the latter that most significantly raises the specter of coercive, autonomy-destroying relationships. One way to ensure that such relationships are less likely to occur would be to place a limit on the size of polyfidelitous families to perhaps no more than four adults.

Does the potential for coercion and difficulties of exit in polyfidelity justify the criminalization of polyfidelity? To begin with, allowing a mature adult to choose to engage in polyamorous relationships that may demand suppression of jealousy seems no worse than entering religious orders that demand suppression of sexuality. These demands may be impossible, and it may be an unwise exercise of an adult's personal autonomy to attempt such suppression, but this is no reason to prohibit the choice. In addition, although utopian/communal visions may even be commonplace in polyfidelity, there is no evidence to suggest that most polyfidelitous families do contain significantly more than four adult members. As such, they are not likely to have reached the tipping point at which individual autonomy is swallowed by the power of the group. Furthermore, it is not illegal for adults to join a cult. For a mature adult to choose to enter into a polyfidelitous family that has cult potential seems no worse than a mature adult entering a monogamous heterosexual marriage that has domestic abuse potential. Again, it is possibly unwise, but that alone is no reason to prohibit the choice.

If polyfidelity does not coerce teenagers into polyfidelitous relationships, and at worst allows adults to choose membership in a group that will demand unusual self-discipline and may become personally coercive, we may still ask what impact polyfidelity has upon children raised in such families. With no more than anecdotal data, these concerns are mostly speculation. On the positive side, polyfidelitous families may be the "village" that Hillary Clinton says is needed to raise a child (Ravenhart and Ravenhart 1997, 11), providing multiple adult parents to meet the varying needs of children. At the same time, we may ask whether there is any threat to children who live with multiple adults not biologically related to them in the "sex positive" culture of polyamory (Strassberg 2003a, 452–53, 510–17). We know that family members and acquaintances are the chief perpetrators of sexual abuse against children in general and that children living with only one parent have an elevated risk of such abuse (Finkelhor 1994). In polyfidelitous families with children, children live with one or more biologically unrelated adults. However, I do not believe there is a significantly increased risk of sexual abuse for such children arising out of their family structure. In many polyfidelitous families, the adults join the family prior to the birth of the child and consider themselves coequal parents of the child. Such parents are very different from the boyfriends or after-acquired husband of a single mother. In addition, the "sex positive" culture of polyamory could also serve to insulate children from such abuse, as "polyfidelity provides multiple sexual outlets for adult family members. Furthermore, polyfidelity would seem unlikely to attract or tolerate latent pedophiles as family members because pedophiles do not have the adult relationship skills sufficient to survive the pressures and demands of polyfidelity" (Strassberg 2003b, 426).

Finally, a larger number of adult parents may minimize such children's exposure to daycare providers and babysitters, who are other potential perpetrators of child sexual abuse.

A final reason for criminalizing polygyny is its central contribution to the creation of isolated theocratic communities that accumulate considerable economic resources, often at the expense of the women and children who help produce those resources (Strassberg 2003b, 409). Such communities substantially evade federal, state, and local regulation in ways that hurt both vulnerable community members and the larger society as a whole. It is clear that polyfidelity poses no such threats. While some practitioners of polyfidelity may value communal living, they are not ideologically homogeneous and show little tendency to band together to create exclusive and truly independent polities (428–29). Indeed, polyfidelity would wither without access to a large population of people not in such relationships from which to find willing and acceptable partners (428).

Understanding the significant differences between fundamentalist Mormon polygyny and polyfidelity makes it possible to consider whether there is a new version of Mormon polygyny that might be called *emerging Mormon polyfidelity*. These polygynous families appear to be financially, socially, and spiritually independent of the fundamentalist communities. Although the husbands may be at least partially seeking the religious gains of polygyny under Mormon theology, they may also be seeking the sexual variety that characterizes polyfidelity. As independents, they must find their own wives because they are not in a position to be handed the teenage daughters of other members of the community. This independence significantly reduces the likelihood of coercion, although there is at least one example of an independent polygynous husband marrying the daughter from a prior marriage of one of his wives. (Kathleen Tracy 2001, describing Tom Green's marriage to LeeAnn Beagley when she was fifteen.) This example reveals that as long as the religious ideology prescribing polygyny is part of the mix, the potential for coercion will be present.

Furthermore, to the extent that husbands in such emerging Mormon polyfidelity must convince adult "mainstream" women who have grown up in a largely monogamous community and are free to choose monogamous marriage that they want to enter into a marriage in which they will share a husband, such husbands must truly have something to offer. The younger the mainstream woman, the less likely she will settle for a polygynous marriage when the possibility of an exclusive monogamous marriage may be around the corner. Polygyny is more likely to be the backup plan for more mature women who have not been able to marry or whose marriages have terminated through divorce or death. However, even these women must be convinced that this particular polygynous marriage is a good solution to their situation. The aspiring husband must offer sexual charisma, financial stability, the opportunity to have children, and/or a community of sister wives who are compatible with each other and can provide parental and even career support. Even if the inducement were religious, the independence of the aspiring husband and the potential wife would seem to ensure that she makes the kind of voluntary, autonomous choice that requires respect and acceptance.

If such autonomously created Mormon polygynous families can remain independent, avoid coercion in bringing new wives into the family and keeping wives from exiting the family, and provide their children with the education, experience, and opportunities that will allow them to create independent families of their own, whether monogamous or polygamous, the connection between polygyny and coercion will be broken. However, if such families were to merge into polygynous communities that controlled the educational and social exposure of their children, or the patriarchs were to try to streamline the process of finding wives by negotiating with other polygynous patriarchs for their young daughters, we would see that these independent polygynists are just a larval stage of a new theocratic community whose practice of polygyny would become coercive. Rather than being emerging Mormon polyfidelists, they would be nascent fundamentalists who want to be in control of their own community rather than be controlled by an existing patriarch.

The mix of theology and sex in fundamentalist Mormon polygyny is extraordinarily potent, offering men as it does eternal and earthly power as well as sexual control and variety. Whether these independent Mormon polygynous husbands can and are willing to maintain a noncoercive family depends on whether they are polyamorists seeking love from women they respect who just happen to be Mormon or whether they are power-hungry fundamentalists whose desire to begin their own kingdoms requires that they temporarily adopt noncoercive strategies. In truth, only time will tell.

In conclusion, I would note that the modern decriminalization of adultery, fornication, and same-sex relationships has been based on the recognition of sex and love as crucial expressions of liberty. I argue that to the extent liberty arguments are made the basis for decriminalizing polygamy, such arguments support decriminalization of pure polyfidelity much more than of fundamentalist Mormon polygyny. Polyamorous relationships are based on love and sexual attraction. Mormon fundamentalist polygyny is about reproduction and patriarchy. It is not clear at this time what independent Mormon polygyny is really based upon. Either it may be polyfidelity in the Mormon context, or it may be an early stage of fundamentalism. Should it be given an opportunity to prove itself, or would decriminalization in this context just ensure the creation of new coercive theocratic communities in which children and adults alike will be deprived of the very constitutional rights that made their communities possible? If the *Brown* decision stands, we may have a chance to find out.

Similarly, if decriminalization of fundamentalist polygyny is sought on religious grounds, I argue that the extraordinary coercive potential of polygyny shaped by and practiced in the context of fundamentalist Mormon theology should take it out of the protection ordinary religious practice receives under the constitution. The free exercise of religion was not meant to support practices that thoroughly destroy the chance for autonomy of children born into and raised within them.

Notes

1.   An earlier version of this chapter was published under Creative Commons copyright (CC BY NC) in *Families: Beyond the Nuclear Ideal* (London: Bloomsbury, 2014).
2.   Brown v. Buhman, 947 F. Supp. 2d 1170, 1215 (D. Utah 2013), at 1215.
3.   Reference re: Section 293 of the Criminal Code of Canada, BCSC 1588 (2011); *Brown*, at 1234.
4.   United States v. Windsor, 133 S. Ct. 2675 (2013); Obergefell v. Hodges, 135 S.Ct. 2584 (2015).
5.   *Brown*, at 1221.
6.   Ibid., at 1234.
7.   Reynolds v. United States, 98 U.S. 145 (1878), at 166.
8.   *Brown*, at 1221.
9.   Employment Division, Department of Human Resources of Oregon v. Smith, 494 U.S. 872, (1990), at 879, quoting United States v. Lee (1982), at 263 n.3, Stevens, J., concurring in judgment.

References

Bailey, Martha. 2015. "Should Polygamy Be Criminalized?" *Social Science Research Network*. http://dx.doi.org/10.2139/ssrn.1509459.
Bennion, Janet. 1998. *Women of Principle: Female Networking in Contemporary Mormon Polygyny*. Oxford: Oxford University Press.

Chambers, David L. 1997. "Polygamy and Same-Sex Marriage." *Hofstra Law Review* 26 (1): 53–83.

Finkelhor, David. 1994. "Current Information on the Scope and Nature of Child Sexual Abuse." *Future of Children* 4 (2): 31–52. http://dx.doi.org/10.2307/1602522.

Foster, Lawrence. 1981. *Religion and Sexuality: Three American Communal Experiments of the Nineteenth Century.* Oxford: Oxford University Press.

Foster, Lawrence. 1997. *Free Love and Community: John Humphrey Noyes and the Oneida Perfectionists.* Chapel Hill: University of North Carolina Press.

Harris, Dan. 2005. "Hundreds of 'Lost Boys' Expelled by Polygamist Community." *ABC News*, June 15. http://abcnews.go.com/WNT/story?id=851753&page=1.

Nearing, Ryam. 1992. *Loving More: The Polyfidelity Primer.* Captain Cook, HI: PEP.

Nearing, Ryam. 1997. "California Book of the Dead." *Loving More Magazine* 9: 22–23.

Northrop, Barry. 1997. "Threesome Makes It Last." *Best of Loving More* 1: 40–42.

Ravenhart, Rachel Wolfe, and Lady Alia-anor Ravenhart. 1997. "Help! I'm Going to Have a Baby." *Loving More Magazine* 9: 10–11.

Slomiak, Mitchell. 1997. "Community: The Dark Side." *Best of Loving More* 1: 18–26.

Song, Sarah. 2007. *Justice, Gender, and the Politics of Multiculturalism.* Cambridge: Cambridge University Press.

Stacey, Judith, and Tey Meadow. 2009. "New Slants on the Slippery Slope: The Politics of Polygamy and Gay Family Rights in South Africa and the United States." *Politics & Society* 37 (2): 167–202. http://dx.doi.org/10.1177/0032329209333924.

Strassberg, Maura. 1997. "Distinctions of Form or Substance: Monogamy, Polygamy and Same-Sex Marriage." *North Carolina Law Review* 75 (5): 1501–624.

Strassberg, Maura. 2003a. "The Challenge of Post-Modern Polygamy: Considering Polyamory." *Capital University Law Review* 31 (3): 439–563.

Strassberg, Maura. 2003b. "The Crime of Polygamy." *Temple Political and Civil Rights Law Review* 12 (2): 353–431.

Tracy, Kathleen. 2001. *The Secret Story of Polygamy.* Naperville, IL: Sourcebooks.

West, C. 1996. *Lesbian Polyfidelity.* San Francisco: Booklegger.

9

POLYGAMY TODAY
A Case for Qualified Recognition

Sarah Song

Which arguments from the nineteenth-century debate on polygamy, if any, are relevant for the contemporary practice of polygamy among fundamentalist Mormons (members of the Fundamentalist Church of Jesus Christ of Latter-Day Saints [FLDS]) in America or any minority group engaging in the practice in liberal democratic societies?[1] Does the concern for equal protection of women support a case for qualified recognition of polygamy?

With regard to Mormon polygamy today, government officials have largely taken a laissez-faire approach, a departure from their approach in the earlier part of the twentieth century. In 1935, the Utah legislature declared cohabitation with "more than one person of the opposite sex" a criminal felony.[2] Although the code is vaguely worded, this law was invoked in several polygamy cases in the 1930s and 1940s. Using the 1935 legislation on cohabitation, Utah and Arizona authorities took several actions against fundamentalists, including a raid on the Short Creek fundamentalist Mormon community in 1935 and raids on various locales on charges of kidnapping, cohabitation, criminal conspiracy, and white slavery in 1944. The charges of kidnapping and conspiracy were not upheld, but on appeal, the US Supreme Court affirmed convictions based on the Mann or White Slave Traffic Act, which forbids the transportation of women across state lines for immoral purposes. The court focused on the question of whether Mormon polygamy was a practice of debauchery and immorality within the reach of federal law. Drawing upon arguments from nineteenth-century decisions against Mormon polygamy discussed above, Justice William O. Douglas, writing for the majority, affirmed that it was. In his dissent, Justice Frank Murphy introduced an unprecedented pluralistic perspective into the nation's highest court. Murphy called polygamy "one of the basic forms of marriage" and argued that it did not constitute sexual enslavement, nor was it "in the same genus" as

DOI: 10.7330/9780874219975.c009

prostitution or debauchery. Citing anthropological findings that monogamy, polygamy, polyandry, and group marriage were four different forms of marriage practiced by different cultures, Justice Murphy argued that Mormon polygamy was "a form of marriage built upon a set of social and moral principles" and ought to be recognized as such (Cleveland v. US).[3]

State and federal authorities have not followed Murphy's lead and gone as far as recognizing polygamy as a legitimate form of marriage; polygamy is still illegal.[4] In practice, however, government officials have increasingly taken a "don't ask, don't tell" approach toward Mormon polygamy. The last major raid against Mormon polygamy took place in 1953 against the Short Creek community in Arizona. There was much public criticism in reaction to photographs of children being torn from their parents and taken to foster homes (Altman and Ginat 1996). Since then, government officials have taken a more tolerant stance. In 1991, the Utah Supreme Court ruled that polygamous families were eligible to adopt. A leader of the Fundamentalist Church of Jesus Christ of Latter-day Saints hailed the Canadian court decision that overturned the ban on polygamy on grounds of religious freedom as a sign that the United States would soon legalize polygamy.[5] This prediction was supported by then Republican governor Michael O. Leavitt's public statement that polygamy might enjoy protection as a religious freedom. After protests from women who had left polygamous marriages, the governor quickly amended his stance, saying that "plural marriage is wrong, it should stay against the law, and there is no place for it in modern society" (Brooke, *New York Times*, Aug. 23, 1998).

In such a laissez-faire legal climate, the number of individuals living in polygamous families in various communities in Utah and Arizona has increased steadily, and the total number of individuals living in polygamous families is estimated to be between 20,000 and 40,000 (Altman and Ginat 1996).[6] In explaining the reasons these communities are growing and the reasons few people exit, anthropologists Irwin Altman and Joseph Ginat suggest that the main reason appears to be religious devotion. Mormon fundamentalists are committed to the founding doctrines regarding plural marriage. In speculating about whether there are sexual motives, Altman and Ginat contend that for men, "any sexual motives must surely pall after a while, as the day-to-day pressures of plural family life cumulate—the financial burdens, the needs of large families, family tensions and conflicts" (Altman and Ginat 1996, 439). They add that the widespread occurrences in American society of serial marriages and divorces, cohabitation of unmarried couples, and affairs and mistresses appear much simpler and more "romantic."

MORMON WOMEN'S PERSPECTIVES

For Mormon women today, as in the nineteenth century, there are strong economic motivations to enter and remain within polygamous relationships. While many women convert to fundamentalism on the grounds that they've discovered the true and underlying basis of Mormonism, many are also divorcées or widows in need of economic support. These women gain "the security of a community and family, the support and assistance of other women, someone to care for their children, and a highly structured set of roles with respect to their husband and children" (Altman and Ginat 1996, 440). Women who enter polygamous marriages tend to be women seeking economic security; for them, conversion to the group is usually followed by striking upward social and economic mobility. Janet Bennion notes that the Mormon fundamentalist group provides "lower-class female recruits" the chance to "ascend to a position of higher marriage (hypergamy)" and a higher level of economic satisfaction than male recruits to Mormon fundamentalism (Bennion 1998).[7] Bennion finds that, compared to women from the mainstream LDS church, Mormon fundamentalist women participate more in social and religious work and also pursue paid work outside the home at higher rates. She argues that polygyny "develops independent women who bear much of the financial responsibility for their families." But her study also finds that men in these communities seek to counteract egalitarian values from the wider society with harsher rules and restrictions for women (Bennion 1998).[8]

If we listen to what Mormon women themselves are saying about polygamy, we find a contested practice. On one side is Tapestry of Polygamy, a group of former polygamous wives, who support the legal ban on polygamy and favor its strong enforcement. They argue that de facto accommodation of polygamy reinforces women's subordination within fundamentalist Mormon communities. On the other side are women living in polygamous relationships, such as members of the Women's Religious Liberties Union, who favor decriminalization of polygamy in the name of religious freedom. They also argue that polygamous arrangements are good for women because they allow them to pursue both career and family by sharing childcare and household responsibilities. A website they maintain denounces forced marriage and incest and, echoing the sentiments of Elizabeth Cady Stanton and Susan B. Anthony, states that "abuse is not inherent in polygamy and can exist in any society" (Batchelor, Watson, and Wilde 2000).[9] Non-Mormons have also made secular arguments in favor of polygamy. In contrasting monogamy and polygamy, one advocate maintains that frequent divorce and remarriage, separation of children from parents, multiplication of step-relationships, and a total breakdown of paternal responsibility suggest that the institution of serial monogamy is in serious trouble and may be no better than polygamy per se (Kilbride 1994).[10]

A CASE FOR QUALIFIED RECOGNITION

What then is the appropriate response to the contemporary practice of polygamy? The charge that polygamous relationships are oppressive is contingent and needs to be investigated by looking at individual relationships and their contexts, just as monogamous relationships should be. The importance of polygamy for Mormon fundamentalists must be weighed against protecting the basic rights of Mormon women and children. On the one hand, liberal democracies should respect people's religious liberty and the liberty to pursue the kinds of intimate relationships that accord with their convictions and desires.[11] Mormon fundamentalists maintain that polygamy is of great importance to their beliefs and way of life. If Mormon women maintain that they have freely chosen to remain in polygamous marriage in accordance with their religious convictions, the state should respect their choices but on the condition that they are free to exit. However, determining whether women have realistic rights of exit is no easy matter; it requires consideration of the sorts of conditions necessary for genuine consent and exit, as well as contextual inquiry to see whether such conditions obtain in any given case.

Exit has recently received considerable attention as a solution to the problem of vulnerable internal minorities. Some liberal political theorists defend toleration of illiberal religious and cultural groups, endorsing a principle of state nonintervention when these groups meet certain minimal conditions necessary for exit.[12] The central claim here is that religious and cultural groups should be let alone so long as membership in these groups is voluntary—not voluntary in the sense that a religious belief and cultural attachments are experienced as choices, but rather in the sense that individual members can, if they wish, exit groups. The appeal of exit as a solution to the problem of vulnerable internal minorities has not only to do with providing vulnerable members with a way to escape internal oppression but also with the transformative potential that the *threat* of exit can have. As Albert O. Hirschman famously argued, the threat of exit can enhance one's voice in decision making (Hirschman 1970). In the context of minority groups, the idea is that if many members can credibly threaten to exit the group on account of their disagreement with particular aspects of group life, the group's leaders would be compelled to reform those aspects. In the Mormon polygamy case, if the threat of exit by women opposed to polygamous marriage was serious enough, it could compel group leaders to reform their marriage practices or to abolish polygamy altogether.

While exit is a real option for members of many religious and cultural minority groups in contemporary America, whether it really is a choice in any particular case depends on the costs of exit and the nature of the group in question. Describing people's convictions and attachments as voluntary seems appropriate against, as Nancy Rosenblum puts it, "a background of fluid pluralism, where other religious homes are open to splitters and the formation of new associations is a real possibility." So long as members are free to exit, religious and cultural associations need not be congruent with public norms and institutions "all the way down" (Rosenblum 1998, 85, 4).

But how far down state intervention will have to go in order to ensure realistic rights of exit for vulnerable internal minorities is an open question. First is the issue of how isolated or open the group is to the wider society. Groups that are relatively isolated and that socialize their members into the inevitability of sex hierarchy, as may well be the case with Mormon fundamentalist communities, are especially worrisome. There is also the issue of the costs of exit—not just the material costs of leaving but also intrinsic and social costs. Leaving means losing not just the cultural or religious affiliations themselves and the intrinsic value they hold for members (intrinsic costs) but also the social relationships afforded by membership (associative costs). In addition, there may be extrinsic costs of educational and employment opportunities or other material benefits associated with membership (Barry 2001).[13] There is not much the state or the wider society can do about intrinsic or associative costs, but it can assist those trying to leave their communities with the extrinsic costs of exit.

Feminist political theorist Susan Okin's criticism of the strategy of exit highlights a different kind of obstacle having to do with the *capacity* for exit, conditions of knowledge and psychology, which require a different sort of response than providing material resources. In many minority groups, there may be strong countervailing pressures that undermine the capacity for exit for women, and girls in particular. Okin highlights three such pressures: girls are much more likely to be shortchanged than boys in education; they are more likely to be socialized in ways that undermine their self-esteem and that encourage them to defer to existing hierarchies; and they are likely to be forced into early marriages from which they lack the power to exit (Okin 1999, 128; 2002, 216–22).

Under such conditions, women and girls within religious groups can hardly be said to enjoy a realistic right of exit.

These concerns suggest the need to think carefully about the sorts of conditions under which women can genuinely make free choices to stay or leave and what the state can do to foster those conditions. Minimal standards necessary to ensure the worth of a right of exit include members' freedom from abuse and coercion; access to decent healthcare, nutrition, and education; and the existence of genuine alternatives among which to make choices, including real access to a mainstream society to exit to (Spinner-Halev 2000).[14] To address the concerns about capacity raised by Okin, education must play a key role. Children should be taught about their basic constitutional and civic rights so they know that liberty of conscience exists in their society and that apostasy is not a legal crime.

Some argue that even these minimal standards are too robust and that the existence of a surrounding market society is all that is required for exit to be a meaningful option (Kukathas 2003).[15] But such an approach overlooks the serious obstacles to exit that the state can help ameliorate and assumes that any state action to address these obstacles would be worse in terms of violating basic individual freedoms (especially freedom of association) than leaving vulnerable members to cope on their own. This minimalist position is right to stress that states have historically oppressed minority groups. But the fact of past oppression of minority groups should not rule out state involvement to address contemporary problems. For some individual members of minority groups, a group's leadership and authority may be experienced as more oppressive than state authorities. Here the state can play a role in protecting the basic rights of individuals. Giving a role to the state does not mean any form of intervention goes; rather, the state's role should be limited to meeting the minimal conditions necessary for exit.

What do these considerations about exit suggest for the contemporary case of Mormon polygamy? A legal regime of qualified recognition of polygamy can, I think, more effectively ensure Mormon women's rights to exit their communities than would outright proscription of polygamy. The current ban on polygamy leaves polygamous wives and their children even more vulnerable to domination by driving polygamous communities into hiding. In May 2001, Tom Green, a husband of five and father of twenty-nine, was convicted on four counts of bigamy, the first prosecution of polygamy since 1953. Green's conviction has caused anxiety among some members of polygamous communities. They fear prosecution of polygamy will discourage a group's most vulnerable members from reporting abuse of women and children. As Anne Wilde, who has been in a polygamous marriage for thirty-two years, put it, "This has pushed people a little further underground." She adds that the Green case had done a major disservice to the estimated 30,000 polygamists who live in Utah and neighboring states by presenting a false image of their chosen way of life. They contend that Green is an anomaly among polygamists for having wives and children in far greater numbers than average polygamist husbands. A more common family includes two to three wives and eight to ten children. Even worse, she says, the separate charge of child rape against Mr. Green for having one wife who was thirteen at the time of their marriage may leave the impression that all polygamist husbands marry under-age girls and abuse children when in fact most do not. Sidney Anderson, director of the Women's Religious Liberties Union, also argues that fear of prosecution for polygamy almost assures that when child abuse does happen, it is more likely to go unreported: "The state is forcing them into an abusive situation, and some men are using it to convince women that they have to live in isolation for the unit to be safe. So women who need help can't get it out of fear." Ms. Anderson argues that the best way to help vulnerable members within polygamous communities is to decriminalize bigamy altogether, which would make it easier for members of plural families to seek help when they need it (Janofsky, *New York Times*, May 24, 2001).

A strategy of qualified recognition of polygamy was pursued in reforming the customary marriage laws in South Africa, and this case is instructive for the case of Mormon polygamy. Drawing on provisions in the South African Constitution, reformers sought simultaneously to respect customary law and protect women's rights (Chambers 2000, 101–24; Deveaux 2003, 780–807).[16] On the one hand, the constitution recognizes the rights of cultural and religious groups, including various systems of customary African law. On the other hand, it specifies equal individual rights and prohibits racial and sexual discrimination, among other forms of discrimination. In the discussions leading up to reform, many different groups were consulted, including the traditional leaders' congress, women's groups, legal-reform groups, and scholars of constitutional and customary law. The actual lived practices of customary marriage were at the center of discussion. The chiefs were persuaded that reforming the customary marriage laws was less likely to erode their authority than retaining traditional customary marriage laws.

What emerged from the deliberations was the Recognition of Customary Marriages Act of 1998. It recognizes all past customary unions as marriages while also reforming customary marriage itself. The law declares women and men formal equals within marriage and grants the state a role in regulating customary marriage. The law requires all marriages to be registered with a government agency, and it requires that divorce and child custody proceedings be conducted by a family-court judge, as opposed to a tribal court. Customary groups are permitted to retain *lobolo* (bride price) as a condition of valid marriage, and polygyny is preserved in a modified form. In order to take a second wife, a man must make a written contract with his existing wife fairly dividing the property accrued at that point and persuade a family court that the contract is fair for all involved.[17]

Qualified recognition of polygamy, as in the case of the modified customary marriage law in South Africa, can offer Mormon women the protection of the law while also respecting their religious commitments. If the law were to recognize polygamy, it could secure legal rights for polygamous wives and ex-wives by regulating the conditions of entry into and exit from such relations. As in the South African case, the state might require a man seeking an additional wife to obtain the consent of his existing wife and to draw up a contract that fairly divides the property they have accrued at that point. If she approved, the couple would then have to obtain the approval of a family court judge. A state that recognizes polygamy could also secure rights for ex-wives and the rights of inheritance for children of polygamous relationships by regulating the terms of property division after divorce. Currently, a polygamous husband in the United States may abandon any wife beyond his first without providing any assistance to her and her children. Securing Mormon wives' exit rights could help strengthen their voice within polygamous relationships.

Utah authorities have moved toward a de facto regime of qualified recognition. They have shifted away from prosecuting polygamy per se toward cracking down on abuses that occur within polygamous marriages. The Utah attorney general publicly advised prosecutors to avoid prosecuting cases of consensual adult bigamy. Instead, Utah authorities have reached a consensus to crack down on child abuse, statutory rape, and incest. In 1998, the Utah legislature raised the age for statutory rape to seventeen from sixteen. In 1999, the legislature raised the minimum marriage age from fourteen to sixteen.[18] The attorney general said he planned to ask the state legislature for money to hire additional investigators for matters relating to "closed societies" so that more traditional crimes do not go unpunished. He favors reducing the charge of bigamy from a felony to a misdemeanor in order to encourage people to provide information about serious crimes in polygamous families (Janofsky, *New York Times*, May 24, 2001).[19] These reforms may stem more from the practical difficulties of prosecuting polygamy: as in the nineteenth century, polygamous men generally obtain marriage licenses only for their first wives, and subsequent marriages are performed secretly. But in addition to these prudential concerns, there are principled arguments in favor of decriminalization. The public-morals argument pressed by nineteenth-century antipolygamy activists, that polygamy was offensive to Christian public morals, does not offer a compelling reason, but the other argument, the concern for equal protection, does. We have good reasons to think that qualified recognition of polygamy can better protect the basic rights of Mormon women and children in polygamous households than can a ban on polygamy.

Notes

1. For discussion of nineteenth-century arguments against polygamy, see chapter 1, "Polygamy in Nineteenth Century America" (Song, chapter 1, this volume).
2. The Utah penal code states, "If any person cohabits with more than one person of the opposite sex, such a person is guilty of a felony" (Utah Criminal Code, chapter 112, Section 103-51-2).
3. Cleveland v. US, 329 US 14 (1946), at 24–29.
4. The Utah Criminal Code states, "A person is guilty of bigamy when, knowing he has a husband or wife or knowing the other person has a husband or wife, the person purports to marry another person or cohabits with another person." Bigamy is a felony of the third degree (Utah Criminal Code, 76-7-101). The Utah Constitution also states, "Perfect toleration of religious sentiment is guaranteed. No inhabitant of this State shall ever be molested in person or property on account of his or her mode of religious worship; but polygamous or plural marriages are forever prohibited" (Article III, § 2).
5. The Canadian case involved a small group in British Columbia affiliated with the fundamentalists of Hildale, Utah, and Colorado City, Arizona (*Salt Lake Tribune*, June 16, 1992).
6. Altman and Ginat estimate between 20,000 and 50,000 (Altman and Ginat 1996, 51, 54).
7. Janet Bennion (1998, 64–65) finds that of the women who converted to the Allred fundamentalist Mormon group, 69 percent (706 women) had graduated from high school, and of that number, 12 percent (143) had earned a college degree. Overall, most women who became plural wives and who worked for wages were low-skilled workers.
8. At least 25 percent of the women Bennion interviewed expressed desire to leave if they could do so without losing their children (Bennion 1998, 134, 136, 151–52).
9. See Batchelor, Watson, and Wilde (2000) and http://www.principlevoices.org.
10. See Philip Leroy Kilbride (1994).
11. Laurence Tribe has long maintained, on civil libertarian grounds, that polygamy should be constitutionally protected and has predicted for the last two decades that *Reynolds* would be overruled (Tribe 1988: 521–28).
12. See William Galston (2002), Chandran Kukathas (2003), Nancy L. Rosenblum (1998), Ayelet Shachar (2001), and Jeff Spinner-Halev (2000, 2005).
13. For discussion of different types of exit costs, see Brian Barry (2001, 150–51).

208   SARAH SONG

14.   Other specific proposals include an exit fund to which group members must contribute to enable members to meet the economic costs of exit should they decide to leave (Spinner-Halev 2000, 77–79) and state regulation of the economic aspects of divorce in the context of legal pluralistic arrangements (Shachar, 2001, 124–25, 134–35).
15.   See, e.g., Kukathas 2003.
16.   Here I draw on David L. Chambers (2000) and Monique Deveaux (2003).
17.   Deveaux, "Deliberative Approach," 112–13.
18.   Utah Statutes, §76, Ch. 5, 401.2; §30, Ch. 1, 9.
19.   Janofsky, "Conviction of a Polygamist" (*New York Times*, May 24, 2001). In contrast to the case of Tom Green, in the more recent case of Warren Jeffs, the leader of the Fundamentalist Church of Jesus Christ of Latter-Day Saints, state authorities are not charging him with bigamy itself but with being an accessory to rape by arranging marriages between under-age girls and older men (Maria Newman, *New York Times*, Sept. 1, 2006, A12).

References

Altman, Irwin, and Joseph Ginat. 1996. *Polygamous Families in Contemporary Society*. Cambridge: Cambridge University Press. http://dx.doi.org/10.1017/CBO97805 11663987.
Barry, Brian. 2001. *Culture and Equality: An Egalitarian Critique of Multiculturalism*. Cambridge: Harvard University Press.
Batchelor, Mary, Marianne Watson, and Anne Wilde. 2000. *Voices in Harmony: Contemporary Women Celebrate Plural Marriage*. Salt Lake City: Principle Voices.
Bennion, Janet. 1998. *Women of Principle: Female Networking in Contemporary Mormon Polygyny*. Oxford: Oxford University Press.
Chambers, David L. 2000. "Civilizing the Natives: Marriage in Post-Apartheid South Africa." *Daedalus: Journal of the American Academy of Arts and Sciences* 129 (4): 101–24.
Deveaux, Monique. 2003. "A Deliberative Approach to Conflicts of Culture." *Political Theory* 31 (6): 780–807. http://dx.doi.org/10.1177/0090591703256685.
Galston, William. 2002. *Liberal Pluralism: The Implications of Value Pluralism for Political Theory and Practice*. Cambridge: Cambridge University Press. http://dx.doi.org/10 .1017/CBO9780511613579.
Hirschman, Albert O. 1970. *Exit, Voice, and Loyalty: Responses to Decline in Firms, Organizations, and States*. Cambridge: Harvard University Press.
Kilbride, Philip Leroy. 1994. *Plural Marriage for Our Times: A Reinvented Option?* Westport, CT: Bergin and Garvey.
Kukathas, Chandran. 2003. *The Liberal Archipelago: A Theory of Diversity and Freedom*. Oxford: Oxford University Press. http://dx.doi.org/10.1093/019925754X.001.0001.
Okin, Susan Moller. 1999. *Is Multiculturalism Bad for Women?* edited by Joshua Cohen, Matthew Howard, and Martha C. Nussbaum. Princeton: Princeton University Press.
Okin, Susan Moller. 2002. "Mistresses of Their Own Destiny: Group Rights, Gender, and Realistic Rights of Exit." *Ethics* 112 (2): 205–30. http://dx.doi.org/10.1086/324645.
Rosenblum, Nancy L. 1998. *Membership and Morals: The Personal Uses of Pluralism in America*. Princeton: Princeton University Press.
Shachar, Avelet. 2001. *Multicultural Jurisdictions: Cultural Differences and Women's Rights*. Cambridge: Cambridge University Press.
Spinner-Halev, Jeff. 2000. *Surviving Diversity: Religion and Democratic Citizenship*. Baltimore: Johns Hopkins University Press.

Spinner-Halev, Jeff. 2005. "Autonomy, Association, and Pluralism." In *Minorities within Minorities*, edited by Avigail Eisenberg and Jeff Spinner-Halev, 157–71. Cambridge: Cambridge University Press. http://dx.doi.org/10.1017/CBO9780511490224.008.

Tribe, Laurence H. 1988. *American Constitutional Law*. 2nd ed. New York: Foundation Press.

10

SHOULD POLYGAMY BE A CRIME?

Martha Bailey

INTRODUCTION

The Canadian province of British Columbia is home to a community of fundamentalist Mormons (members of the Fundamentalist Church of Jesus Christ of Latter-Day Saints) who practice plural marriage. This community has attracted extensive negative media coverage, and there have been calls to address identified problems in the community in part by enforcing the criminal law prohibition of polygamy (Bramham 2008).[1] Charges eventually were laid against two patriarchs of the fundamentalist group. However, after the appointment of a special prosecutor to pursue the charges was quashed because of irregularities, these charges were stayed. Rather than attempting again to lay criminal charges, the British Columbia government instead sought an advisory opinion from its Supreme Court, a trial court that also has jurisdiction to hear and consider questions referred to it by the provincial government (Blackmore v. British Columbia 2009).[2]

Two questions have been put to British Columbia's Supreme Court:

(1) Is section 293 of the Criminal Code of Canada consistent with the Canadian Charter of Rights and Freedoms?

(2) If not, what particular or particulars and to what extent? What are the necessary elements of the offense in section 293 of the Criminal Code of Canada? Without limiting this question, does section 293 require that the polygamy or conjugal union in question involved a minor, or occurred in a context of dependence, exploitation, abuse of authority, a gross imbalance of power, or undue influence? On November 23, 2011, the British Columbia trial court upheld Canada's anti-polygamy law (*Reference re: Criminal Code* 2010, para. 9).

Although some of this paper touches on the main question in the reference, it does not use constitutional analysis. Instead of considering whether it is constitutionally permissible for Canada to criminalize

DOI: 10.7330/9780874219975.c010

polygamy, I assess the wisdom of criminalization. My conclusion is that criminalization is unwise. Regardless of whether the existing provision passes constitutional muster, I argue that Canada should put aside its efforts to criminally sanction polygamy and instead focus on addressing directly the harms often associated with polygamy.

The starting point for my argument that polygamy should not be criminalized is that Canada is a monogamous country and I assume it will remain so. Only monogamous marriages may take place in Canada. The Civil Marriage Act defines marriage as between two people (Civil Marriage Act 2005).[3] A married person cannot marry again unless the existing marriage is dissolved by death or divorce, and any marriage by a person who has a prior subsisting marriage is void. Bigamy is a crime. My view is that Canada's "cultural commitment to monogamous marriage" is sufficiently protected by the civil laws of marriage and the criminal prohibition of bigamy (Berger 2008).[4] Advocates of maintaining Canada's criminal provision on polygamy seem to mistakenly assume that without this provision, Canada would become a polygamous country or would somehow be endorsing polygamy, but this is not the case. There are many monogamous countries in the world, including Britain, Canada's "mother country," that do not criminalize polygamy. The criminal provision on polygamy is not needed to bolster Canada's character as a monogamous country.

Furthermore, the provision is problematically broad and inconsistent with the general approach in Canada to moral offenses. Supporters of the provision argue that it may assist us in addressing the harms associated with polygamy, particularly harms relating to the exploitation and abuse of women and children. My view is that Canada's criminal provision on polygamy is not an effective tool for addressing those harms and may even exacerbate some problems.

My discussion of Canada's polygamy law begins with a review of other moral offenses addressed in the Criminal Code. This review provides context to the discussion and is intended to support my claim that the polygamy provision is inconsistent with Canada's general approach to moral offenses. I then examine the polygamy provision and identify problems of overinclusiveness. In the next section, I consider whether the polygamy provision should be retained in order to address problems relating to closed communities, to prevent harms to children or women, or to maintain current immigration policies that deny admission to those who would practice polygamy in Canada. My conclusions are that the polygamy provision is not effective in dealing with problematic closed communities or preventing harms to children or women. The provision does play a role in the immigration system because of the way the immigration statute is structured, but current immigration policy could be maintained by an amendment to the immigration statute. In a final section of the paper, I identify some terminological confusions that have arisen in discussions about polygamy and offer some clarifications.

THE CRIMINAL LAW AND SEXUAL ACTIVITIES

In *Lawrence v. Texas* (2003),[5] the US Supreme Court overruled its prior decision in *Bowers v. Hardwick* (1986)[6] and held that the Texas statute criminalizing sodomy was unconstitutional because it violated the due process clause. In his vehemently dissenting opinion, Justice Scalia darkly warned the majority that "state laws against bigamy, same-sex marriage, adult incest, prostitution, masturbation, adultery, fornication, bestiality, and obscenity are likewise sustainable only in light of *Bowers's* validation of laws based on moral choices." This (rather surprising) list of moral offenses dates from the early years of American settlement. As Justice Jack L. Landau commented in *State v. Ciancelli*: "Early colonists, particularly new England puritans, devoted an extraordinary amount of energy to the regulation not only of public immorality, but also of entirely private sexual conduct, including adultery, fornication, buggery, and—with particular zeal bestiality" (2002).[7]

Canada has never had the same appetite for criminalizing private sexual activity as seemingly have at least some of the US states. Neither adultery nor fornication (nor masturbation!) were criminalized here, except insofar as such activity harms children. And back in 1968, Parliament, agreeing with Pierre Trudeau that "there's no place for the state in the bedrooms of the nation," repealed the old criminal prohibition of sodomy. For the most part, Canada does not criminalize noncommercial sexual activities carried out between two consenting adults in private.[8]

As for noncommercial private sexual activities involving *more* than two consenting adults, the only explicit prohibition is in regard to anal intercourse, which must involve the presence of only two people to avoid sanction under s. 159. Even this limitation must be viewed in light of the Supreme Court of Canada ruling that group sex (perhaps involving anal intercourse?) among consenting adults who had joined a private swingers club for the purpose of exchanging partners and participating in group sex was not "indecent," and therefore the operator of the club was not guilty of keeping a "common bawdy-house."[9] The chief justice described the club activities as follows:

A number of mattresses were scattered about the floor of the apartment. There people engaged in acts of cunnilingus, masturbation, fellatio and penetration. On several occasions observed by the police, a single woman engaged in sex with several men, while other men watched and masturbated. Entry to the club and participation in the activities were voluntary. No one was forced to do anything or watch anything. No one was paid for sex. While men considerably outnumbered women on the occasions when the police visited, there is no suggestion that any of the women were there involuntarily or that they did not willingly engage in the acts of group sex. (R. v. Labaye 2005)[10]

However unsavory, the swingers club activities did not amount to "indecency" within the meaning of the Criminal Code. The chief justice concluded that "consensual conduct behind code-locked doors can hardly be supposed to jeopardize a society as vigorous and tolerant as Canadian society" (R. v. Labaye 2005).[11]

Clearly then, Canada is tolerant of private noncommercial sexual activities among consenting adults. The major exception to this general rule of tolerance is incest. According to the Criminal Code, "Everyone commits incest who, knowing that another person is by blood relationship his or her parent, child, brother, sister, grandparent or grandchild, as the case may be, has sexual intercourse with that person" (Criminal Code n.d.).[12] Incest is a crime even when the act takes place in private between consenting adults (R. v. R.P.).[13]

At first blush, the Criminal Code provision on incest seems to mirror the law governing capacity to marry. If it did so, it would support extending to Canada the following description of US regulation of sexual activity: "Historically, criminal law and family law have worked in tandem to produce a binary view of intimate life that categorizes intimate acts and choices as either legitimate marital behavior or illegitimate criminal behavior" (Murray 2009).[14] But this statement, however applicable to the United States, has never been true of Canada, where the space for sexual activities that are "neither marital nor criminal" has always been larger than in some US states (Murray 2009).[15] For example, adultery is not a crime, but adulterers by definition are not married to one another and are not free to marry because of the prior existing marriage. Even in regard to incest, there is space for sexual activities that are neither criminal nor marital.

In order to identify the "law-free" zone of incestuous relationships, it is necessary to turn to the Marriage (Prohibited Degrees) Act, which provides an exhaustive list of the relatives one may not marry: "No person shall marry another person if they are related lineally, or as brother or sister or half-brother or half-sister, including by adoption" (S. C.

1990).[16] This statute substantially reduced the restrictions on marrying relatives. Today, stepfathers and adult stepdaughters (or stepsons), aunts and adult nephews (or nieces), and so forth, are not subject to any criminal sanctions for engaging in sexual activity, and their family relationship is not an impediment to marriage.[17] But there remains a law-free zone of relationships neither sanctioned as marriages nor criminalized. The current restrictions on marriage include adoptive relationships, whereas the Criminal Code provision applies only to blood relationships. Therefore adoptive parents or grandparents and their (adult) children or grandchildren, or adoptive siblings, are not subject to criminal sanctions for having sexual intercourse, but they are not able to marry.

In summary, Canada, for the most part, does not intrude into the bedrooms of the nation by imposing criminal sanctions for private, noncommercial sexual activity among consenting adults. Behaviors such as adultery, group sex, and sexual relations between adoptive fathers and their adult children may be considered immoral or repugnant to many or most Canadians, but these activities are not crimes. That sexual activity is not criminalized does *not* mean the activity is necessarily legalized in the sense of governed by marriage law or otherwise deemed acceptable or in any way endorsed. In Canada, it is *not* the case that "sexual acts and choices are categorized as either legitimate (marriage) or illegitimate (crime)" (Murray 2009).[18] There is a law-free space within which parties may engage in sexual activity without criminal sanction but are not permitted to marry.

THE CRIMINAL LAW AND CONJUGAL RELATIONSHIPS

The Criminal Code includes five offenses under the heading Offences against Conjugal Rights. These five offenses are bigamy (s. 290), procuring a feigned marriage (s. 292), polygamy (s. 293), pretending to solemnize marriages without legal authority (s. 294), and solemnizing a marriage that contravenes the law (s. 295).

Putting aside the provision on polygamy, these "offences against conjugal rights" have long historical roots, stemming from a time in English history when the legal and social significance of marriage was far greater than it is today. The rules regarding the creation of legal marriages were uncertain and in flux. Families, the state, and the church were accorded far greater control over marriages. Divorce was largely unavailable. In this context, clandestine marriages and irregular marriages (bigamous, incestuous, or involving minors) were a problem.[19] Drawing on criminal provisions first enacted in Britain from the early seventeenth century, Canada first enacted its own criminal laws on bigamy shortly after confederation in 1869 (*Offenses* 1869),[20] on procuring or assisting in procuring a feigned marriage in 1886 (An Act to Punish 1886),[21] on solemnizing a marriage without legal authority in 1886 (An Act Respecting s.1 1886),[22] and on solemnizing a marriage that contravenes the law in 1886 (An Act Respecting s.1 1886).[23]

Canada's bigamy law now provides:

(1) Every one commits bigamy who (a) in Canada, (i) being married, goes through a form of marriage with another person, (ii) knowing that another person is married, goes through a form of marriage with that person, or (iii) on the same day or simultaneously, goes through a form of marriage with more than one person; or (b) being a Canadian citizen resident in Canada leaves Canada with intent to do anything mentioned in subparagraphs (a)(i) to (iii) and, pursuant thereto, does outside Canada anything mentioned in those subparagraphs in circumstances mentioned therein.

(2) No person commits bigamy by going through a form of marriage if (a) that person in good faith and on reasonable grounds believes that his spouse is dead; (b) the spouse of that person has been continuously absent from him for seven years immediately preceding the time when he goes through the form of marriage, unless he knew that his spouse was alive at any time during those seven years; (c) that person has been divorced from the bond of the first marriage; or (d) the former marriage has been declared void by a court of competent jurisdiction.

(3) Where a person is alleged to have committed bigamy, it is not a defense that the parties would, if unmarried, have been incompetent to contract marriage under the law of the place where the offense is alleged to have been committed.

(4) Every marriage or form of marriage shall, for the purpose of this section, be deemed to be valid unless the accused establishes that it was invalid.

(5) No act or omission on the part of an accused who is charged with bigamy invalidates a marriage or form of marriage that is otherwise valid.

Bigamy was first made a criminal offense in England in 1603.[24] Prior to this it was an ecclesiastical offense. England's criminal provision in bigamy law was aimed at deceptive conduct. It punished those who bigamously married an innocent victim and also couples who sought social acceptance or some other advantage by entering into a bigamous marriage. In these cases, the existence of a prior marriage was kept secret from the innocent spouse or society at large or both.[25] The bigamy law did not address open polygamy, although polygamy was practiced and discussed in Europe at the time (Chapman 2001).[26] England did not criminalize polygamy in the sense of open, ongoing cohabitation of multiple parties, only bigamy.

Canada's criminal provision on polygamy was not imported from England or France. It was first enacted in 1890 in response to the criminalization of polygamy in the United States and the potential move of American Mormons to Canada (An Act Further 1890).[27] Parliamentary debates and the wording of the provision itself indicate that the law was aimed at Mormons. Indeed, one early unreported case apparently ruled that it applied only to Mormons (R. v. Liston 1893),[28] although in fact the law was subsequently applied to a native Canadian who had two wives in accordance with tribal customary law (The Queen 1899).[29] The references to religion have been expunged, and the current Canadian polygamy provision states:

> (1) Everyone who (a) practices or enters into or in any manner agrees or consents to practice or enter into (i) any form of polygamy, or (ii) any kind of conjugal union with more than one person at the same time, whether or not it is by law recognized as a binding form of marriage, or (b) celebrates, assists or is a party to a rite, ceremony, contract or consent that purports to sanction a relationship mentioned in subparagraph (a)(i) or (ii), is guilty of an indictable offense and liable to imprisonment for a term not exceeding five years.
>
> (2) Where an accused is charged with an offense under this section, no averment or proof of the method by which the alleged relationship was entered into, agreed to or consented to is necessary in the indictment or on the trial of the accused, nor is it necessary on the trial to prove that the persons who are alleged to have entered into the relationship had or intended to have sexual intercourse.

The provision is very broad. It does not contain the limitation included in the US Uniform Model Penal Code provision on polygamy, which states,

> A person is guilty of polygamy, a felony of the third degree, if he marries or cohabits with more than one spouse at a time in purported exercise of the right of plural marriage. The offense is a continuing one until all cohabitation and claim of marriage into (a) any form of polygamy; or (b) any kind of conjugal union with more than one person at the same time; or (c) what among the persons commonly called Mormons is known as spiritual or plural marriage; or (d) who lives, cohabits, or agrees or consent to live or cohabit, in any kind of conjugal union with a person who is married to another or others in any kind of conjugal union . . . is guilty of a misdemeanor, and liable to imprisonment for five years and to a fine of five hundred dollars.

On its face, the Canadian provision applies to visitors to Canada who have a valid foreign polygamous marriage. Canada is a monogamous country, but its public policy against polygamy does not require exposing such visitors to the risk of criminal prosecution. There is no obvious state interest in prosecuting transient parties to a polygamous marriage.[30] The provision applies to all parties to the relationship. It is not limited to blameworthy patriarchs who use their position of authority to acquire multiple wives. It applies to the women as well, and a policy not to charge the women may answer this concern. Yet the provision does cast the women as outlaws. There is reason to believe that some polygamous families may be isolated and suspicious of government intervention. Casting all members, including the victims, as criminals may exacerbate the isolation and suspicion and thereby impede efforts to provide assistance to vulnerable members.

The provision applies to cases involving adults who freely choose to carry on conjugal relationships with multiple parties. It is not limited to cases involving minors or in which any of the parties lack the capacity to consent for any reason. In addition, it appears to criminalize consensual egalitarian polyamorous relationships (Criminal Code 2010).[31] In light of the fact that the state has largely withdrawn from the bedrooms of the nation, it is difficult to see the rationale for intervening in cases of polygamy involving only consenting adults. Such intervention is particularly hard to justify because the crime described in section 293 is difficult to distinguish from adultery, which is not a crime. Because Canadians can carry on adulterous relationships or join swingers clubs without criminal penalty, it cannot credibly be claimed that carrying on conjugal relationships with multiple parties is so violative of our social norms that, like incest, it must be criminalized even when it involves only consenting adults (R. v. Labaye 2005).[32]

CLOSED COMMUNITIES

Closed communities isolated from mainstream society, particularly those led by patriarchs who control the resources and sexuality of the members and sustained by religious or cult beliefs, have a sorry history (Barlow 2006).[33] Whether or not polygamy is a feature of such closed communities, there may be concerns about abuse of vulnerable people, particularly children, trapped in such communities, and fragile souls who may be drawn to such groups. Governments wanting to address apparent abuses in such communities are greatly challenged. Efforts to rescue vulnerable people from closed communities may have the effect of drawing the group closer together; some ham-fisted government interventions have been self-defeating or of questionable effect (Reavis 1995).[34] Even those within the group who perceive problems and would like outside assistance may be distressed by what they perceive as overly zealous or unfair targeting of the community. The reactions of closed communities that practice polygamy to aggressive criminal enforcement efforts are referred to in the handbook for law-enforcement officials published jointly by the Utah and Arizona attorneys general:

> The fundamentalists adapted to a secret, underground lifestyle to avoid prosecution and what they perceived as persecution from the "world." Mass arrests were made in some polygamous communities in 1935 and 1944, culminating in the largest raid of that era occurring in 1953, when more than 100 officers descended upon short creek (now Hildale, Utah and Colorado City, Arizona) in an aggressive crusade to stamp out polygamy. The husbands were arrested, while the panicked women and children were bussed to southern Arizona. Images of crying children being torn from the arms of polygamous mothers triggered a public relations backlash. Recently, a community-wide raid took place in the FLDS community near Eldorado, Texas, in April of 2008. Although this raid did not occur in Utah or Arizona, many of the families involved had recently relocated to Texas expressly to distance themselves from perceived persecution. These events have resulted in deep scars among fundamentalist Mormons and helped foster a fear of government agencies and a distrust of "outsiders." (Utah Attorney 2009)[35]

The current strategy outlined in the Utah/Arizona handbook is to increase efforts to enforce laws when child abuse, domestic violence, or fraud is alleged, rather than prosecuting for bigamy, or polygamy, per se (Utah Attorney 2009).[36] Instead of focusing on the polygamous "lifestyle," the states are working to reduce the fear and distrust of government so that they can provide needed services and education to those remaining in or making the transition out of the polygamous community. The advantage of this strategy is that it may help decrease the secrecy and isolation that can shield abusers and prevent victims from seeking help.

The question in Canada is whether section 293 is a useful tool to deal with potential problems in closed polygamous communities. Because living in a conjugal relationship with more than one person seems no worse than adultery, which is not a crime, those who consider polygamy consistent with their religious beliefs are likely to perceive section 293 as evidence of public hostility to their religion. The history of the criminal offense and its terms support the narrative of religious persecution among polygamous groups. Prosecuting for polygamy, rather than dealing directly with child abuse, domestic violence, fraud, or other crimes, is likely to appear as persecution and may increase secrecy and isolation. If there are no grounds for child-protection proceedings or for criminal charges, other than charges of living in a conjugal relationship with more than one person, I suggest that it would be better to adopt the approach outlined in the Utah/Arizona handbook and focus on providing needed services and education for those remaining in the community or for those who want to transition out.

HARM TO CHILDREN

A child might be harmed by polygamy as a result of growing up in a polygamous household and being exposed to polygamy, by becoming a "child bride" in a polygamous union, or by becoming a superfluous "lost boy" who is ejected from a polygamous community (Bramham 2008).[37] Preventing such harms would be a justification for criminalization. Section 293, however, does not target any of these potential harms directly. There is no reference to children in the provision, no requirement that there be any children involved for there to be a conviction. The current section 293 applies whether children are present or not and whether children are harmed or not. The provision is overly broad because it applies to cases involving no children and only consenting adults.

There are provisions in the Criminal Code that directly target harms to children and that might apply to children in polygamous communities. Section 172 criminalizes adultery, sexual immorality, habitual drunkenness, and other forms of vice carried on in the home of a child if the effect is to endanger the morals of the child. These behaviors generally carry no criminal penalty but do so when it can be shown that they endanger children. As for cases of minors becoming wives in polygamous unions, the Criminal Code imposes sanctions for sexual activity with children and, in particular, for sexual touching of minors by those in a position of trust or authority toward the child, or those with whom the young person is in a relationship of dependency, or those in a relationship with a young person that is exploitive of that young person (Criminal Code 1985).[38]

In addition to the Criminal Code provisions, there is also child protection legislation, which allows authorities to apprehend children who are in need of protection.[39] The current criminal and child protection legislation appear to address potential harms to children in polygamous families.

GENDER EQUALITY

Canada has obligations under the charter, the Convention on Civil and Political Rights, and the Convention on the Elimination of All Forms of Discrimination against Women to ensure gender equality and eliminate discrimination against women. The Committee on the Elimination of Discrimination against Women issued a General Recommendation 1994, stating:

> States parties' reports also disclose that polygamy is practiced in a number of countries. Polygamous marriage contravenes a woman's right to equality with men, and can have such serious emotional and financial consequences for her and her dependents that such marriages ought to be discouraged and prohibited. The committee notes with concern that some states parties, whose constitutions guarantee equal rights, permit polygamous marriage in accordance with personal or customary law. This violates the constitutional rights of women, and breaches the provisions of article 5 (a) of the convention. (General Recommendation 1994)[40]

Rebecca Cook and Lisa Kelly noted that "beyond international human rights treaty law, it is clear that customary international law requires the prohibition or at the least restriction of polygyny. Surveying state practice, it is evident that the majority of states prohibit the practice" (Cook and Kelly 2006).[41] Canada, like most Western countries, does not permit polygamous marriages under their marriage laws. Furthermore, Canada, like many Western countries, criminalizes bigamy.

It is not at all clear that a criminal prohibition against living in a conjugal relationship with more than one person is necessary, and many monogamous Western countries have not enacted such a law. If polygamous marriages are not permitted under a country's civil marriage laws, and if bigamy is a crime, the country has established that it is a monogamous country that "prohibits" polygamy in compliance with human-rights norms. There are no reports of international human-rights bodies that I know of suggesting that monogamous countries that do not permit polygamous marriages and do criminalize bigamy must also criminalize the practice of carrying on a conjugal relationship with more than one person in order to comply with their human rights obligations.

In polygamous countries, polygamy is legal and endorsed by the state, which extends the status of marriage and incidents of marriage to those who enter into this unequal form of marriage. Legalized polygamy is part of a package of laws, policies, and practices that maintain gender inequality in polygamous countries. The package often includes one-sided divorce laws and unequal access to education and economic opportunities for women. The obligation under the UN human rights conventions is to get rid of or at the very least restrict state-sanctioned legal polygamy. This obligation does not require that carrying on a conjugal relationship with more than one person be criminalized. The Committee on Elimination of Discrimination against Women is not admonishing Britain, Hong Kong, Jamaica, New Zealand, or any of the many other monogamous countries that do not criminalize the practice of carrying on a conjugal relationship with more than one person to do so.

IMMIGRATION POLICY

Canada's immigration laws protect Canada's monogamous character by excluding multiple spouses from the family reunification program and from the list of family members who can immigrate with a successful applicant.[42] In addition, applicants who qualify independently may be deemed "inadmissible" for "criminality"—applications will be turned down if there are reasonable grounds for an immigration officer to believe that an applicant will commit an offense under section 293.[43] Section 293, then, provides a basis for determining that an applicant is inadmissible for criminality. Canada could more directly carry out its policy of not permitting immigration of polygamists by including in the list of those who are inadmissible to Canada anyone who is coming to Canada to practice polygamy. This direct approach is used in other countries, such as the United States.[44]

If it were not a crime to carry on a conjugal relationship with more than one person at a time, it would not follow that there would be a constitutional right to marry more than one person at a time or that more than one person could be sponsored for immigration as a "conjugal partner." A person with standing could bring a constitutional challenge to Canada's marriage law, which permits only monogamous marriages, or to the exclusion of polygamous parties from the category of eligible family members under the immigration law. I think it is unlikely that any such challenge would be successful, but this issue is distinct from the issue of retaining section 293. Protecting Canada's monogamous marriage law and immigration policy from constitutional challenges does not depend on making the practice of living in a conjugal relationship with more than one person a criminal offense.

ADDENDUM ON TERMINOLOGY

This final section identifies some relevant terms that are used in different ways, thereby giving rise to some confusion.

Decriminalization and *legalization*. *Decriminalization* refers to repealing the criminal offense of polygamy. Some people use the term *legalization* as a synonym for *decriminalization*, that is, to mean repeal of section 293. Others use *legalization* to mean changing the marriage laws to allow polygamous marriages to take place. It is important to clarify that decriminalization does *not* mean changing the marriage laws to allow polygamous marriages to take place. Repealing section 293 would not change the civil laws, which do not permit polygamous marriages to take place in Canada.

Prohibit, ban, and *criminalize*. Sometimes the terms *prohibit* or *ban* are used as synonyms for *criminalize*, but other times these terms are used to describe the effect of civil-marriage laws that do not permit polygamy. This can lead to misunderstandings. For example, a government report says that "in the United Kingdom, polygamy is also prohibited" (Cook and Kelly 2006).[45] This may lead readers to think that polygamy is a crime. But Britain does not have a criminal offense of polygamy, only bigamy.

Polygamy and *bigamy*. The Law Reform Commission of Canada noted that polygamy consists in the maintaining of conjugal relations by more than two persons: "When the result of such relations is to form a single matrimonial or family entity with the spouses, this is regarded as polygamous marriage. . . . The maintaining of more than one monogamous union by the same person corresponds with the popular notion of bigamy. . . . In legal terms, however, [polygamy and bigamy] have a more specific meaning. In particular bigamy, which is defined in relation to the legal institution of marriage, is distinguished from polygamy by the requirement of formal marital ties" (Law Reform 1985).[46]

As the terms are used in the Criminal Code and in this paper, *bigamy* is going through a form of marriage while married to someone else. *Polygamy* is the practice of living in a conjugal relationship with more than one person at the same time. Some use the term *polygamy* to mean *bigamy*. For example, a reporter wrote that "polygamy" is illegal in Britain and punishable by imprisonment for up to seven years,[47] but polygamy is not a criminal offense in Britain, and it is bigamy that is punishable by imprisonment for up to seven years.

It is particularly important to be specific as to what is meant by *ban, prohibit*, and *criminalize* and by *polygamy* and *bigamy* in the comparative law context. Policymakers may well look to what other jurisdictions have done in relation to polygamy. The material cited above might give the impression that Britain has a criminal offense of polygamy, when in fact it does not. Many countries maintain their monogamous character without creating a criminal offense of polygamy, and it is helpful to know that.

Recognition. Confusion may arise in regard to *recognition* of polygamous marriages. It is important to emphasize the distinction between *recognition* in the sense of a state extending status to polygamous unions under its domestic laws and *recognition* in the sense of a state acknowledging a status created by a foreign law. Canada does not *recognize* polygamous unions by extending status to such unions under its domestic laws, but it does *recognize* valid foreign polygamous marriages, as do most Western countries. The recognition of valid foreign polygamous marriages does not vitiate Canada's character as a monogamous country or suggest endorsement of polygamy. Incidents of marriage—the rights and obligations, benefits and burdens that flow from marital status—are extended to valid foreign polygamous marriages only to the extent that doing so does not violate Canada's public policy. Canada's commitment to monogamy does not require a blanket refusal to extend the incidents of marriage to those validly married in polygamous countries. Any such blanket refusal would disproportionately affect the women because it would effectively strip them of the marital rights they reasonably expected to enjoy as the result of entering into a legally valid marriage in their home country.

Notes

1. In particular, Daphne Bramham (2008), a columnist for the *Vancouver Sun*, has written extensively about the fundamentalist community and published *The Secret Lives of Saints: Child Brides and Lost Boys in a Polygamous Mormon Sect.*
2. Blackmore v. British Columbia (Attorney General (2009), 247 C.C.C. (3d) 544. *Reference re: Criminal Code* 2009. See British Columbia's *Constitutional Question Act* 1996.
3. The Civil Marriage Act 2005 stipulates that "marriage, for civil purposes, is the lawful union of two persons to the exclusion of all others."
4. Benjamin L. Berger describes the criminalization of polygamy as "a use of the criminal law to protect a cultural commitment to monogamous marriage" in "Moral Judgment, Criminal Law and the Constitutional Protection of Religion" (2008) 40 S.C.L.R. (2d) 513 at 549.
5. Lawrence v. Texas (2003) 539 U.S. 558 at 590.
6. Bowers v. Hardwick (1986) 478 U.S. 186, 106 S.Ct. 2841, 92 L.Ed.2d 140.
7. State v. Ciancelli (2002) 181 Or.App. 1, 45 P.3d 451 at 456.
8. By the phrase "noncommercial sexual activities carried out between two consenting adults in private," I am intending to exclude sexual activities that are commercial, public, or nonconsensual, or that involve animals or minors. And my use of the term *sexual activity* is meant to refer to the activity itself, not to the making of images or records of such.

9. R. v. Labaye, 2005 SCC 80, [2005] 3 S.C.R. 728 (hereafter, *Labaye*); R. v. Kouri, [2005] 3 S.C.R. 789, 2005 SCC 81. The Criminal Code s. 197 defines a "common bawdy-house" as "a place that is (a) kept or occupied, or (b) resorted to by one or more persons for the purpose of prostitution or the practice of acts of indecency," and under s. 210 keeping a common bawdy-house is an indictable offence.

10. *Labaye*, paras. 7 and 8.

11. *Labaye*, para. 71.

12. According to the Criminal Code, s. 155(1), section 155(4), "In this section, 'brother' and 'sister', respectively, include half-brother and half-sister."

13. R. v. R.P. (1996), 149 N.S.R. (2d) 91, 105 C.C.C. (3d) 435 (C.A.).

14. Murray (2009, 1256).

15. Murray (2009, 1257) argues that, in light of cases such as *Lawrence v. Texas*, the United States is now developing a larger "law-free" zone of sexual activity that is not criminal and not marital. This would move the United States closer to the situation in Canada.

16. S.C. 1990, c. 46, s. 2(2).

17. The Marriage (Prohibited Degrees) Act was enacted after extensive public consultation and objections from religious organizations. In response, Senator Joan Neiman stated: "Those religions which wish to maintain a large number of prohibitions are free to do so, and are free not to give their sanction to adherents who do not comply. In a pluralistic society like Canada the general law should not be constrained by any particular religious views." The Senate took the view that individuals and organizations could govern themselves by their own values, but that the law of the land should be as unrestricted as possible. It was pointed out that "socially undesirable marriages . . . take place for many, many reasons and we cannot and do not attempt to legislate to prevent those marriages." Canada, Senate Debates (1985), 1744–50 at 1749.

18. Murray (2009, 1302).

19. Lawrence Stone (1995); Law Reform Commission of Canada (1985, 7–8); Lemmings (1996, 339); Outhwaite (1995).

20. Offences against the Person, S.C. 1869 (32–33 Vict.), c. 20, s. 58.

21. An Act to Punish Seduction, and Like Offences, and to Make Further Provision for the Protection of Women and Girls, S.C. 1886 (49 Vict.), s. 52, s. 3 (this provision was based on existing provisions enacted in provinces).

22. An Act Respecting Offences Relating to the Law of Marriage, R.S.C. 1886 (49 Vict.), c. 161, s. 1 (this provision was based on existing provisions enacted in provinces).

23. An Act Respecting Offences Relating to the Law of Marriage, R.S.C. 1886 (49 Vict.), c. 161, s. 3 (again, this provision was based on existing provisions enacted in provinces).

24. 1 Jac. 1. c. 11.

25. The deceptive nature of bigamy, which is misuse of a ceremony that would otherwise be valid to create a state-sanctioned union, was emphasized in *R. v. Friar* (Ont. Co. Ct., 1983), unreported, Borins J., as cited in *R. v. Sauve*, [1997] A.J. No. 525 (Prov. Ct.) at par. 3, put it: "The essential gravity of the offence remains the deception which the bigamist exhibits, in some cases, where he has said nothing about the original marriage to the new partner; but, perhaps, more importantly which he exhibits in all cases by the falsification of state records in the application for the marriage license."

26. Samuel Chapman (2001, 26–27).

27. An Act Further to Amend the Criminal Law, S.C. 1890, c. 37, s. 11 (1890). The provision read, "Everyone who practices, or, by the rites, ceremonies, forms, rules or customs of any denomination, sect or society, religious or secular, or by any form of contract, or by mere mutual consent, or by any other method whatsoever,

and whether in a manner recognized by law as a binding form of marriage or not, agrees or consents to practice or enter."

28. R. v. Liston (1893) (Toronto assizes, unreported).

29. The Queen v. Bear's Shin Bone (1899), 4 Terr. L.R. 173, 3 C.C.C. 329.

30. On this issue it may be useful to consider that most countries do not permit same-sex marriage and many impose criminal penalties on same-sex relations. Canada may be more successful in persuading the latter to be tolerant, at least to the point of not criminalizing same-sex married couples visiting from Canada, if we refrain from criminalizing their visiting polygamous families.

31. In the reference case now before the British Columbia Supreme Court, the attorney general of British Columbia is arguing that, properly interpreted, is constitutional, and it has submitted that "on its face and when interpreted in light of its purpose, legislative history, social context, and Canadian and international human rights norms, the prohibition should be interpreted as follows: Section 293 prohibits marriages or marriage-like relationships involving more than two persons that purport to be (a) sanctioned by an authority having power or influence over the participants and (b) binding on any of the participants." The attorney general has further submitted that "the Criminal Code prohibition was and is addressed to the overwhelmingly dominant form of polygamy, and the one most closely associated with demonstrable and apprehended social harms: that is, a patriarchal polygyny that is intergenerationally normalized and enforced through more or less coercive rules and norms of non-state social institutions. Section 293 leaves the balance of multi-partner human sexual behavior, that which is unrelated to the harms the prohibition seeks to address, unaffected" (*Reference re: Criminal Code* 2010, para. 8). Whatever may be the submissions of the attorney general on the proper interpretation, the provision on its face does not carry the limitations that are suggested. The attorney general appears to be inviting the court to effectively rewrite the provision in order that it pass constitutional muster.

32. Justices Bastarache and LeBel in *Labaye* at para. 109 said that "according to contemporary Canadian social morality, acts such as child pornography, incest, polygamy and bestiality are unacceptable regardless of whether or not they cause social harm. The community considers these acts to be harmful in themselves." Insofar as this statement suggests that polygamy as defined in the Criminal Code is so violative of social norms that criminalization is justified, I respectfully disagree.

33. See, e.g., Kate Barlow (2006), *Abode of Love: Growing Up in a Messianic Cult*, about the nineteenth-century English group, Agapemone, formed by a defrocked clergyman who claimed to be guided by the Holy Ghost.

34. In the extreme case of the 1993 FBI assault on David Koresh's Branch Davidians in Waco, Texas, well-meaning but clumsy government efforts ended in tragedy. See Reavis (1995).

35. Utah Attorney (2009), 8.

36. Ibid., 9.

37. The terms are borrowed from Bramham (2008).

38. Criminal Code (n.d.) s., 153.

39. For example, see Child, Family and Community Service Act, R.S.B.C. 1996, c. 46.

40. General Recommendation No. 21 (13th session, 1994).

41. Cook and Kelly 2006, part VA.

42. The Immigration and Refugee Protection Regulations (SOR/2002-227), s. 117(9) c), state, "(9) A foreign national shall not be considered a member of the family class by virtue of their relationship to a sponsor if . . . (b) the foreign national is the sponsor's spouse, common-law partner or conjugal partner, the sponsor has an existing sponsorship undertaking in respect of a spouse, common-law partner

226   MARTHA BAILEY

or conjugal partner and the period referred to in subsection 132(1) in respect of that undertaking has not ended; (c) the foreign national is the sponsor's spouse and (i) the sponsor or the foreign national was, at the time of their marriage, the spouse of another person, or (ii) the sponsor has lived separate and apart from the foreign national for at least one year and (A) the sponsor is the common-law partner of another person or the conjugal partner of another foreign national, or (B) the foreign national is the common-law partner of another person or the conjugal partner of another sponsor."

43.   The Immigration and Refugee Protection Act, S.C. 2001, c. 27, I-2.5, s. 36(2)(d) states, "A foreign national is inadmissible on grounds of criminality for committing, on entering Canada, an offence under an Act of Parliament prescribed by regulations." This must be read in light of s. 33, which states that "the facts that constitute inadmissibility under sections 34 to 37 include facts arising from omissions and, unless otherwise provided, include facts for which there are reasonable grounds to believe that they have occurred, are occurring or may occur." See, e.g., Ali v. Canada (Minister of Citizenship and Immigration), [1998] No. 1640 (T.D.); Awwad v. Canada (Minister of Citizenship and Immigration), [1999] No. 103; [1999] A.C.F. no 103; 162 F.T.R. 209; 85 A.C.W.S. (3d) 892.

44.   See, e.g., Immigration and Nationality Act, 8 U.S.C. 1182, s. 212(15)(A): "Any immigrant who is coming to the United States to practice polygamy is inadmissible."

45.   Cook and Kelly 2006, part V4.

46.   Law Reform Commission of Canada (1985, 13).

47.   Martiuk (*Calgary Herald*, Feb. 15, 2008). See also Hall (*Detroit Free Press*, Sept. 5, 2009) and 4 Am. & Eng. Enc. L. (2d ed.) 39: "Bigamy, or polygamy, therefore consists in the making of the unlawful contract and the abuse of the formality which the law has enjoined as requisite to the creation of the marital relation. And it is the abuse of this formal and solemn contract, by entering into it a second time when a former husband or wife is still living, which the law forbids because of its outrage upon public decency, its violation of the public economy, as well as its tendency to cheat one into a surrender of the person under the appearance of right."

References

American Law Institute, Model Penal Code, article 230.1(2).

An Act Further to Amend the Criminal Law. 1890. S.C., c. 37, s. 11.

An Act to Punish Seduction, and Like Offences, and to Make Further Provision for the Protection of Women and Girls. 1886. S.C. (49 Vict.), s. 52, s. 3.

An Act Respecting Offences Relating to the Law of Marriage. 1996. R.S.C. (49 Vict.), c. 161, s. 1.

Barlow, Kate. 2006. *Abode of Love: Growing Up in a Messianic Cult.* Fredericton, NB: Goose Lane Editions.

Berger, Benjamin L. 2008. "Moral Judgment, Criminal Law and the Constitutional Protection of Religion" 40 S.C.L.R. (2d) 513, p. 549.

Blackmore v. British Columbia (Attorney General). 2009. 247 C.C.C. (3d) 544.

Bowers v. Hardwick. (1986) 478 U.S. 186, 106 S.Ct. 2841, 92 L.Ed.2d 140.

Bramham, Daphne. 2008. *The Secret Lives of Saints: Child Brides and Lost Boys in a Polygamous Mormon Sect.* Toronto: Random House Canada.

British Columbia's *Constitutional Question Act.* 1996. R.S.B.C., c. 68.

Chapman, Samuel. 2001. *Polygamy, Bigamy and Human Rights Law.* Bloomington, IN: Xlibris.

Cook, Rebecca, and Lisa Kelly. 2006. "Polygyny and Canada's Obligations under International Human Rights Law." Research report for Department of Justice Canada.

Civil Marriage Act. 2005. c. 33, C-31.5, s. 2.

Criminal Code. n.d. s. 155(1). Section 155(4).

General Recommendation. 1994. No. 21 (13th session).

Immigration and Refugee Protection Act. 2001. S.C., c. 27, I-2.5, s. 36(2)(d).

Lawrence v. Texas. (2003) 539 U.S. 558 at 590.

Law Reform Commission of Canada. 1985. "Bigamy." Working Paper 42, Law Reform Commission of Canada, Ottawa.

Lemmings, David. 1996. "Marriage and the Law in the Eighteenth Century: Hardwicke's Marriage Act of 1753." *Historical Journal (Cambridge, England)* 39 (2): 339–60. http://dx.doi.org/10.1017/S0018246X00020276.

Murray, Melissa. 2009. "Strange Bedfellows: Criminal Law, Family Law, and the Legal Construction of Intimate Life." *University of Iowa Law Review* 94: 1253–56.

Offences against the Person. 1869. S.C. (32–33 Vict.), c. 20, s. 58.

Outhwaite, R. B. 1995. *Clandestine Marriage in England, 1500–1850.* London: A&C Black.

Queen v. Bear's Shin Bone. 1899. 4 Terr. L.R. 173, 3 C.C.C. 329.

Reavis, Dick. 1995. *The Ashes of Waco: An Investigation.* New York: Simon and Schuster.

Reference re: Section 293 of the Criminal Code of Canada. 2009. BCSC 1668.

Reference re: Section 293 of the Criminal Code of Canada. 2010. BCSC 1308, para. 8.

R. v. Friar (Ont. Co. Ct., 1983), unreported, Borins J., as cited in *R. v. Sauve,* [1997] A.J. No. 525 (Prov. Ct.), par. 3.

R. v. Labaye, 2005 SCC 80, [2005] 3 S.C.R. 728 ("*Labaye*"); *R. v. Kouri,* [2005].

R. v. Liston (1893).

R. v. R.P. (1996), 149 N.S.R. (2d) 91, 105 C.C.C. (3d) 435 (C.A.).

S.C.R. 789, 2005 SCC 81.

Smith v. Smith 1952.2 S.C.R. 312.

State v. Ciancelli. (2002) 181 Or.App. 1, 45 P.3d 451 at 456.

Stone, Lawrence. 1995. *Uncertain Unions and Broken Lives.* New York: Oxford University Press.

Utah Attorney General's Office and Arizona Attorney General's Office. August 2009. *The Primer: A Handbook for Law Enforcement and Human Services Agencies Who Offer Assistance to Fundamentalist Mormon Families.* Family Support Center.

11

(MIS)RECOGNIZING POLYGAMY

Kerry Abrams

INTRODUCTION

There is a burgeoning awareness that polygamy may require legal recognition. The increased liberality of law regarding LGBT families, culminating last summer in the US Supreme Court's overturning of state bans on same-sex marriage, has prompted scholars, judges, activists, and legislators to ask the question, "if same-sex marriage, why not polygamy?" In December 2013, a federal judge struck down the part of Utah's antipolygamy statute that criminalizes cohabitation between a married person and someone other than their spouse. Activists have argued that the constitution requires recognition of polygamy or, conversely, that recognition is a mistake that will lead to the further entrenchment of women's subordination (Strassberg 2003). Debates about polygamy usually focus on decriminalization and the related question of whether polygamous family structures are inherently subordinating women. Recently, however, a handful of scholars have shifted from arguing about decriminalizing to theorizing what full-blown recognition would entail, analogizing polygamous relationships to business partnerships or corporations and arguing that business law provides a framework for the legal recognition of intimate relationships between more than two adults (Davis 2010; Drobac and Page 2007; Ertman 2001).[1]

This essay considers the legal recognition of polygamy from a different perspective. Instead of tackling the normative question of whether recognition is a desirable goal or what legal form such recognition should take, it instead questions whether full recognition is a feasible, or even necessary, goal for polygamists and their allies. It argues that full recognition of polygamy is more difficult than commonly understood for two reasons: (1) our current family law protects family privacy to an extent that would be difficult with polygamous relationships, and (2) the current law of marriage involves public benefits not infinitely divisible among multiple parties. The essay then argues

DOI: 10.7330/9780874219975.c011

that, despite these obstacles, we may see legally supported polygamous families in the near future, but not through the outright recognition of polygamy as a form of marriage. Instead, full recognition may not be necessary because elements of polygamous relationships are already being recognized through alternative means. Legal mechanisms, such as the enforcement of contracts for adult relationships, recognition of nonmarital cohabitants, registration schemes such as domestic partnership and reciprocal beneficiaries, and recognition of multiparent families are already beginning to make the simultaneous recognition of multiple relationships possible. Focusing solely on decriminalization misses the larger issue: polygamous marriage is an outdated way of thinking about adult relationships because marriage itself no longer captures the reality of many adult lives. Legal scholars may "misrecognize" the problem of polygamy when they focus on decriminalization and full recognition rather than scrutinizing the ways in which polygamy is already partially and unintentionally recognized by law. Rather than resisting polygamy as a threat to traditional marriage or embracing it as a civil rights issue, we instead could use it as an opportunity to reevaluate the law of marriage and its relationship to public benefits and legal parentage.

Part 1 of the essay begins by observing that, from a legal perspective, polygamy is a species of marriage. In order to define polygamy and understand how it might be recognized, we must first define marriage and understand what is at stake in the state's recognition of personal, intimate relationships. Part 2 considers in detail the benefits and obligations conferred by civil marriage and explores how those benefits and obligations might—or might not—apply to polygamous marriages. It argues that providing recognition to polygamous marriage would dramatically change how state family law works by opening up ongoing marriages to state intervention. It then observes that these difficulties extend to the public benefits associated with marriage, which would be difficult to replicate with multiple spouses. Part 3 shows that despite the difficulties with full recognition of polygamy, partial recognition does occur, sometimes leading to unintended consequences. Part 4 then argues that although the many obstacles to recognition of polygamy identified in parts 2 and 3 may prevent full recognition, understanding polygamy as a form of marriage may be a distraction. As marriage declines in importance and is no longer the fundamental ordering principle of family law, trying to determine whether polygamy "counts" as marriage misses the mark. Polygamous families, if they want it, will be able to obtain recognition in many ways without being legally married, and these other means may actually be more attractive to them than opening up traditional marriage to include multiple spouses.

WHAT IS MARRIAGE?

In order to consider the project of legally recognizing polygamy, we must first articulate the assumptions built into the notion of legal recognition of an intimate relationship. In the United States, as in most Western countries, monogamous marriage has long been the centerpiece of legal recognition of the family. Yet "marriage" is in the eye of the beholder and, indeed, can mean many different things depending on context. The definition of marriage has also shifted over time, with some features becoming increasingly important and some decreasing in importance or even falling away altogether.

Sex and Procreation

Traditionally, marriage was the legal status that provided a space for state-approved sexual relationships and the procreation of children. Fornication and adultery were criminal acts, and nonmarital children suffered numerous legal disabilities (Grossman and Friedman 2011). This bundling together of marriage, sex, and procreation meant that access to marriage was a necessary precondition for state-sanctioned sexual and procreative activity. In the famous case of *Zablocki v. Redhail*, where a man challenged a Wisconsin law barring him from marriage because he was in arrears on his child support payments for a nonmarital child, the US Supreme Court was explicit about the link between marriage, sex, and procreation:

> It is not surprising that the decision to marry has been placed on the same level of importance as decisions relating to procreation, childbirth, child rearing, and family relationships . . . it would make little sense to recognize a right of privacy with respect to other matters of family life and not with respect to the decision to enter the relationship that is the foundation of the family in our society . . . if [Redhail's] right to procreate means anything at all, it must imply some right to enter the only relationship in which the State of Wisconsin allows sexual relations legally to take place.[2]

In the last fifty years, however, this tight link between marriage, sex, and procreation has unraveled. The US Supreme Court has also struck down laws discriminating against nonmarital children, bolstered the constitutional parentage rights of nonmarital fathers, and overturned laws criminalizing nonmarital sex.[3] The state's moral interest in linking these three issues also declined. While in 1986 the court could compare homosexual activity to "possession in the home of drugs, firearms, or stolen goods," by 2003 it insisted, in upholding the right of people to engage in sodomy, that "our obligation is to define the liberty of all, not to mandate our own moral code."[4] These changes in law track changes in social behavior. Between 1970 and 2000, the number of cohabiting couples rose from 523,000 to 5.5 million (Grossman and Friedman 2011, 125). Between 1980 and 2011, the percentage of births that were nonmarital rose from 18.4 percent to 40.7 percent.[5]

Although marriage, sex, and procreation have unraveled, they have not become completely unbundled. Marriage still provides legal advantages to parents and children. A child born within a marriage, for example, is still presumed in many states to be the legal child of its birth mother's spouse, regardless of whether there is actually a genetic relationship between them (Appleton 2012). Some states still criminalize adultery. And many people still consider marriage to be a desirable, if not necessary, precondition for childrearing (Cahn and Carbone 2010). But "love, marriage, and the baby carriage" no longer always occur in that order, or even together at all (McClain 2007).[6]

Privatized Dependency

Another purpose of marriage has been the privatization of dependency (Fineman 2004). At common law, a married woman's legal being was suspended; she was "covered" by her husband—hence the term *coverture* to describe the law of marriage. In turn, husbands were required to support their wives (Grossman and Friedman 2011, 59–61). Modern family law views marriage differently; husbands and wives no longer have distinct and separate roles. But marriage law still encourages financial dependency and presumes that spouses will care for one another and provide for one another. Family law doctrines such as community property assume that under ordinary circumstances, couples will pool their resources; remedies such as maintenance (alimony) can require spouses to continue to fulfill their duty to support one another even after divorce. Marriage also can affect access to welfare benefits. Benefits can be terminated through marriage by imputing the income of a spouse to a recipient; conversely, some benefits under Social Security become available only through marriage. Underlying all of these rules is the assumption—and, sometimes, legally enforceable rule—that spouses have a duty to support one another. This duty, in turn, prevents married people from becoming a drain on the state. In the United States, the extent to which the law relies on marriage to privatize dependency is much more extreme than in most other Western nations. Health insurance, for example, is not provided by the government but rather through employers to both employees and employees' spouses—hence the oft-repeated phrase that someone is *married to healthcare*.[7] The notion of privatized dependency is also at least partially responsible for the other public benefits granted to (or requirements imposed on) married couples: eligibility for lawful immigration status, a fast track to citizenship, exemptions from the estate tax, and joint income tax filing are all examples of how the state presumes that married couples share a financial interdependence not shared by cohabiting couples, friends, roommates, or siblings.

Public Commitment

Despite its roots in the regulation of sex and procreation and the privatization of dependency, legal marriage has a cultural force that goes far beyond the bundle of rights and duties it encompasses. As the US Supreme Court put it in a case establishing the right of prison inmates to marry, marriages are "expressions of emotional support and public commitment," and "many religions recognize marriage as having spiritual significance." Even if the state were to stop attaching public benefits and private duties to marriage, many people would likely want to marry to demonstrate their commitment to each other or to their religious communities. Marriage confers the state's seal of approval on a particular type of adult intimate relationship.[8]

Bundling

Marriage is a status that bundles all of these elements together. The benefits associated with the status change over time, but the status remains intact. The core element that remains the same is the bundling together of private obligations, public benefits, and religious, social, and state approval. When a plaintiff sues for the right to marry, the right claimed is entry into this preferred status with which various financial benefits and mutual obligations have been bundled. Take away any of these individual rights (e.g., the marital exemption from the estate tax, or the right to sponsor a spouse for immigration status) and the status still retains its importance but with a different combination of rights embedded in it. But take away the right to the status itself and the denial of the rights within it becomes an issue of constitutional magnitude (Sunstein 2005). In marriage, the whole really is more than the sum of its parts.

PRIVACY, MARITAL BENEFITS, AND POLYGAMY

Legally and culturally, then, marriage has many meanings. If polyga-mous groupings were to be recognized as legal marriages, what would this recognition look like? At first glance it appears simple. Multiple spouses could enter into legally sanctioned marriages by seeking licenses and marrying ceremonially through state-approved procedures. Plural marriages would be recognized as well at divorce or death. But recog-nizing multiple spouses at divorce or death creates a host of potential difficulties.

Divorce, Plural Marriage, and Family Privacy

Normally, state family law regulates marriage primarily at entry and exit (divorce). Between entry and exit, however, state intervention is the rare exception rather than the norm. The law intervenes in cases of criminal violence between spouses, but courts are inclined to stay out of spouses' midmarriage financial agreements, their injuries to each other, and their failures to support or provide services to each other. A spouse who is having marital problems cannot sue for enforcement of the marital contract; the only remedy is divorce.

Recognition of polygamous marriage, however, could dramatically alter this norm for the participants in polygamous marriages because in polygamy, there is no "mid-game" (Davis 2010, 1990). Polygamous relationships can be extremely unstable—think, for example, of FLDS (Fundamentalist Church of Jesus Christ of Latter-Day Saints) member Alex Joseph's eight divorces—and the frequent, if not constant, entry and exit of new spouses would create many more occasions and oppor-tunities for state intervention (Emens 2004, 317). This ongoing state oversight would alter marriage, at least in the case of polygamy, in sev-eral important ways. Each time a new person entered or exited a mar-riage, the change would alter the interests of existing spouses in their marital or community property. At exit, just as in any other divorce, a court would have to approve a division of marital property. In marriages with plenty of wealth, this process would be costly for the court system because spouses might engage in protracted litigation where so much property was at stake. In marriages with little wealth, the divorce itself might be simpler, but the effects on the public fisc would be more prob-lematic. Women's income decreases dramatically upon divorce, and, indeed, young women appear to be worse off if they marry and divorce than if they never marry at all (Hamilton 2012). Similarly, a court would have to determine eligibility for and the amount of maintenance to be

awarded at multiple points during a multiperson marriage, and the formula for determining maintenance would have to be altered to include
the reality of multiple mutually obligated parties.[9]

Being in a legally recognized polygamous marriage, then, could
involve much more state intrusion than being in a legally recognized
monogamous marriage. People who stay in a monogamous marriages
for fifty years experience family privacy—a lack of state intrusion—for
each of those fifty years. Their interactions with the state regarding their
families are limited to specific instances, such as filing joint tax returns,
obtaining a child's birth certificate, or exercising their authority to make
medical decisions on behalf of an incapacitated spouse. But a person
who stays in a polygamous marriage for fifty years may see many husbands or wives come and go and experience the state's intrusion into
the details of those comings and goings at multiple and unpredictable
moments: Whose fault was it? Who owns what? How much support must
the existing spouses pay the one who is leaving and for how long? Who
has custody of the children? This family-state dynamic is much different
from what we are accustomed to and might be undesirable to many people—including polygamous families themselves. Similar observations
have been made about the law of inheritance (Davis 2010).

Polygamy and Marriage-Based Public Benefits

The state law of marriage, divorce, and inheritance is not the only legal
context within which and through which polygamy could be recognized.
Marriage is a status category of central importance in the allocation of
benefits in the modern welfare state. Tax benefits and burdens, food
stamps, welfare payments, social security, pensions, health insurance,
and immigration status all take marriage to be a stable and useful category for determining eligibility, noneligibility, and axes of dependency
among individual people.

Marriage is often assumed to be largely private and contractual;
spouses agree to take responsibility—financial and emotional—for
one another. But many of the benefits of marriage are conferred by
the state, and they cannot be easily divided among multiple spouses. A
bank account could, in theory, be divided into thirds just like a pie if
one member of a polygamous trio divorced the other two. This dividing
up might be unfortunate for a spouse who would, under monogamous
circumstances, have received half the pie instead of one-third, but we
might justify it as the fruits of a joint venture to which that spouse is presumed to have contributed one-third of the profits.

Public benefits, in contrast, are not carved from "pies" owned by a partner to the marriage. Take, for example, the social security retirement system. The social security system protects low-earning married retirees with high-earning spouses at the expense of couples who earn similar amounts over their lifetimes and single people. For example, a retiree can claim either 100 percent of her own social security entitlement (determined, in part, by how much she earned over her lifetime) or, alternatively, if she is married, the equivalent of 50 percent of her spouse's entitlement. This 50 percent is in addition to the 100 percent her spouse claims. The family where one spouse opts for the 50 percent instead of her own entitlement (presumably because it is more than her own entitlement) receives 150 percent of the higher-earning spouse's entitlement; this additional money has to come from somewhere, and it comes from the income paid into the system by the many single people or worried married people who will not be claiming a spousal benefit.

When a spouse elects to take the equivalent of 50 percent of her spouse's entitlement rather than 100 percent of her own, she is not taking part of a pie earned by her spouse; her spouse still gets to keep his or her whole pie. Instead, the availability of the spousal entitlement is a cash incentive, given to families who structure themselves into a breadwinner/homemaker model at the expense of those who do not (Liu 1999). Social security benefits are not simply marriage-based benefits; they are benefits that reward a particular type of marriage.

Were the federal government to recognize polygamy, it would have to decide what to do about multiple spouses. Imagine first a family of five spouses: one breadwinner spouse and four homemaker spouses who either made no income during their lifetimes or income so insubstantial that 50 percent of the breadwinner spouse's entitlement would exceed 100 percent of their own. Would they each have the option of taking the equivalent of 50 percent of the breadwinner spouse's payout? In other words, would that family receive 300 percent of the breadwinner spouses's entitlement (100 percent of that spouse's entitlement going to him or her, and 50 percent of the entitlement going to each of four spouses)? Or, instead, would the earning spouse have the opportunity or obligation to designate only one spouse, by premarital contract or other means, who would collect that portion of the payout, leaving three of the four spouses entirely without retirement income? Or perhaps the spousal entitlement would be divided into equal shares, with each homemaker spouse receiving 12.5 percent of the breadwinner spouse's entitlement. Our current system already recognizes "serial polygamy." As Nancy Polikoff has pointed out, the politician Newt Gingrich has been married three times, and since each marriage lasted longer than ten years, each wife is eligible to receive the spousal benefit, which means his family could end up costing taxpayers 250 percent of his entitlement (Polikoff 2008). Recognition of polygamy would expand this form of federal subsidy beyond multiple serial marriages to multiple simultaneous ones.

Even more complex would be cases in which a polygamous family contained more than one breadwinner spouse. Could more than one spouse take the equivalent of 50 percent of more than one spouse's social security entitlement? Or would the non-earning spouses simply split 50 percent of each of the earning spouses' pensions? Currently, spouses cannot take social security retirement from more than one spouse; if they meet the requirements, because of divorce, based on more than one spouse, they must choose one. But polygamy might put a wrench in this system; if a reason underlying the spousal entitlement rule is that we think that marriage privatizes dependency and that married couples pool their resources, then why shouldn't spouses in a family with two breadwinners and three homemakers also get credit for pooling their resources? As in state family law, frequent divorce would further complicate this picture, making it likely that polygamous families would create complex webs of breadwinner and homemaker spouses, married and divorced in various combinations over time, a possibility that the social security system would be very ill-equipped to handle.

Social security is just one example of how marital benefits are not always analogous to dividing up a pie. Indeed, the flexibility of the size of the pie explains, at least in part, Utah's codification of "purporting to marry" or cohabiting with a second person as criminal bigamy (partially struck down in *Brown*). Utah's legislators were concerned that FLDS women were claiming to be single and collecting welfare benefits, including food stamps, based on their household size and income without considering their husbands' incomes. Thus, the legislature made it a crime to "purport to marry" or cohabit with another if that person was already married. One way of understanding this prohibition is that the pie available in public benefits had been fraudulently increased; by appearing to be fatherless, husbandless families, the individual households headed by wives were eligible for more than their fair share of state largesse. Of course, if the women had been single mothers, they would have been entitled to this support, and it is unclear why the existence of a spiritual husband necessarily makes him available for support. In this light, the law looks like a back-door attempt to reintroduce the "spouse in the house" rules struck down in the late 1960s by the

US Supreme Court. A lurking concern may have been that as a practical matter, most of the wives were turning over their welfare checks to their husbands; thus, the financial transaction ultimately looked like the "hub" of a plural marriage collecting from "the spokes" payments that were in turn provided by the state—payments that the "hub" was not entitled to even if the "spokes" were.[10]

PARTIAL RECOGNITION

Full recognition of polygamy seems, at this juncture, to be politically unlikely; the legal obstacles, as outlined above, add to this unlikelihood. But what about partial recognition? Could polygamy be recognized for some purposes but not others? To some extent, partial recognition already occurs in the United States. Some polygamous wives, for example, have had the marriage law of their countries of origin, where polygamy was legal, recognized in the context of inheritance. Other countries, however, have far more experience with recognition of polygamy for some purposes and not others. This partial recognition might at first glance seem like an attractive option since it could protect vulnerable second, third, or fourth wives in some circumstances without incentivizing polygamy by recognizing it for all purposes. When we take a close look at how partial recognition has played out, however, it seems less desirable because it is difficult for the government to predict how the particular combination of recognition and nonrecognition rules will play out. To consider how partial recognition works in various contexts, let's examine how a decision about recognition of polygamy for immigration status works in tandem with recognition of polygamy for welfare purposes.

Whether a country recognizes polygamy for immigration purposes may seem relatively unimportant if the polygamists one has in mind are FLDS constituents. (Note, however, that the early LDS church attracted plural wives by advertising in Europe and offering to pay the immigration expenses of interested women.) Immigrants are likely to be the group that is most invested in the legal recognition of polygamy. For these polygamists, primarily Muslims from other countries seeking a better life abroad, immigration recognition would appear to be crucial. In fact, in its opinion upholding Canada's antipolygamy law, the Supreme Court of British Columbia expressly mentioned the likelihood that polygamists would see Canada as an attractive target of immigration as a factor important to its decision.[11]

The United States bans outright immigration by those who "intend to practice polygamy in the United States." "Practicing polygamists" are also ineligible for naturalized citizenship on the grounds that they are, by definition, not people of "good moral character." These rules effectively deny second and subsequent wives the security that immigration status would confer. Thus, these wives usually enter the country on tourist visas, overstay, and become subject to deportation if detected and apprehended. As Claire Smearman (2009) has shown, the law is calibrated to confer protection on a husband and one wife. Because the husband may sponsor his children for lawful immigration status regardless of whether he is married to their mothers, second and subsequent wives may find themselves trapped in a relationship in which they may lose access to their children, either because the husband sponsors the children for lawful immigration status and leaves the wife behind or because the wife will be subject to deportation if she attempts to leave her husband and gain custody of the children. And because unauthorized immigrants are not eligible for welfare, she would have difficulty striking out on her own. Thus may nonrecognition for immigration purposes have unintended and very painful consequences for some of those living in polygamy.[12]

In contrast, the United Kingdom and France have each partially recognized polygamy, but neither country's experience indicates that it has found a method of partial recognition clearly superior to the United States'. Like the United States, both of these countries are modern welfare states that give public benefits, including unemployment insurance and housing subsidies, to impoverished citizens and residents. And both are attractive destination countries for immigrants. But when a country partially recognizes polygamy, there can be unintended consequences.

The United Kingdom: No (at Least Officially) to Immigration, Yes to Welfare

The majority of families practicing polygamy in the United Kingdom are Muslim immigrants from Pakistan and, to a lesser extent, India and Bangladesh, although recent news reports indicate that polygamy is making a revival among second- and third-generation Muslims whose parents or grandparents emigrated from those countries. In the United Kingdom, individuals cannot legally enter into a polygamous marriage, but those who enter into a polygamous marriage abroad and then reside in the United Kingdom do not face criminal penalties. Recognition beyond this limited decriminalization is partial. Husbands cannot sponsor more than one wife for immigration status. Immigration law does provide, however, some legal avenues for entry of new wives: husbands sometimes sponsor new wives for immigration status by claiming them as nannies for their children or as caretakers for sick relatives. Some women come on visitors' visas and overstay, so they are technically unauthorized but difficult to locate or deport. Finally, a husband can divorce his first wife but continue to live with her and be married to her under Islamic law and then sponsor an additional wife whom he legally marries (and he could continue to do this serially). The UK Immigration Rulebook requires that the new wife in this last circumstance be given entry clearance, even where the divorce of the previous wife "is thought to be one of convenience," the husband is still living with the previous wife, and "to issue the entry clearance would lead to the formation of a polygamous household." Taken together, these rules have made it fairly easy for husbands from countries where polygamy is practiced to expand their families by marrying new wives in Islamic (*Nikah*) ceremonies and then bringing them to the United Kingdom.[13]

Once present, wives in polygamous families have several options for obtaining welfare benefits. One is to simply admit that their family is polygamous and apply for income support benefits or jobseeker's benefits ("the dole"). Although polygamous marriages are not recognized for immigration status, the United Kingdom does recognize them for income-support benefits and jobseeker's benefits. In late 2007, the Department for Work and Pensions (DWP), after a multiagency investigation, issued new guidelines for income support, stating, "Where there is a valid polygamous marriage the claimant and one spouse will be paid the couple rate. . . . The amount payable for each additional spouse is presently £33.65 pounds ($66.41)." This payment may be made directly into the husband's bank account if his wives agree. A Department of Works and Pensions spokesman justified the rule by arguing that it did not "reward" polygamy since second wives are worse off than single women, who are eligible for a greater jobseeker's allowance (£60 per week) than is a second wife (£33.65 per week). A husband with many wives may also be eligible for additional housing benefits and council-tax benefits in order to reflect the larger housing space needed for his family.[14]

Thus, the United Kingdom *partially* recognizes polygamy. It is illegal to enter into a plural marriage in the United Kingdom, but the country recognizes those formed legally elsewhere. The country does not confer on polygamous spouses eligibility for immigration benefits, but it does confer housing, unemployment, and welfare benefits, and there are alternative immigration routes. The British government estimates that there are 1,000 polygamous families living in Britain, but social workers interviewed by journalists estimate that the actual number is closer to 20,000. This difference is likely reflected by the government's focus on polygamous families who are living together and potentially eligible for benefits. Families who choose not to live together can actually benefit more from the welfare system than can those who choose recognition, and the majority of polygamous families in the United Kingdom are likely not seeking recognition at all. As in Utah, many women in polygamous marriages simply live apart from their husbands and seek welfare benefits at the higher single rate. This practice has recently been the subject of several media exposés, with some critics recommending a requirement that those who enter into *Nikah* marriages register as married with the government, which would open the door to criminal sanctions against those who marry more than one spouse.[15] The increased number of third-generation Muslims in the United Kingdom who are practicing polygamy may have resulted in part from the relatively lax approach the United Kingdom has taken toward public benefits.

France: No to Welfare, Yes to Immigration (at Least at First)

A contrasting example of this dynamic occurred in France. Until recently, France opted for a fairly open immigration policy. Prior to 1993, France legally recognized foreign polygamous marriages for immigration purposes as long as they were valid in the country in which they were performed (Starr and Brilmayer 2003, 245). France has a large immigrant population, due in part to its colonial presence in much of Africa, including Morocco, Tunisia, Algeria, and Guinea and in part to its post-war immigration policy, which encouraged the migration of guest workers in boom times and their deportation when the economy went bust (Scales-Trent 1999, 720). Taken together, these factors brought to France a much larger population of polygamous immigrants than that found in the United Kingdom. Indeed, many experts estimate that there were 200,000 people living in polygamous families in France by the 1990s (721). The majority of these families are immigrants from sub-Saharan Africa, and there is a sizeable population of such immigrants from Algeria and Morocco as well.

Like the United Kingdom, France recognizes polygamous marriages entered into in a jurisdiction where polygamy is legal. And just as the United Kingdom allows foreigners to follow the law of their domicile in marriage customs, France too recognizes polygamy if authorized by a noncitizen's personal status (Scales-Trent 1999, 721). Polygamous families are recognized by the systems that allocate some public benefits but not by others. For example, according to Judy Scales-Trent (1999), family allowances are available based on the number of children in a family, but the father is the beneficiary of these allowances. Thus, he can claim and collect a family allowance for children from multiple wives. In contrast, a second wife in a family in which the first wife also is living in France cannot receive benefits that might otherwise be thought to accrue directly to her, such as health insurance with maternity coverage, since these benefits can only be assigned to one wife. This form of partial recognition enables men to create large families with multiple wives and children but places the second and subsequent wives in vulnerable, even perilous, positions.

Prior to 1993, then, France recognized polygamy in a partial and fractured way. Polygamy was recognized for immigration purposes and for family benefits flowing to fathers to support children from multiple wives, but it was not recognized in connection with personal benefits that could be paid directly to second and subsequent wives. During Charles Pasqua's term as interior minister, France began to adopt a much more conservative stance toward immigration. In 1993, France passed several new immigration laws, known as the Pasqua Laws, which limited spousal visas and working papers to only one spouse (Starr and Brilmayer 2003, 247). The Pasqua Laws also made the children of second spouses ineligible for the family allowance benefit. In other words, France moved from a partial recognition system to a system in which recognition was far more minimal than before. Indeed, the only recognition after the Pasqua Laws, at least prospectively, was that a polygamous marriage entered into elsewhere was not a crime. Retrospectively, however, the Pasqua Laws reshaped the formerly fractured recognition of polygamy in surprising ways. The law made the ban on recognition of polygamy for immigration and welfare purposes retrospective as well, but to avoid a clash with international human-rights norms, it gave families a loophole. If the husband divorced all of his wives but one and physically separated the household so that each wife lived separately, the wives would not be deported and would not lose their working and residence papers. Because French law lacked the power to invalidate any Muslim marriage, families were thus able to maintain their marital status for religious purposes so long as they were legally divorced and not cohabiting. French authorities have been strict about enforcement; renting apartments in the same building is not sufficient to constitute the "decohabitation" required by law (Starr and Brilmayer 2003, 248).

Partial recognition always occurs against the backdrop of a particular legal and cultural context, and it is the context that matters as much or perhaps even more than the formal recognition. The French experience differs from the English one in important ways. First, and most obviously, the total number of immigrants practicing polygamy is much higher in France.[16] Causation is difficult to infer from bare immigration statistics. Given the colonial relationships between France and many African countries and given its guest-worker-driven immigration policy, polygamist immigrants might have migrated there regardless of France's stance on polygamy. But it seems at least possible that its early recognition of polygamy, at least for immigration-status purposes, may have prompted larger numbers of polygamists to move there, whether they were polygamist immigrants choosing France as a destination country or deciding to practice polygamy upon their arrival. Important too are the different attitudes toward assimilation taken by the United Kingdom and France. The United Kingdom has generally approached immigration and citizenship through an integrationist policy, encouraging the maintenance of cultural ties and distinguishing integration from a more coercive assimilation. In contrast, France has more aggressively demanded that immigrants conform to French culture, an approach famously debated in the press when a Muslim woman who wore the *niqab* was refused citizenship in 2008 (Mullally 2010, 194–97).

Recognition of polygamy, then, can take multiple forms, and the forms can fluctuate depending on the social, cultural, economic, and legal terrain on which polygamy is practiced. In a country with a robust welfare system, full recognition may well require extending benefits to polygamous families. Indeed, the expansive view most Western democracies now take toward extramarital sex and childrearing may well require some form of recognition, in that the children of polygamous mothers are difficult to distinguish from the children of unmarried mothers, at least in terms of their moral claim to state support. In some ways, recognition in a strong welfare state is an easier proposition than it is in a country like the United States, where public benefits are still largely tied to marriage and, in particular, to incentivizing a division of labor within marriage.

ARE WE ALL POLYGAMISTS NOW?

So far, this essay has focused on the ways in which full recognition of polygamy would substantially change the law of marriage and the ways in which partial recognition could have unintended consequences. There is a third, and important, piece to the puzzle. Some of the benefits and obligations of marriage can be granted even without formal recognition of a relationship as a marriage. This form of recognition is becoming increasingly common in nonpolygamous families. When we add together the various forms of recognition of functional families, what we end up with may look very much like formal recognition of polygamy, or formal recognition of polygamy for some purposes, making full recognition less important.

Recognition of Nonmarital Adult Relationships

In many jurisdictions, cohabiting couples are treated like married couples for some purposes. Often, this form of recognition treats the couple as married for joint property purposes but not state benefits, although the reverse is sometimes true. Take, for instance, Washington state. Under Washington case law, if a couple is in a "committed intimate relationship," property obtained during that relationship will be treated as community property to be equitably divided upon dissolution of the relationship, just as property obtained during marriage would be at divorce. The factors courts consider in determining whether a couple is in a committed intimate relationship include continuous cohabitation, duration of the relationship, purpose of the relationship, pooling of resources and services for joint projects, and the intent of the parties. This recognition maps fairly neatly onto the theory of marriage as privatized dependency, expanding recognition beyond married couples to all who intend to become mutually dependent. The American Law Institute Principles of Family Dissolution suggest a similar rule that would make both property division and maintenance available to committed couples.[17]

Other jurisdictions allow unmarried adults to contract into relationships that mimic some, but not all, of the elements of marriage. California famously adopted this contractual approach in *Marvin v. Marvin*, a case involving the actor Lee Marvin and his long-term girlfriend Michele Triola, who went by Michele Triola Marvin.[18] Similarly, New Jersey has recognized contractual relationships, and courts have enforced contracts even where the contract is oral and implied rather than written and express.[19]

In addition to all of these judicially created doctrines recognizing nonmarital adult relationships, some jurisdictions have adopted legislatively created statuses. Most famously, many states and countries have passed civil-union, domestic-partnership, and reciprocal-beneficiary legislation that allows same-sex couples, and in some instances different-sex couples, or specifically senior-citizen couples, to enter into binding, legally recognized relationships without marrying. The primary feature these schemes share is that the couples must opt in by registering; they cannot accidentally become "civil unioned." Other jurisdictions, however, have legislatively adopted standards that resemble the judicially adopted "committed intimate relationships" rule. New Zealand, for example, recognizes marriages, civil unions, and "de facto relationships." A de facto partner is entitled not only to property division at dissolution but also access to alimony payments and inheritance rights (Atkin 2009). New Zealand also extends joint tax treatment, social assistance, and immigration benefits to people in de facto relationships. Some Canadian provinces have adopted similar schemes.[20]

So what do these instances of recognition of nonmarital relationships have to do with polygamy, which is, after all, a form of marriage? Some of them may provide a back door to recognition of multiple intimate relationships without using the *marriage* or *polygamy* labels. In the *Marvin* case, for example, Lee Marvin and Michele Triola had lived together from 1965 to 1970 and presented themselves to the world as a married couple. But Marvin was legally married to another woman through 1967. The court nevertheless held that if she could demonstrate that she and Marvin had entered into a contract, Triola could recover on the contract. Similarly, *Roccamonte*, a New Jersey case, involved a married man and his single female partner who lived together for thirty years while the man remained married to his wife. The court found that the couple had entered into an agreement that he would support his girlfriend for life, despite the financial effect this agreement could have on his ability to also support his existing wife. The New Zealand legislation uses "emotional connection," not monogamy, to determine whether a "de facto relationship" exists; multiple relationships, and de facto relationships combined with marriages or civil unions, are certainly possible.[21] (In contrast, Washington state will not recognize a committed intimate relationship if either party is married to someone else; similarly, civil unions and domestic partnerships are generally available only to the unmarried.) In those jurisdictions that do allow for the possibility of multiple legally recognized relationships, the state's refusal to recognize polygamy may be irrelevant to the day-to-day lives of polygamous families. In these instances, the state *does* recognize multiple affective adult relationships, or at least partially recognizes them (granting, for example, property division but not immigration benefits, or inheritance rights but not welfare access). With a menu of options available, individuals, couples, and groups of affiliated people can largely tailor their relationships to their own needs and purposes. In fact, they might actually be better off than if they were all legally married to each other. Remaining single, for example, might make some eligible for welfare benefits, and the group could devise strategies for using the law to shape the varying relationships among family members through cohabitation contracts or establishing eligibility for recognition of nonmarital status relationships.

Recognition of Multiple Parent-Child Relationships

In addition to the recognition of nonmarital relationships, many jurisdictions are also increasingly recognizing multiple parent-child relationships. As recently as 1989, US Supreme Court Justice Scalia could declare, "California law, like nature itself, makes no provision for dual fatherhood."[22] That is no longer so. In 2013, the California legislature passed a statute that allows more than two parents to be declared the legal parents of a child. The Dutch legislature is considering a similar move. The United Kingdom has long allowed an additional adult, beyond a child's two parents, to obtain "parental responsibility" without full legal parenthood. Delaware's "de facto-parent" doctrine allows a child, under certain circumstances, to have full legal parenthood. A Pennsylvania court recognized a genetic mother, her former lesbian partner, and their sperm donor as the legal parents of a child. The District of Columbia allows a sperm donor to contract with a child's intending parents so that all three retain legal parentage. Several states in the United States have allowed "third parent adoption," in which both genetic parents retain legal parent status but allow a third party (often the partner or spouse of one of the parents) to adopt the child as well. And many states now allow a parent to relinquish a child for adoption but retain visitation rights. Some of these jurisdictions are actually allowing three or more parents to be legal parents; others (like the United Kingdom and the postadoption-contract-agreements states) only allow two parents but give partial recognition, through the right to enforceable visitation, to a third adult.[23]

As discussed previously, the law has already come very far from when it considered marriage to be the solely appropriate space for parenting. The dismantling of illegitimacy as a salient legal category and the decriminalization of extramarital sex went far to disaggregate sex from marriage from procreation. Sex and procreation have become further disaggregated as a practical matter through sperm and egg donation, in-vitro fertilization, and surrogacy. The recent recognition of multiple parenthood takes this disaggregation one step further. It's not just that a couple doesn't have to be legally married to be a child's parents but that the individuals claiming parenthood don't have to be a couple at all. They could be a sperm-donor friend of a lesbian couple; they could be a married heterosexual couple and the wife's ex-husband; they could be three friends who decide to have a baby.

A Menu of Options

Taken together, complete or partial recognition of multiple adult relationships and complete or partial recognition of multiple-parenting relationships could provide many of the benefits of recognition of polygamy while avoiding some of the problems. The state could decide, for example, that public benefits such as Social Security or estate-tax exemptions would only apply to married couples or, perhaps, require individuals to designate their "plus one" for benefits that are not pie-like in their ability to be divided. But individuals could contract or register their way into legally recognized relationships with multiple adult partners in order to foster financial and emotional interdependency or to ensure their children are emotionally and financially supported (or both). For some polygamists, this form of self-selecting specific forms of recognition might be preferable to wholesale recognition of polygamy as a form of marriage. Contract regimes, especially, enable spouses in plural marriages to negotiate the terms of each relationship within the group. Functional tests, such as the New Zealand "de facto-relationship" law, on the other hand, would be more difficult to use for planning purposes. Since the relationship is recognized only when a claim for benefits is made or a relationship dissolves, it would be difficult to know in advance whether the requirements for a de facto relationship had been met; it is the *facts* in de facto, after all, that determine whether the relationship passes muster, not only the parties' intent. This uncertainty might make this form of recognition less attractive to polygamists.

It is important to acknowledge that the law in this area is developing. We are not all polygamists—not yet. Many jurisdictions do not recognize multiple parenthood; many more do not recognize nonmarital intimate relationships as having a meaning beyond a personal one. But the direction the law is moving in is toward increased recognition of sexual and parenting relationships independent from marriage (and independent from each other) and toward abolishing the "rule of two," both for intimate adult relationships and for the number of parents a child can have. If this trend continues—and it seems likely that it will, given the increased number of LGBTQ families and blended stepfamilies creating families in which multiple parents are a reality—opening up the category of *marriage* to polygamists may not be the legal avenue most likely to provide recognition for polyamorous groups. And many people who benefit from these new doctrines may not think of themselves as polygamous, or even polyamorous, at all. They may be blended families who are coparenting children, married adults having affairs, or even roommates or siblings who want to create legally binding, mutual financial arrangements. In twenty years, we may well wake up to discover that the partial recognition of alternative family structures has crept into our lives and realize that whether the law recognizes polygamy as a form is entirely irrelevant.

CONCLUSION

This essay has evaluated the recognition of polygamy and concluded that polygamy is likely to pose numerous challenges to recognition. Polygamy is particularly fraught because it exposes the ways in which the law of marriage already does not adequately reflect the needs of many families, and then exacerbates these inadequacies. Of course, this legal analysis is no substitute for an ethical one. It is, however, a necessary consideration in any ethical analysis. Abstract ethical concepts can fall apart in the implementation of legal rules. Refusing to recognize polygamy, as in the example of US immigration policy, can put plural wives in an untenable situation, forcing them to choose between staying in an abusive or unwanted marriage and losing custody of their children. Partial and full recognition, however, can have unintended consequences as well by encouraging dependency and fostering subordination within the family, and by sending mixed messages to individuals in polygamous families. And polygamous families may not use partial or full recognition in the way lawmakers might expect; they may prefer contractual relationships or nonrecognition to control by the state.

Thinking hard about recognition forces us to articulate what core values (if any) marriage protects in the first place. A careful analysis of what recognition of polygamy might look like demonstrates how difficult it would be to transform the work currently done by marriage law to a polygamous context. In contrast, the work that family law *beyond* marriage law is currently doing may be where polyamorous relationships are most likely to be recognized, in part or in full. Instead of arguing about decriminalization—which appears at this point to be constitutionally required—legal reformers should pay closer attention to how partial or full recognition of multiple adult-adult and adult-child relationships would help or hinder the family lives of all people, those who consider themselves polygamists and those who do not.

Notes

1. See Brown v. Buhman, Memorandum Decision and Order Granting in Part Plain-
    tiffs' Motion for Summary Judgment, Case 2:11-cv-00652-CW-BCW (D. Utah, Dec.
    13, 2013) (striking down cohabitation clause in Utah statute); http://gaymarriage
    .procon.org/view.resource.php?resourceID=004857 (listing states that have adopt-
    ed marriage equality).
2. Zablocki v. Redhail 434 U.S. 374 (1978).
3. See, e.g., Trimble v. Gordon, 430 U.S. 762 (1977) (nonmarital children); Caban v.
    Mohammed, 441 U.S. 380 (1979) (nonmarital fathers); Lawrence v. Texas, 539 U.S.
    558 (2003) (nonmarital sex).
4. *Bowers v. Hardwick* 478 U.S. 186 (1986); Lawrence v. Texas.
5. US Department of Health and Human Services (2013, 9).
6. Several states still criminalize adultery although the constitutionality of these
    provisions is in dispute. See Peter Nicolas (2011, 97, 108, noting that twenty-four
    states still have criminal adultery laws on their books); Hobbs v. Smith, No. 05 CVS
    267, 2006 WL 3103008, at #1 (N.C. Super. Ct. Aug. 25, 2006) (striking down a law
    criminalizing fornication and adultery on grounds that it violated substantive due
    process rights).
7. The effect of the Patient Protection and Affordable Care Act (popularly known as
    Obamacare) on the relationship between health insurance and marriage is complex
    and largely still unknown. Most married couples are likely still better off than
    singles, assuming whatever premiums they pay to their employers are lower than
    those they would pay buying insurance using an exchange. For uninsured couples,
    however, marriage may make access to health insurance more difficult because
    it could push their family income over the eligibility line for a subsidy. See Mary
    Chastain (2013).
8. Turner v. Safley, 482 U.S. 78 (1987) (inmate restrictions on marriage); Windsor v.
    United States (seal of approval).
9. In the Recognition of Customary Marriages Act of 2008, South Africa developed an
    approach to multiple spouses that allows a first wife to demand a division of family
    property and registration of a property regime governing a new polygamous mar-
    riage if her husband marries an additional wife. Failure to give the first wife notice
    has been interpreted to invalidate the additional marriage (see Mbatha and Joffe
    2012).
10. See Utah Code § 30-1-4.5 (Supp. 2005); see also Brown v. Buhman, Memorandum
    Decision and Order Granting in Part Plaintiff's Motion for Summary Judgment), case
    No. 2:11-cv-0652-CW (C.D. Utah, Dec. 13, 2013) (striking down "cohabitation" lan-
    guage in a Utah statute as violating the free exercise clause for the First Amendment
    and the due process clause of the Fourteenth Amendment); State v. Holm, 137 P.3d
    726 (Utah 2006) (upholding constitutionality of a Utah statute despite holding in
    Lawrence v. Texas); King v. Smith, 392 U.S. 308 (1968) (striking down an Alabama
    law that made ineligible for dependent child benefits children of mothers who
    "cohabited" with a man, even where that man was married to someone else).
11. Reference re: Section 293 of the Criminal Code of Canada, 2011 BCSC 1588s,
    paras. 557–76.
12. INA §212(a)(10)(A) ("practicing polygamy"); INA § 101(f) ("good moral charac-
    ter"). As Claire Smearman has shown, there is a way around the prohibition. The
    inadmissibility grounds do not apply in asylum cases. And although in order to
    adjust status to become a permanent resident after one year, an asylee must show
    that she is admissible, §209(c) of the INA permits DHS officers to waive the require-
    ment "for humanitarian purposes, to assure family unity, or when it is otherwise in

the public interest," thus potentially opening the door to LPR status for polygamists (Smearman 2009, 437).

13. Immigration Law of 1988, cited in Malik (2008). Prior to 1988, husbands could sponsor a second (or subsequent) wife if both parties had a domicile in a country that allowed polygamy (Reid, *Daily Mail.com*, Sept. 24, 2011; Wintour, *Guardian*, Nov. 7, 1987).

14. Income support is an income-related means-tested benefit for low-income people. To be eligible, a person must have savings of under £16,000, work fewer than sixteen hours per week, and have a reason that they are not actively seeking work, such as illness, disability, or the care of children ("Parental Rights" 2014). Jobseeker's benefits have similar financial eligibility requirements but require that the recipient be actively seeking employment (Malik 2008). See also Jonathan Wynne-Jones (*Sunday Telegraph*, Feb. 3, 2008), who discusses the four departments—Treasury, DWP, HM Revenue and Customs, and the Home Office—involved in the review and their consensus that recognizing multiple marriages conducted overseas was "the best possible" option. See also Tom McTague (*Mirror* [London], Dec. 28, 2011), who states that a man and his "first wife" can jointly claim £105.95 in dole payments made up of a £67.50 single-person payout and a couple's top-up of £38.45, and "subsequent" wives get £38.45 top-up. See also Tom Savage (*Daily Star*, Aug. 29, 2007). The council-tax benefit is essentially a rebate against the council tax (a tax loosely analogous to local property taxes in the United States) for eligible low-income homeowners.

15. Sue Reid (*Daily Mail Online*, Sept. 24, 2011), Baronness Flather (*Daily Mail.com*, Sept. 16, 2011).

16. To compare: in 2010, the two largest immigrant groups in the United Kingdom after Irish immigrants were Indians and Pakistanis, 693,000 and 431,000, respectively, in a country with a population of 62,300,000 (Office for National Statistics 2010). Estimates of the number of immigrants and citizens practicing polygamy in the United Kingdom range from 1,000 to 20,000 families. The 2011 population of metropolitan France was 65,821,885, with 713,334 immigrants from Algeria, 653,826 from Morocco, 234,669 from Tunisia, and 669,401 from sub-Saharan Africa. The government estimates that 200,000 immigrants and citizens are practicing polygamy in France.

17. American Law Institute, Principles of the Law of Family Dissolution (2002), Ch. 6, Domestic Partners, Sec. 6.02-03. The leading case on committed intimate relationships in Washington state is Connell v. Washington, 127 Wn. 2d 339, 898 P.2d 831 (1995). Washington stops short of granting *all* marital benefits to couples in committed intimate relationships. Such couples are not eligible for alimony, and separate property remains separate (which differentiates them from married couples in Washington, for whom divorce courts may consider all property—including property obtained before marriage and inherited during marriage—as property to be equitably divided upon divorce.) See also ALI Principles.

18. Marvin v. Marvin (Cal. 1976).

19. See *Roccamonte* (NJ 2002).

20. See New Zealand Property (Relationships) Act 1976, Public Act 1976 No. 166, as amended 1 Feb. 2002, Part 2C (meaning of de facto partner), 2D (meaning of de facto relationship).

21. Ibid.

22. Michael H. v. Gerald D. 491 U.S. 110 (1989).

23. See Michael H. v. Gerald D. (holding California law allows for only one father); Jacob v. Shultz-Jacob, 923 A.2d 473482 (Pa. Super. Ct. 2007); 13 Del. Code sec. 8-201(c) (setting forth de facto parent status that allows for the possibility of three

or more parents); "Parental Rights and Responsibilities" (2014), explaining parental responsibility; Nancy Polikoff (2012 blog post at http://beyondstraightandgay
marriage.blogspot.com/2012/07/where-can-child-have-three-parents.html), discussing various jurisdictions.

References

Appleton, Susan Frelich. 2012. "Illegitimacy and Sex, Old and New." *American University Journal of Gender, Social Policy and the Law* 20 (3): 347–84.

Atkin, Bill. 2009. "Wider Perspective: The Legal World of Unmarried Couples: Reflections on 'De Facto Relationships' in Recent New Zealand Legislation." *Victoria University of Wellington Law Review* 39: 793–811.

Cahn, Naomi, and June Carbone. 2010. *Red Families v. Blue Families: Legal Polarization and the Creation of Culture.* New York: Oxford.

Chastain, Mary. 2013. *Married Couple Considers Divorce to Save Money on Obamacare.* *Breitbart.* http://www.breitbart.com/big-government/2013/11/09/married-couple-may-divorce-to-save-money-on-obamacare.

Davis, Adrienne D. 2010. "Regulating Polygamy: Intimacy, Default Rules, and Bargaining for Equality." *Columbia Law Review* 110 (8): 1955–2046.

Drobac, Jennifer A., and Antony Page. 2007. "A Uniform Domestic Partnership Act: Marrying Business Partnership and Family Law." *Georgia Law Review (Athens, Ga.)* 41 (2): 349.

Emens, Elizabeth. 2004. "Monogamy's Law: Compulsory Monogamy and Polyamorous Existence." *New York University Review of Law and Social Change* 29 (2): 277.

Ertman, Martha M. 2001. "Marriage as a Trade: Bridging the Private/Private Distinction." *Harvard Civil Rights-Civil Liberties Law Review* 36 (1): 79.

Fineman, Martha Albertson. 2004. *The Autonomy Myth: A Theory of Dependency.* New York: New Press.

Grossman, Joanna L., and Lawrence M. Friedman. 2011. *Inside the Castle: Law and the Family in 20th Century America.* Princeton: Princeton University Press. http://dx.doi.org/10.1515/9781400839773.

Hamilton, Vivian. 2012. "The Age of Marital Capacity: Reconsidering Civil Recognition of Adolescent Marriage." *Boston University Law Review. Boston University. School of Law* 92 (6): 1817.

Liu, Goodwin. 1999. "Social Security and the Treatment of Marriage: Spousal Benefits, Earnings Sharing, and the Challenge of Reform." *Wisconsin Law Review* 1999 (1): 1.

Malik, Talal. 2008. "UK Legally Recognises Multiple Islamic Wives." *Arabian Business.com.* http://www.arabianbusiness.com/uk-legally-recognises-multiple-islamic-wives-121789.html.

Mbatha, Likhapha, and Lisa Fishbayn Joffe. 2012. "Recognition of Polygamous Marriages in the New South Africa." In *Gender, Religion, and Family Law: Theorizing Conflicts between Women's Rights and Cultural Traditions,* edited by Lisa Fishbayn Joffe and Sylvia Neil, 190–210. Waltham, MA: Brandeis University Press.

McClain, Linda C. 2007. "Love, Marriage and the Baby Carriage: Revisiting the Channeling Function of Family Law." *Cardozo Law Review* 28 (5): 1233.

Mullally, Siobhan. 2010. "Gender Equality, Citizenship Status, and the Politics of Belonging." In *Transcending the Boundaries of Law: Generations of Feminism and Legal Theory,* edited by Martha Fineman, 192. Abingdon, VA: Routledge.

Nicolas, Peter. 2011. "The Lavender Letter: Applying the Law of Adultery to Same-Sex Couples and Same-Sex Conduct." *Florida Law Review* 63 (1): 97–128.

Office for National Statistics. 2010. *Statistical Bulletin: Annual Mid-year Population Estimates, 2010.* http://www.ons.gov.uk/ons/publications/re-reference-tables.html?edition=tcm%3A77-231847.

"Parental Rights and Responsibilities" 2014. *Gov.UK.* https://www.gov.uk/parental-rights -responsibilities/what-is-parental-responsibility.

Polikoff, Nancy. 2008. *Beyond (Straight and Gay) Marriage: Valuing All Families under the Law.* Boston, MA: Beacon.

Scales-Trent, Judy. 1999. "African Women in France: Immigration, Family, and Work." *Brooklyn Journal of International Law* 24 (3): 705.

Smearman, Claire A. 2009. "Second Wives Club: Mapping the Impact of Polygamy in U.S. Immigration Law." *Berkeley Journal of International Law* 27 (2): 382.

Starr, Sonja, and Lea Brilmayer. 2003. "Family Separation as a Violation of International Law." *Berkeley Journal of International Law* 21 (2): 213.

Strassberg, Maura. 2003. "The Crime of Polygamy." *Temple Political and Civil Rights Law Review* 12 (2): 353.

Sunstein, Cass R. 2005. "The Right to Marry." *Cardozo Law Review* 26 (5): 208.

US Department of Health and Human Services. 2013. National Vital Statistics Report 62 (1). http://www.cdc.gov/nchs/data/nvsr/nvsr62/nvsr62_01.pdf.

CONTRIBUTORS

JANET BENNION (Janet.Bennion@lsc.vsc.edu) is a professor of anthropology at Lyndon State College and author of *Polygamy in Primetime* (University of Brandeis Press 2012), *Women of Principle: Female Networking in Contemporary Mormon Polygyny* (Oxford University Press 1998), and *Desert Patriarchy* (University of Arizona Press 2004). She conducted ethnographic fieldwork among the Apostolic United Brethren of Utah and Montana and the Firstborn LeBaron family of Chihuahua, Mexico.

LISA FISHBAYN JOFFE (fishbayn@brandeis.edu) is the associate director of the Hadassah-Brandeis Institute of Brandeis University, where she directs the Project on Gender, Culture, Religion and the Law. The mission of the GCRL Project is to produce scholarship that explores the tension between women's equality claims and religious laws. She has edited the anthologies *Gender, Religion and Family Law: Theorizing Conflicts Between Women's Rights and Cultural Traditions* (with Sylvia Neil, Brandeis University Press 2012) and *Women's Rights and Religious Law* (with Fareda Banda, Routledge Press, forthcoming 2016). She is editor of the Brandeis Press series on Gender, Culture, Religion and the Law and is cofounder of the Boston Agunah Taskforce.

* * *

KERRY ABRAMS (kerryabrams@virginia.edu) is a professor of law at the University of Virginia School of Law. She is the author of numerous articles and essays, including "Polygamy, Prostitution, and the Federalization of Immigration Law" (*Columbia Law Review* 2005), "Immigration Law and the Regulation of Marriage" (*Minnesota Law Review* 2007), and "Marriage Fraud" (*California Law Review* 2012).

MARTHA BAILEY (baileym@queensu.ca), LLB (University of Toronto), LLM (Queen's University), and DPhil (Oxford University) is a professor of law at Queen's University, Canada. She teaches and researches in the areas of international family law, comparative law, and private international law.

LORI G. BEAMAN (lbeaman@uottawa.ca) is the Canada Research Chair in the Contextualization of Religion in a Diverse Canada, professor in the Department of Classics and Religious Studies at the University of Ottawa, and the principal investigator of the Religion and Diversity Project, a thirty-seven member international research team whose focus is religion and diversity (see www.religionanddiversity.ca). Her publications include "Deep Equality as an Alternative to Accommodation and Tolerance" (Nordic Journal of Religion and Society 2014), "Battles over Symbols: The 'Religion' of the Minority Versus the 'Culture' of the Majority" (*Journal of Law & Religion* 2012/13), and *Defining Harm: Religious Freedom and the Limits of the Law* (UBC Press 2008).

JONATHAN COWDEN has a PhD in political science from Yale University and is the author of numerous articles. He also has an MSW and currently works as a social worker in San Jose.

SHOSHANA GROSSBARD (sgrossba@mail.sdsu.edu) is a professor of economics at San Diego State University and the University of Zaragoza. She is founding editor of *Review of Economics of the Household* and author of *On the Economics of Marriage* (Westview Press 1993) and *Marriage and the Economy* (Cambridge University Press 2003). She tweets at @econoflove.

MELANIE HEATH (mheath@mcmaster.ca) is an associate professor of sociology at McMaster University. Her research interests include studying the consequences of family, gender, and sexual politics on social inequality. Her current research, funded by an SSHRC Insight Grant, compares polygamy's criminalization in Canada, the United States, France, and Benin to shed light on how governments seek to balance competing rights of equality, sexual and familial intimacy, and religious freedom in regulating polygamy. She is author of *One Marriage under God: The Campaign to Promote Marriage in America* (New York University Press 2010).

DEBRA MAJEED (debramajeed@gmail.com) is a professor of religious studies at Beloit College. She has published in the *Journal of Feminist Studies in Religion*, the *Encyclopedia of Women and Religion in America*, the *Encyclopedia of Women in Islamic Cultures*, and *Delving Deeper Shades of Purple: Charting Twenty Years of Womanist Approaches in Religion and Society*, among others. Her first book, *Polygyny: What It Means When African America Muslim Women Share Their Husbands*, was published in 2015 by University Press of Florida.

ROSE MCDERMOTT (rose_mcdermott@brown.edu) is a professor of political science at Brown University. She is coeditor of two books and author of three books and over ninety articles in a wide variety of topics. She was an expert witness for the attorney general of Canada on the polygyny reference trial in British Columbia in 2011. She is the past president of the International Society of Political Psychology.

SARAH SONG (ssong@law.berkeley.edu) is a professor of law and associate professor of political science at the University of California, Berkeley, and the author of *Justice, Gender, and the Politics of Multiculturalism* (Cambridge University Press 2007).

MAURA IRENE Strassberg (maura.strassberg@drake.edu) is a professor of law at Drake University Law School. She is the author of three polygamy-related articles: "A Difference of Form or Substance: Monogamy, Polygamy and Same-Sex Marriage" (*North Carolina Law Review* 1997); "The Challenge of Post-Modern Polygamy: Considering Polyamory" (*Capital University Law Review* 2003); and "The Crime of Polygamy" (*Temple University Policy and Civil Rights Law Review* 2003).

INDEX

www.ingramcontent.com/pod-product-compliance
Lightning Source LLC
Chambersburg PA
CBHW032124020426
42334CB00016B/1056